A Strong Dose of Myself

By the same author

Poetry

Walking Under Water
Tenants of the House
Poems, Golders Green
A Small Desperation
Selected Poems
Funland and Other Poems
Collected Poems 1948–1976
Way Out in the Centre

Plays

Three Questor Plays
The Dogs of Pavlov
Pythagoras

Prose

Ash on a Young Man's Sleeve
O. Jones, O. Jones
A Poet in the Family

A Strong Dose of Myself

Dannie Abse

Dannie Abse.

Hutchinson
London Melbourne Sydney Auckland Johannesburg

Hutchinson & Co. (Publishers) Ltd

An imprint of the Hutchinson Publishing Group

17–21 Conway Street, London W1P 6JD

Hutchinson Group (Australia) Pty Ltd
30–32 Cremorne Street, Richmond South, Victoria 3121
PO Box 151, Broadway, New South Wales 2007

Hutchinson Group (NZ) Ltd
32–34 View Road, PO Box 40-086, Glenfield,
Auckland

Hutchinson Group (SA) Pty Ltd
PO Box 337, Bergvlei 2012, South Africa

First published 1983
This collection © Dannie Abse 1983

Photoset in Linotron Ehrhardt by
Rowland Phototypesetting Ltd,
Bury St Edmunds, Suffolk.

Printed in Great Britain by
The Anchor Press Ltd and
bound by William Brendon & Son Ltd,
both of Tiptree, Essex.

ISBN 0 09 151260 3

Contents

Introduction

Thoreau advised visiting lecturers in the USA to give audiences 'a strong dose of yourself. That's what they want – it doesn't matter what sort of damn fool you happen to be!'

I have had similar, if less blunt advice, especially between 1972 and 1982, from BBC producers who kindly invited me to provide talks or from editors who commissioned me to contribute to their magazines. A number of them, though ignorant of Thoreau's frank, cheerful suggestion, had read either *Ash on a Young Man's Sleeve* (1954) or *A Poet in the Family* (1974) and thought that I might be prepared to write further autobiographical texts. After a while, thanks to such intermittent promptings, I began to keep this book in mind.

I do hope the reader will find a pattern in this mosaic and I am encouraged by the knowledge that autobiography can take very many forms. Rockwell Gray has remarked in the *Kenyon Review*: 'There is no longer the assumption that one must have reached a ripe old age to write autobiography as a retrospective summing up: the venture may be engaged in at almost any age and, potentially, as many times as one chooses. . . . It may be concerned with the present and future as with the past. Not bound to any particular structure, stylistic or tonal model, autobiography is . . . the most protean of enterprises.'

I must acknowledge – apart from the BBC – the *Jewish Quarterly*, the *Listener, London Magazine, Planet, Poetry Wales, PN Review* and *Punch*. I am grateful also to Robson Books for allowing me to reprint a piece from *My Medical School*; The Woburn Press for 'The Experiment' which originally served as a preface to my play *The Dogs of Pavlov*; and Mr Lionel Monteith of the Lincoln Clinic who invited me to deliver the second J. R. R. Tolkien lecture ('Pegasus and the Rocking Horse') at the Institute of Psychoanalysis in London on 29 April 1981.

Other pieces, one-third of the number, have not appeared in print before and were especially written for this volume; in short, were commissioned by myself.

My thanks, finally, to Michael Burn for allowing me to quote a poem of his from *Open Day and Night* (Chatto and Windus); to David Wright for poems from *To the Gods, the Shades* (Carcanet New Press); to Cary Archard of the Poetry Wales Press for his practical encouragement; and to my wife, Joan, for laughing in the right places.

D.A.

Part One

Return Ticket to Cardiff

We were wandering Welsh Jews. I was born in Whitchurch Road, Cardiff, but after a year or two we were on the move. To 289 Albany Road, Cardiff. A few years later the wanderlust possessed my parents again and we shifted three minutes away to 237 Albany Road. A few years of stability and doors slamming before we trekked another 500 yards to 66 Albany Road.

Was this an advance? We were nearer to the Globe Cinema now, where for 4d. on a Saturday morning I could watch Tom Mix or Rin Tin Tin from the classy balcony and gob down on the kids who'd paid only 2d. in the stalls. But my parents remembered the good old days at 289 Albany Road so, soon, we made Pickfords happy and moved back threequarters of a mile in that direction to 66 Sandringham Road. 'Sixty-six is our lucky number,' my father said doubtfully.

Why did we move so frequently from rented house to house? Because the bathroom needed redecorating and had begun to look like a grudge; because, though the jokes remained the same, my father's fortunes changed; because the mice had taken to chewing aphrodisiacs; because of Dai or Ken or Cohen the Crooner – for truly, sometimes, it is easier to move house than to get rid of certain guests.

I liked Cardiff. Until I was eighteen all that I felt attracted to, all that I loved was circumscribed by its boundaries. Yet I must have had some curiosity about other cities, other countries, for I recall asking my mother, 'Where does England begin?' She promptly pointed to a nearby convenient railway bridge that crossed over Newport Road: 'By there,' she said. Though she was twenty-five miles wrong I thought for years that this side of the bridge was Wales where dark-haired men were human-size, 5 feet 8½ inches like I am now, whereas eastward – 'over there' – the wrong side of that significant bridge, strode alien flaxen-haired Englishmen affected with pituitary trouble.

South of our district, too, lived dangerous giants of a sort. Why else was I not allowed to go beyond Splott to the docks? 'People get knifed in Tiger Bay,' my mother warned me. Frankly, it was none too safe north of Albany Road either, for Philip Griffiths lurked there ready to bash me simply because he was a year older than I was or because I preferred Eldorado ice cream to Wall's, or because I considered J. C. Clay a better bowler than Verity. Worse, after dark, coming home that way I had to pass St Margaret's Church graveyard where ghosts, magnified amoebae, slipped their chains so that between lamp-posts I would have to run faster than my own long shadow.

No, west was best. The direction of a 2A tram to Victoria Park where Billy the Seal swam in pond water that needed a wash and where nearby, in a house called Mon Repos, lived Margaret Williams who wore no knickers.

West is best. I'd go that way 'into town' when mitching from school so that I could hide in the echoing acoustics of the National Museum where I would stare for hours at the illuminated tanks of tropical fish or at the glass-eyed stuffed animals caught forever in petrified movement. West was the direction of pleasure. Summer holidays and occasional Sundays my father would drive us to the nearby grey sullen sea of Penarth or Cold Knap or Ogmore-by-Sea or Porthcawl. Or back to where my mother was born – Ystalyfera – where she would converse in Welsh while the rest of us would listen without passports.

West was also the direction of religion. For I would have to travel that way to reach Windsor Place Synagogue and to that piece of holy ground near the secretive River Taff. That ground, where even tries were converted, was called Cardiff Arms Park, and there huge crowds would religiously sing 'Land of My Fathers', a national anthem that is half a dirge and half a battle cry.

I suppose most youngsters vacillate between fear and happiness. Midway is boredom. And boredom, too, is big on the map of Cardiff, for it is a rainy city where children press their noses against window glass and whine, 'Mama, what shall I do now? What can I play now?' But when the sun is out, what a handsome city Cardiff is. When I return there now and loiter a bit – say at Roath Park Lake where I regularly swam as a boy until I got a duckshit rash – I am surprised how naturally beautiful are those places I once played in. I never realized this as a schoolboy. Few of us when young are enraptured by nature as Wordsworth was. (Don't your children sitting in the back seat of the car – when you cry, 'Look! Look!' at a sunset or some dizzy vista – continue to quarrel or read their comics?) I certainly did not realize how charming are the corners of Cardiff.

But it's a long time ago now since, standing below Cardiff Castle, I was Robin Hood halfway up the tower – which I remember one guide saying was built in the sixteenth century, oh aye, during Queen Victoria's reign. And it's a long time since I first stood on the terraces of Ninian Park when Cardiff City was bottom of Division 3 (South) and the brass band played 'Happy Days are Here Again' while I imagined myself to be their new signing about to change the soccer destiny of Wales.

Such triumphs would make 'them' put up a blue plaque for me like they did for Ivor Novello on that house he once occupied in Cowbridge Road. But they would have a problem. Which house would they choose? Would it be 289, 237 or 66 Albany Road? Or 66 Sandringham Road, or 66 Vaughan Avenue in Llandaff, or that house in Windermere Avenue half bombed during the Second World War (while I was in it) or 198 Cathedral Road? (Cathedral Road was once the 'Arley Street of Cardiff, mun).

Well, since I'm dreaming why shouldn't I go the whole hog? Let them put blue plaques on the lot. Yes, so many blue plaques with the words: 'Family Abse, wandering Welsh Jews, lived here.'

2

It was a pilot programme for London Weekend Television titled *Friends of John Betjeman*. I could not claim to be a friend of Sir John. I had not previously met him. No matter; here I was in the studio invited to read a few poems of my own and to chat with John Betjeman about verse that he had selected. The technicians were messing about. It would be an hour yet before we'd wear artificial smiles and the programme would begin. 'The first poem I've chosen,' said Sir John, 'is by Hood.' He didn't mean Robin Hood. It so happened that I had recently read a strange long poem by Thomas Hood called 'Miss Kilmansegg and Her Precious Leg'. I asked Sir John whether he knew it. He knew it very well. With surprising passion he turned to me as if I had given him something he had wanted all his life. 'How *very* good of you to know that poem,' he cried out. 'Oh, thank you, thank you very much.' Suspiciously, I

smiled. But John Betjeman was being quite sincere; he was sincerely
grateful that another individual had read and liked a poem he knew
and cared for. He continued to thank me rhapsodically and his eyes
glittered with pleasure as we discussed the merits of Thomas Hood's
poetry. 'The poem I've chosen of Hood's,' said Sir John, 'is "I
remember, I remember the house where I was born". Some may
think it sentimental but it isn't, it isn't and I don't care if it is!' Staring
straight ahead he chanted those extraordinary lines that, at first, I
thought twee until I really listened. Then I realized how the rhythm
of the poem lulled me and half disguised the terrible pessimism and
depression that engined the remembrances:

> I remember, I remember,
> The house where I was born,
> The little window where the sun
> Came peeping in at morn;
> He never came a wink too soon,
> Nor brought too long a day,
> But now, I often wish the night
> Had borne my breath away!
>
> I remember, I remember,
> The roses, red and white,
> The violets, and the lily-cups,
> Those flowers made of light!
> The lilacs where the robin built,
> And where my brother set
> The laburnum on his birthday, –
> The tree is living yet!
>
> I remember, I remember,
> Where I was used to swing,
> And thought the air must rush as fresh
> To swallows on the wing;
> My spirit flew in feathers then,
> That is so heavy now,
> And summer pools could hardly cool
> The fever on my brow!
>
> I remember, I remember,
> The fir-trees dark and high;
> I used to think their slender tops
> Were close against the sky:
> It was a childish ignorance,
> But now 'tis little joy

To know I'm farther off from heav'n
Than when I was a boy.

I couldn't remember the house where I was born. All I knew about 161 Whitchurch Road in Cardiff was that my parents labelled it 'The Smoky House'. That was because the chimney needed sweeping and since we were about to move my mother never bothered to summon the sweep. I don't recall the house being smoky. I do recall (my first memory I think) that I was being looked after by my big brother Wilfred. He is with me and I am somewhere (in a pram?) and looking through railings at green stuff (a park?). Well, Cardiff is a city of pram-filled parks and perhaps anyone born in Cardiff has a similar early memory. What else? I remember, I remember bugger all.

After the programme John Betjeman remarked, 'One day you should go back and visit the house where *you* were born.' I nodded. Why not? One day I would. I'd knock on the door of the smoky house in Whitchurch Road. 'Here I am,' I'd say. I would knock on the door of 289 Albany Road too. Audaciously, perhaps, I'd visit all those Cardiff houses we had once lived in. Middle-aged I would breathe in air I had once breathed out. The more I thought about it the more I resolved to go back to my own beginnings. I even fixed a date for that nostalgic mission: Monday, 29 May, the bank holiday. Then if I hadn't changed my mind, if my enthusiasm had not entirely evaporated, I would travel the twenty-three miles from Ogmore-by-Sea to the Smoky House which, like a hero, I would enter unarmed.

29 May proved to be a rare day, perfect weather. Do you remember what you did on that blue, beautiful bank holiday, 29 May 1978? Remember the mirages on the roads? Perhaps you were in one of those innumerable cars that travelled to Ogmore-by-Sea? If so, I could have passed you as I travelled eastward from Ogmore, where I think I was conceived, to Cardiff where I know I was born.

Frankly, 161 Whitchurch Road, a plain two-storeyed, semi-detached house, would hardly excite anyone, least of all Sir John. I sat in the car in the bank-holiday-empty Whitchurch Road at 10.30 a.m. and gave the Smoky House the eye. It didn't look as if it would last long enough to have that blue plaque on its grey facade: 'Dannie Abse, Cardiff City FC supporter, was born here, poor chap.' I quit the car and approached the front door. There, I was baffled. Two bells! The Smoky House had been turned into two self-contained flats. Which bell to ring, bottom or top? Eeny meeny miney mo – bottom bell. I was lucky: a young, dazzlingly pretty woman with dark, closely cut, curly hair wearing very short tennis shorts opened the door. Yes, I thought, it *is* worth knocking on doors, banging on bells, being a commercial traveller, a vote canvasser, a Jehovah's Witness. I explained my mission and, yes, I could come in and look around providing her flatmate agreed. Would I excuse her while she consulted her flatmate? Her flatmate, another young woman in her twenties, appeared and I smiled at her, my teeth cleaned. Hesitatingly, the other young lady agreed. Perhaps I did look like a burglar casing the joint. Three inquisitive cats also materialized, six unblinking yellow eyes. The grate, I noted, had been converted into an electric fire – no more smoky chimneys. In the front room I loitered, trying to feel something, anything. Here my parents, no doubt, entertained the occasional important visitor and brought out the best crockery or offered him or her a glass of sherry with a dainty slice of dried-up Madeira cake? I felt nothing.

The attractive curly-haired girl – her name was Veronica – led me into the bit of a garden in the back where a couple of dozen worn-out bluebells and a dusty lilac tree waited to be appreciated. Vaguely I wondered whether the tree was older than I (the tree is living yet!), then Veronica opened the back door of the garden. A lane and, immediately the other side of that narrow lane, railings. Railings! Railings of a park! I heard a click in my head and Veronica said, 'That's called Maitland Park.'

So now I knew the name of my first memory, and appropriately as I stood there a young couple pushed a baby across the grass towards a building with a red-tiled roof. Despite the trees, I could read the words painted meaninglessly – doubtless by some erring kids – across this roof: 'ANDY, PAT, PAUL'. Just that. And I thought, were these names mere graffiti or plaques? And was there any difference?

3

On the way to 289 Albany Road I stopped the Austin Maxi outside Marlborough Road Elementary School where I had first, wide-eyed and reluctant, begun my so-called education. The school had been bombed during the war but now it looked much the same. It was curiously quiet waiting there in the spreading sunlight – no high, piping, pre-pubertal voices sang 'Ash Grove' or 'Men of Harlech'. And then visions, visions, clear, not even behind glass! Those boys there, playing with coloured glass alleys in the gutter, well, one of them was me and it was almost half a century ago.

'Swap you three of these for your blood alley!' said Philip Griffiths.

And of course that vision faded as soon as it appeared, leaving me though with that sense of vertigo that any grown man may experience when he contemplates Time Past or No Time At All. The uneasiness such as one might feel on staring at a night sky and apprehending infinity. But the sky was blue, blue, blue, and the two streets were empty that were called Marlborough Road and Agincourt Road. When a woman came out of one of the houses she smiled at me knowingly as if she knew why I was there. I didn't have to say to her, 'I went to school here, you know. George Thomas who's now the Speaker in the House of Commons used to teach me – though that's not why I'm so ignorant!'

As a matter of fact, Mr Thomas was particularly kind to me. 'Order, Order,' Mr Thomas now shouts in the House of Commons at all those squealing MPs and 'Order, Order,' shouted the same Mr Thomas, sir, when I first started in the Big Boys.

Before I reached 289 Albany Road I stopped the car again, this time outside St Margaret's Church. Gosh, I was tall enough to look over the graveyard wall. And I had always thought of it as so high, higher than the walls of Troy. Still, I could only *just* see over it: if some one had spotted me from the churchyard he would have only seen the top of my head, my forehead, eyebrows and my eyes, that's all. And, of course, underneath, the appropriate caption, 'Wot, no ghosts?'

Nobody was about. I walked through the gate, across the pathway strewn with multicoloured confetti, then on the turf towards the dark high cedar tree. Where were all the stone angels, stone tablets behind which I had once played hide and seek? As the song goes, where had all the flowers gone? There were a few graves, not many. Most of the daisy-spotted turf lay back, tidy, unmarked. I read one tilting stone visiting card:

> *In Memory of Sig Thomas John of this Parish formerly of the 43rd Reg. He fought under Generals Moore and Wellington through all the late war in the Spanish Peninsula. He was also engaged at Waterloo. Died October 10, 1864, aged 83 years.*

'Thomas John,' I said, 'You're dead.'
'Absent, sir,' he replied.

There were only fifteen graves left in St Margaret's Church. Who had taken the rest away? Who had selected those to remain behind to play for St Margaret's Dead First XV? Here perhaps was the hooker:

In Memory of John Roberts of the Town of Cardiff who died March 11th,
1851.

Before I could say, 'Heel, John,' a telephone sounded from inside
the shut church. It rang and rang. Nobody answered. I watched two
butterflies the same colour as the daisies crookedly float beyond the
cypress tree further and further until they disappeared over the wall
from no-man's-land into the District of Roath. Soon I, too, quit St
Margaret's churchyard.

I was disappointed to find nobody in at 289 Albany Road. I banged
the knocker, rang the bell, uselessly. All the blinds were ominously
drawn upstairs and downstairs. In an empty milk bottle a rolled note
read, 'No milk today.' A note so peremptory, so curt. Why? Had the
owners of 289 gone away for the bank holiday, or had there been a
death in the street? Those drawn curtains, those blinds baldly down.

In the thirties, when there had been a death they blinded the
windows of the house. I remember, I remember, when next-door
Jumbo Thomas's father died. Yes, the blinds had been drawn then
and six black horses had pulled a black hearse away leaving nothing
behind, not even manure. Again I felt the edges of panic as I
remembered. This surely is what the slow movements of all those
quartets, Mozart, Beethoven, Schubert, are about: *loss*. The sound
of loss.

Odd to return to where one was born, to visit a graveyard with most
of the graves gone and now a house that seemed to proclaim it was
mourning for someone. Not for me, surely, not for the boy I was? But
I felt the grey hair on my head rise when I noticed across the road
(where there used to be, behind a white wall, handsome Roath Court
House) a bold sign: 'ROATH COURT FUNERAL HOME'. This was too
apt. *Home*. What a word to use. I fled. No point in visiting any of the
other houses I once had lived in, that had once been home. Nothing
around here remains the same, I thought, except – there beyond St
Margaret's Church – the secret minnow-smelling brook in Waterloo
Gardens moving in the old direction.

The Crowning of Kid Brother

Recently, I sat down to dinner with several friends. They began to talk about birthdays. To my ordinary dismay, I soon discovered that I was the oldest in that room. *Me*. Impossible! Older than those balding heads the other side of the table, that haggard-looking lot? Surely it was only a few subversive summers ago that my mother hummed in the Welsh weather, 'Danny Boy'. Then I *was* a boy, unlike my brothers, Wilfred and Leo, who, almost nine and seven years older than I, were already men. They shaved. They swore. They went out with women. They were privy to secrets I did not know. They had opinions that mattered.

Maybe others who are the last-born also find it difficult to accustom themselves, as I do, to proliferating grey hairs – and have to convince themselves that they can express an opinion about religion or politics without that opinion being immediately discounted. I have one sister. I was only seven when she left home, so, because she hardly knew me as a young teenager, she is likely to respect my opinions. But Wilfred and Leo, they knew me, and today, affectionate as they are, and though allowing me one province of expertise – poetry – about everything else, I sense they won't, they can't, really take me seriously.

After all, when they were aged eighteen and sixteen and arguing the toss about Karl Marx and Sigmund Freud, I was reading the *Gem* and the *Magnet*. In those days, they knew I was a ten-year-old idiot who could not even pronounce *dialectical materialism*, so the hell with it. I wasn't worth talking to. Why should things be different now? I hear their castigating voices still: 'Not "emeny", *enemy*,' said Wilfred. 'Not "cimena", *cinema*,' cried Leo. 'Not "Goath", *Goethe*.'

We youngest children should, by rights, have outsize inferiority feelings. Haven't we all been ridiculed by older siblings? 'Who wrote this, and about whom?' Leo asked me, in his best inquisitor voice:

> Just for a handful of silver he left us,
> Just for a riband to stick in his coat.

I looked around furtively. Yards of silence stretched. 'By Browning,' my brother thundered triumphantly, 'and it's about Wordsworth selling out, becoming poet laureate. Any fool knows that.'

Worse, our ignorance is not merely about literature but about life itself. 'You washed your hair while you were having a bath? In the same bathwater?' Wilfred said, appalled. 'You always do? You mustn't do that. That's not the way to do things. You're ten now, at your age you should know that.'

It was always so, the youngest ignorant and chided by elder brothers. Evidence of it is there in the history books, in the Bible, too, and in those fairy stories that begin, 'Once upon a time, there was a king who had three sons. Two were intelligent, but the youngest was stupid and called Dummling.' The nice thing is – nice if you're the youngest, that is – Dummling, in those fairy stories, always scores in the end. He is helped by earthly magical forces – an animal, a toad, a white cat – and, near the last page, scoops the prize and the Fair Lady. Wonderful. Even when the youngest is a girl, downtrodden, enslaved, wronged and vulnerable, she is finally favoured – seen by all the world as being the virtuous one – and her situation is magically transformed. I close my eyes. The reel of years revolves backwards, and I hear Cordelia say, 'Wasn't I right, Daddy?' Further back still, I see the headlines of a prewar *South Wales Echo*. It reads, 'Cinderella Wins.'

Alfred Adler wrote much about children, according to their order of birth. For instance, he says that the eldest child likes to look back and speak of the good old gone days. Well, the first-born was once, of course, the only child. That was the perfect time, when he was the sole star and had the undivided attention of his parents – when he was the tops, the Colosseum, the Louvre museum … Mickey Mouse. No little beastly Leo to shout, 'Look at me, Dada,' or Dannie Boy yelling, 'Look at me, Mama.' No wonder eldest children are supposed to be admirers of the past, pessimists of the future.

According to Adler, they are also likely to be authoritarian by nature. After all, they would still be the sole star, if some swine hadn't changed the rules. So later, grown up, conservative, they think, 'Everything should be done by rule, and no rule should ever be changed. Power should be preserved in the hands of those who are entitled to it.'

I can imagine all you first-born being irritated by such an analysis. I, being last-born, can find it plausible. I can think to myself, 'What a perspicacious fellow this Dr Alfred Adler is!' Only when he begins talking about the youngest in the family do I find him utterly superficial and wrong-headed! 'No, no,' I say, when he argues that we, the youngest, have been spoilt. 'Pooh, pooh,' I growl, when he maintains that we, the youngest, are often inordinately ambitious, wishing to excel in everything. That's nonsense; I know that from my own experience. When a boy, I only wanted to play cricket for Glamorgan, football for Cardiff City. A really ambitious, nasty chap would have wanted to play cricket for England, football for Wales. True, I daydreamed of being a great pianist, dramatist, physician, poet – who would be applauded by men, adored by women. Perhaps I ought to admit, also, that, now and again, I wanted to live for ever. But such trifling ambitions are hardly inordinate or unusual, surely?

Dr Adler argues that many of the youngest in the family are lazy. What a fool this Adler is! The laziness, apparently, stems from such a vaulting ambition that it just cannot be realized. Since we cannot, say, climb to the top of the mountain, we just lounge about on the lowest slopes, yawning. All kinds of other accusations may be made against the youngest of the family, if that is true. For example, red-hot ambition will inevitably lead to treachery. Sure as eggs, the youngest will betray his elder brother for a mess of pottage, or for the crown of England.

Has it always been thus, all the way back to Jacob? I recall how that smooth conman, his hands wrapped in hairy skins, sat before his blind father, Isaac, and muffling his voice, said, 'I am Esau, thy first-born.' Isaac replied, 'The voice is Jacob's voice, but the hands are the hands of Esau.' No, Jacob could not even adequately impersonate his twin brother's voice. As an actor, he would not even have been cast as an extra in some Hollywood Bible epic; but he fooled Isaac all right, who must have wanted to be fooled, and he betrayed his twin brother, Esau. He was in rivalry with big, hairy brother from the start.

The Bible tells us that the first twin born was Esau, 'and after that came his brother out, and his hand took hold on Esau's heel.' *Esau's heel*, my foot! So Jacob was grasping his brother's heel, right from the beginning, trying to pull him back, or just lazily hanging on for an easy ride.

Supposing we, the youngest children, admit that we are unattractively ambitious, slothful and spoilt, and given to acts of betrayal, surely some benefits must have ensued from our placing in the order of things? I inherited from Wilfred more than his medical textbooks, which always had written on their flyleaf, '*Nil desperandum*'; from Leo I inherited more than a political anger serviced by the paradox of slums and cripples in a world of colours.

I think any youngest child, especially if there is a gap of some years between him and the next, is bound to feel some sense of what it means to be an outsider. What young, sleepy child has not heard, at the top of a dark landing, the sound of music downstairs, the happy voices of brothers and sisters and their friends, enjoined in a loud party – laughter in another room – and not felt excluded? But isn't that, eventually, a cause for celebration rather than lament? I should like to think I have some sympathy for the mavericks and outsiders of our society, for the injured and the snubbed, for the derelicts and the deranged, for those who fail and fall all too humanly; and if I do possess such sympathies, are they not rooted in that shadowy locus at the top of the stairs?

Feeling too much sympathy for the underdog, though, has its ludicrous complications. If you want a man losing to win, and he begins to win, should you then start supporting his adversary instead? First, I am shouting for young David, armed only with a sling as he confronts that toweringly tall champion, Goliath. 'On my right, Goliath, from Gath, height six cubits and a span.' Goliath, his chest huge under the decorated metal armour, will lift a powerful arm to acknowledge the wild cheers of the Philistines, while I weakly shout, 'Boo,' and 'Rubbish.' 'On my left, in his little socks, David, the shepherd boy, height around three cubits and half a span,' and I'm on my feet cheering. But after the whistle blows, and after the stone sinks so shatteringly through Goliath's forehead, my voice evaporates. In silence, I begin to feel sympathy for that ex-champion, that pituitary giant now horizontal on the ground.

When David pulls out Goliath's sword from Goliath's sheath and cuts off Goliath's head, while David's supporters are shouting, 'Easy! Easy!' I begin to consider the shame of Goliath, who will be known throughout time as a loser, as a big lout beaten and humiliated by a mere boy. And, thinking that, I become most myself, the youngest in the family. You see, the youngest, I believe, always wants a draw – eight draws on a Saturday!

Come to think of it, to claim that one has a gift to feel sympathy for underdogs and outcasts implies that one is superior to such people. My claims, I now perceive, are mere boasts. Back to Adler! He suggests that boasting is only one way of hiding unadmitted feelings of inferiority. It seems I have a hell of an inferiority problem – all, no doubt, the result of being the youngest son.

Frankly, though, I prefer Freudian interpretations of human quirkiness – Freud rather than Adler. A psychoanalytic view, for instance, of that Dummling fairy story, demonstrates that the youngest son is victor because he is nearest to his own animal nature. The three sons are seen as representing the superego, the ego, and the id. The youngest son (the id) is in touch directly with his own elemental force, as symbolized by that powerful toad or by that white cat. Though stupid, he is a poet fundamentally, a dreamer in touch with the source of his dreams.

I like that, and the fact that I write poetry may have something to do with my liking. Besides it is all probably true: poets are thought of, by the public, as being shameless, lawless creatures and forever young. Mr X, though he may be over forty, is always described as 'one of Britain's *young* poets'. Even when he is the funeral side of fifty, he is likely to be called 'one of Britain's *younger* poets'.

Poets and the youngest children of families never grow old. We may become grey-haired or bald, we may be wizened, our hands may tremble, our voices become thin as reeds, but this is all just a master disguise. All you have to do, to see us as we really are, is to touch us with a wand. You are fooled, father Isaac. Give us your blessing.

Sorry, Miss Crouch

Whenever my father tucked the violin under his chin and dragged the wavering bow across the strings, his whole countenance would alter. Often with eyes half closed like a lover's, he would lean towards me and play Kreisler's 'Humoresque' with incompetent daring. He was an untutored violinist who, losing patience with himself, would whistle the most difficult bits. I always liked to hear him play the wrong notes and whistle the right ones; and, best of all, I liked his response to my huge, small applause: he would solemnly and elaborately bow. After this surprising theatrical grace he would generally give me an encore.

That August evening he gave me several encores: 'Men of Harlech', 'My Yiddisher Mama' and 'Ash Grove'. Afterwards he said, 'You'll be ten next month – wouldn't you like music lessons?'

I was being offered a birthday present. Psss. I wanted a three-spring cricket bat, like the one M. J. Turnbull, the captain of Glamorgan, used, not music lessons. I didn't want to play a violin.

'The piano,' my father said. 'We have a first-class piano in the front room and nobody in the house uses it. Duw, it's like having a Rolls-Royce without an engine. Useless. If your mother wants something for decoration she can have an aspidistra.' He replaced his violin in its case. 'Yes,' he continued. 'You can have lessons. You'd like that, wouldn't you, son?'

'No, don't want any,' I said firmly.

'All right,' he said, 'we'll arrange for Miss Crouch to come and give you piano lessons every Thursday.'

When my mother told me I could have a cricket bat as well, I was somewhat mollified. Besides, secretly I was hoping Miss Crouch would look like a film star. Alas, several Thursdays later I discovered I disliked piano lessons intensely and mild, thin, tut-tutting Miss Crouch did not resemble Myrna Loy or Kay Francis. The summer was almost over and on those long Thursday evenings I wanted to be out and about playing cricket with my friends in the park. So, soon, when Miss Crouch was at the front door, her pianist's hand on the bell, I was doing a swift bunk at the back, my right, cunning cricket hand grasping the top of the wall that separated our garden from the back lane. My running footsteps followed me all the way to Waterloo Gardens with its minnow-smelly brook and the pointless shouts of other children in the cool suggestions of a September evening. In the summerhouse my penknife wrote my first poem – I expect it's still there – 'MISS CROUCH IS A SLOUCH'.

My father was uncharacteristically stern about me ditching Miss Crouch. For days he grumbled about my lack of politeness, insensitivity and musical ignorance. 'He's only ten,' my mother defended me. On Sunday, he was so accusatory and touchy that when all the family decided to motor to the seaside I said cleverly, 'Can't come, I have to practise for Miss Crouch on the bloomin' piano.' They laughed, I didn't know why. And now even more annoyed, I resolutely refused to go to Ogmore-by-Sea.

'We'll go to Penarth,' my father said, a little more conciliatory. 'I'll fish from the pier for a change.'

'Got to practise scales,' I said, pushing my luck.

'Right,' my father suddenly snapped. 'The rest of you get ready, that boy's spoilt.'

My mother, of course, would not hear of them leaving me, the baby of the family, at home on my own. However, I was stubborn and now my father was adamant. Unwillingly, my mother, at last, planted a wet kiss on my sulky cheeks and the front door banged with goodbyes and 'We won't be long.' Incredible – hard to believe such malpractice – but they actually took me at my word, left me there in the empty front room, sitting miserably on the piano stool. 'What a rotten lot!' I said out loud and brought my two clenched fists onto the piano keys to make the loudest noise the piano, so far, had ever managed to emit. It seemed minutes before the vibrations fell away, descended, crumbled, into the silence that gathered around the tick of the front-room clock. Then, as I stood up from the piano stool, the front door bell rang and cheerfully I thought, 'They've come back for me. This time I'll let them persuade me to come to Penarth.' I'd settle for special icecream, a banana split or a peach melba. Maybe I'd go the whole hog and suggest a knickerbocker glory. Why not? It hadn't been *my* idea to learn the piano as a birthday present. Not only that, *they* had abandoned me, and in their ten minutes of indecision I could have *died*. I could have been *electrocuted* by a faulty plug. I could have fallen down the stairs and broken *both my legs*. It would have served them right.

I opened the front door to see my tall second cousin. Or was Adam Shepherd my third cousin? Anyway, we were related because he called my mother Auntie Katie and he, in turn, was criticized with a gusto only reserved for relatives. Father had indicated he was the best-looking member of the Shepherd family (excluding my mother, of course), but he was girl-mad. 'Girl-mad,' my mother would echo him. 'He needs bromides.'

Standing there, though, he looked pleasantly sane. And, suddenly, I needed to swallow. I would have cried except big boys don't cry. 'What's the matter?' he asked, coming into the hall, breathing in its sweet biscuity smell. I told him about Miss Crouch and my birthday, about piano scales and how I had scaled the wall, about them leaving me behind, the rotters.

'Get your swimming stuff,' Adam interrupted me. 'We'll go for a swim in Cold Knap, it'll be my birthday present to you.'

'Can we go to Ogmore, Adam?' I asked.

Less than a half-hour later in Adam Shepherd's second-hand bull-nosed Morris we had chugged out of Ely and now were in the open country. Adam was really nice for a grown-up. (He was twenty-one.)

'Why do girls drive you crazy?' I asked him.

It was getting late but people were reluctant to leave the beach. There was going to be one of those spectacular Ogmore sunsets. Adam and I had dressed after our swim and we walked to the edge of the sea. There must still have been a hundred people behind us, spread out like a sparse carnival on the rocks and sand. We were standing close to the small waves collapsing at our feet when suddenly a man began singing a hymn in Welsh. Soon a group around him joined in. Now those on the other side of the beach also began to sing. Everybody on the beach, strangers to each other, all sang *together*. When the man who had begun singing sung on his own the hymn sounded sad. Not now. The music was thrilling and I wished I could play the piano – if only one could play without having to practise.

Adam kept telling me that those on the beach were behaving uncharacteristically. 'Like stage Welshmen,' he said. 'This is like a pathetic English B film. It's as if they've been rehearsed.' But then

Adam himself joined in the hymn. In no time at all, somehow, he was next to a pretty girl who was singing like billyo. I had noticed how he'd been glancing at that particular girl even before we went swimming.

'You look like a music teacher,' he said to the girl and he winked at me. Consulting me, he continued, 'She doesn't look like Miss Crouch, I bet?'

'Miss Crouch, who's she?' the girl asked.

Their conversation was daft. I gave up listening and threw pebbles into the waves. I thought about what Adam said – about the singing, like a film. I had been to the cinema many times. I'd seen Al Jolson. And between films, when the organ suddenly rose triumphantly from the pit, it changed its colours just like the sky was slowly doing now – the Odeon sky. Amber, pink, green, mauve. My mother had a yellow chiffon scarf, a very yellow scarf, and she sometimes wore with it an amber necklace from Poland. I don't know why I thought of that. I thought of them anyway, my parents, and soon they would be returning from Penarth. It was getting late. I went back to Adam and to the girl whom he now called Sheila. 'I'm hungry, Adam,' I said. 'We ought to go home.'

Adam gave me money to buy icecream and crisps so I left them on the beach and I climbed up on the worn turf between the ferns and an elephant-grey wall. At the top, on the other side of the road, all round Hardee's Café, sheep were pulling audibly at the turf. One lifted its head momentarily and stared at me. I stared it out.

I took the icecream and crisps and sat on a green wooden bench conveniently placed outside the café. Down, far below, the sea was all dazzle, black and gold. Nearer, on the road, the cars, beginning to leave Ogmore now, had their side lamps on. Fords, Austin Sevens, Morris Cowleys, Wolseleys, Rovers, Alvises, Rileys, even a Fiat. I was very good at recognizing cars. Then I remembered my parents and felt uneasy. If they returned from Penarth and found me missing, after a while they'd become cross. I'd make it up to them. I'd practise on the piano. I'd tell them about the singing at Ogmore. They'd be interested in that. 'Everybody sang like in a film, honest.'

When I returned to the beach the darkness was coming out of the sea. All the people had quit except Adam and Sheila. It seemed she had lost something because Adam was looking for it in her blouse. They did not seem pleased to see me. Unwillingly they stood up and, for a moment, gazed towards the horizon. A lighthouse explosion became glitteringly visible before being swiftly deleted. It sent no long message to any ship, but another lighthouse, further out at sea, in the distance, nearer the Somerset coast, brightly and briefly replied.

'They'll be worried 'bout me,' I said to Adam.

'They'll be worried about him at home,' Adam told Sheila. She nodded and took Adam's hand. Then my big cousin said in a very odd, gentle voice, 'You go to the car. We'll follow you shortly.'

So I left them and when I looked back it was like the end of a film for they were kissing and any second now the words THE END would appear. I waited inside the car for *hours*. Adam was awful. Earlier he had been nice, driven me to Ogmore, swum with me, messed around, played word games. Icecream. Crisps. It was the girl, I thought. Because of the girl he had gone mad again, temporarily. When he did eventually turn up at the car, on his own, pulling at his tie, he never even said, 'Sorry!'

Returning to Cardiff from Ogmore usually was like being part of a convoy. There'd be so many cars going down the A48. And we'd sing in our car – 'Stormy Weather' or 'Mad About the Boy,' or 'Can't Give You Anything But Love, Baby'. But it was late and there were hardly any cars at all. Adam didn't even hum. He seemed anxious. 'Your father and mother will bawl me out for keeping you up so late,' he said.

Yes, it was *years* after my bedtime. If I hadn't been such a big boy I would have had trouble keeping my eyes open.

'We'll have to tell them we've been to Ogmore,' said Adam gloomily. 'We'll have to say the car broke down, okay?'

Near Cowbridge, we overtook a car where someone with a hat pulled down to his ears was sitting in the dickey. We followed its red rear light for a mile or two before passing it. Then we followed our own headlights into the darkness. There was only the sound of the tyres and the insects clicking against the fast windscreen.

Adam wished we were on the phone. So did I. David Thomas, my friend, was on the phone. So were Uncle Max and Uncle Joe, but they were doctors. You needed a phone if you were a doctor. People had to ring up and say, 'I'm ill, doctor, I've got measles.' I wished we had a phone rather than a piano.

'Have you a good span?' I asked Adam.

'Mmmm?'

'To play an octave?'

At last we arrived in Cardiff, into its mood of emptiness and Sunday night. Shops dark, cinemas and pubs all closed. At Newport

Road we caught up with a late tram, a number 2A, which with its few passengers was bound for the terminus. Blue-white lights sparked from its pulley on the overhead wires. After overtaking it we turned left at the white wall and passed St Margaret's Church and its graveyard where sometimes David Thomas and I would play hide-and-seek.

'Albany Road,' I said.

'Right,' said Adam. 'Don't worry. Don't say too much. I'll come in and explain about us having a puncture.'

'What puncture, Adam?' I asked.

He parked the car, peered at his wristwatch under the poor lamplight. 'Christ, it's twenty to eleven,' he groaned. He needn't worry, I thought. When I told them that from now on I'd practise properly they would let us off with a warning.

When Adam rang the bell the electric quickly went on in the hall to make transparent the coloured glass of the lead lights in the front door. Then the door opened and I saw my mother's face . . . *drastic*. At once she grabbed me to her as if I were about to fall down. 'My poor boy,' she half sobbed.

In our living room she explained how worried they had all been. They made an especial point of returning early from Penarth and I had . . . 'Gone . . . *gone*,' said my mother melodramatically. Later it seemed they had all searched for me in the streets, the back lanes, the park, and she had even called at David Thomas's house to see if I was there.

'You didn't have to run off just because you don't like piano lessons,' my mother said, scolding us.

'I don't like piano lessons,' I said, 'but –'

'He didn't run off,' Adam said, interrupting me. 'We had a puncture, Auntie.'

When my mother told Adam that, as a last resort, they had all gone to the police station, and that's where they were now, Adam became curiously emotional. He even made an exit from our living room backwards. 'Gotter get back,' he muttered, 'I'm sorry, Aunt Katie.' Poor Adam, girl-mad.

Before I went to bed my mother gave me bananas and cream and she mashed up the bananas for me like she used to – as if I were a kid again.

'I'll speak to your father about the piano when he comes in,' my mother said masterfully. 'Whatever he says, no more piano lessons for you. So don't fret. No need to run away again.'

I was in bed and asleep before the family returned from the police station. And over breakfast my father, at first, didn't say anything – not until he had drunk his second cup of tea. Then he declared authoritatively, 'I'm not wasting any more good money on any damn music lessons for you. As for the damn piano, it can be sold.' My father said this looking at my mother with rage as if she might contradict him. 'If this dunce, by 'ere,' he continued, 'can't learn the piano from a nice lady, a capable musician like Miss Crouch, well not even Solomon could teach him.'

My mother laughed mockingly. 'Ha ha ha, Solomon! Solomon was wise but he never played the piano. Ha ha ha, Solomon indeed, ha ha ha. Your father, I don't know.'

'Why are you closing your eyes?' I asked my father.

It was time to go to school. I had to kiss Dad on the cheek. As usual, he smelt of tobacco and his chin was sandpaper rough. But he ruffled my hair, signifying that we were friends once more.

'I hate Mondays,' I said.

'Washing day. I loathe them too,' said my mother.

Miss Crouch never came to our house again. And it was almost a week before Dad took down his violin and played 'Humoresque'. I didn't listen properly. I was waiting for him to finish so that I could ask him if, after we had sold the piano, we could have a telephone installed instead – like they had in David Thomas's house.

A Skull in the Wardrobe

Half the family are doctors. There is my eldest brother Wilfred, my father's brother Max, my mother's brother Joe. There are my two Ammanford cousins and also two other cousins from Cardiff, Michael and Jack. So when the family meets on those rare ceremonial occasions of celebration or lament, it is less a family gathering than a medical conference.

In 1937, when I, a small boy, said, 'I wouldn't mind being a vet' – the cat lay motionless on its cushion on the carpet, its electric eyes staring at nothing, and would not sip even a little of the warm milk I was offering it – my brother Wilfred said masterfully that I might as well become, like so many others in the family, a doctor. 'Sick people,' he maintained with the authority of one who had read *Twelve Great Philosophers*, 'are more important than sick animals.' I stared unhappily at the cat while my father, overhearing our conversation, teased, 'You think this duffer has enough intelligence to become a doctor?' My eldest brother replied without irony, 'All you need is average intelligence to become a doctor. He'll manage it. We ought to think seriously about putting his name down for the new West-minster Hospital medical school that they are planning.'

My mother used to say, 'Dannie never thinks of tomorrow.' She was wrong. I did and I do. But I rarely think of the day after tomorrow. That is why, perhaps, I have always resisted the idea of buying life insurance and that is certainly why, also, since the question of what-are-you-going-to-be-when-you-grow-up had been solved, I thought more of being a medical student than a doctor.

Wilfred had just qualified. For years I had heard about medical student experiences and pranks. Had not Wilfred cured a baffling case of hysterical blindness through hypnosis? (Wilfred was going to be a psychiatrist.) And only eighteen months earlier Wilfred had been doing his midwifery and the telephone had sounded *after midnight*. That's how important it was to be a medical student.

True, on that occasion, Wilfred had to go to a house in Zinc Street to deliver a baby. The voice commanding him to do so had, apparently, been Welsh and urgent and hoarse. So my big brother, hero Wilfred, with his little black bag, climbed on to his bicycle and made for Splott. He did not know that Mr and Mrs Jones of Zinc Street had only just married, were still on their blissful honeymoon, and had no immediate plans to have a baby. He did not know that the hoarse, urgent, Welsh voice was that of another medical student conning him.

It was raining in the district of Roath, Cardiff, where we lived then and from where Wilfred set out, and it was raining in the district of Splott, Cardiff, when he arrived on his bicycle, flustered and damp, at a dark door in Zinc Street. Clutching his little black bag he banged at the front door till a light went on upstairs, then a light in the hall, and finally the door opened to a sleepy, burly, tall lock forward in pyjamas asking, 'Mmmm?'

'Where's your wife, Mr Jones?' asked Wilfred.

'Upstairs in bed,' replied the burly man, surprised.

And he was even more surprised when Wilfred said, 'Good,' as he pushed past him and ran up the stairs enthusiastically.

Yes, I thought, it may be fun to become a medical student, to mess around like that, and save every now and then one or two lives! I fancied myself walking down Queen Street with a stethoscope sticking, like a credential, out of my pocket.

Some years later, in 1941, during my last year in school when I was studying those pre-medical subjects, biology, chemistry and physics, I was to hear much more about the crises and practical jokes of 'med' students. Three of my friends – a year older than I – were already at the Welsh National School of Medicine. When I joined them at their students' union to play poker they were full of medical gossip: how Spud Taylor after a rectal examination on a woman had diagnosed, to the delight of the other students, an enlarged prostate; better still, how Tonker Davies had cut off a penis from one of the cadavers in the anatomy room, put it in his trouser pocket before going to a student dance and, eventually, when the last waltz was being played – 'Any umbrellas, any umberellas, don't mind the rain' – Tonker had pulled it out of his trousers much to the consternation of his partner!

Such was the tenor of the conversations of these friends of mine, these first-year medical students. Their talk was frequently anecdotal in that way, bawdy or about sport. They were never philosophical while sober. As the record turned on the Medical Students' Union radiogram and Dinah Shore sang 'Body and Soul' or 'Smoke Gets in Your Eyes' or 'Sophisticated Lady', I never heard any of those poker players vulnerably say why he wanted to become a doctor or confess to aspirations of doing good in the world. They pondered on nothing more awesome than a Royal Flush. Or so it seemed. As for me, though I was beginning to write poetry (I was told it was 'just a phase'), I felt happy in the company of such friends. I certainly did not feel like the composer Berlioz who had written, 'Become a doctor! Study anatomy! dissect! witness horrible operations . . . Forsake the empyrean for the dreary realities of earth! the immortal angels of poetry and love and their inspired songs for filthy hospitals, dreadful medical students . . .'

No, I wanted to become one of those dreadful medical students myself. My regret was that I could not stay at home and study at the Welsh National School of Medicine. Finally, though, I did not so much leave home as home left me! For, during a February air raid (the night turned luminous green because of flares), it seemed some German pilot mistook Roath Park Lake for Cardiff Docks and bomb after bomb whistled down to cause explosions followed by lonely silences. The house next door disappeared and part of our house collapsed. Injured, I was taken to Bridgend Cottage Hospital where I was looked after by one of my Ammanford cousins. 'Look after this boy,' he kept winking at the nurses, 'he's valuable, he's going to become a doctor.'

Nineteen months later, in September – that month of cool suggestions and pleasant sunlight a shade too yellow – I arrived in wartime London, the train doors in Paddington station banging behind me like gunshot reports. My cases made my arms long for they contained not only predictable contents but my brother's weighty medical textbooks and the half-skeleton he had bequeathed me.

These I unpacked in a boarding-house room in Swiss Cottage. I put the femur, tibia, the armbones, the wired foot, the wired hand and the skull in the wardrobe and the textbooks – on the flyleaf of each was written, 'D. Wilfred Abse, *Nil Desperandum*' – on the mantelpiece. I was ready 'to go', ready to begin my studies at King's College in the Strand where Westminster Hospital students, along with those from Charing Cross Hospital, King's College Hospital and St George's Hospital, spent their pre-clinical years.

King's College in the Strand was cold, shabby, capacious and murky. It sounded of footsteps on linoleum and stone. Even when no one was about, the place sounded of ghosts in slippers. It smelt of stone and the nineteenth century. Because of air raids, most students, other than the medics, had been evacuated to provincial cities, so it was more obviously empty, stony, murky than ever. My first ordeal was to firewatch on the roof of King's one moonless night when the air-raid siren had sounded. The second ordeal, a daytime one, was to enter the anatomy dissecting room and to be assigned one half of a male body.

The formalin that preserves the cadavers pricks the eyes and has a reeking odour that seeps insidiously, pervasively, into one's clothes. And the cadavers themselves seemed so helpless and naked! Still I did not bolt as Berlioz had done in his day. 'Robert,' wrote Berlioz, 'asked me to accompany him to the Dissecting Room at the Hôpital de la Pitié. When I entered that fearful charnel-house, littered with fragments of limbs, and saw the ghastly faces and cloven heads, the bloody cesspools in which we stood, with its reeking atmosphere, the swarms of sparrows fighting for scrapings and rats in the corners gnawing bleeding vertebrae, such a feeling of horror possessed me that I leapt out of the window as though Death and all his hideous crew were at my heels.'

Revulsion does not endure. I remember how, a few weeks after the commencement of our anatomy course, I observed one student, who earlier had been particularly fastidious, drop his lit cigarette accidentally into the open cavity of a dead abdomen; then, unthinkingly, he picked his cigarette up, put it back in his mouth and went on dissecting with no sense of disquiet or disgust. The medical student soon forgets that the body he is dissecting was once alive. It becomes a model. Later I was to learn, during my clinical years, the live patient in the same way would often become a 'case'.

I did not enjoy anatomy; it was a chore to commit to memory the coloured plates of the anatomy book, to recall in detail, and as clearly as an eidetic image, the Rembrandt painting one had made for oneself by laying bare muscles, tendons, arteries and nerves of a body that gradually became smaller and smaller as it was dissected away. That I had to spend so many hours in the anatomy room, that students everywhere had to learn in minute detail the anatomy of the human body (and embryology) seemed ridiculous to me. By the time we qualified most of us would have forgotten all but the most important details. Now I know that this cloudy remembrance of the subject makes us no worse doctors, for the knowledge we acquired so obsessively, and at such pains, and that we lost with such felicity, is quite useless for the most part in the general practice of medicine. Even those who, as postgraduates, specialize in surgery, have to relearn the subject.

It amuses me, as I write this, to try and remember the vessels and nerves close to the ankle – I have worked in a chest clinic for years – but all I can recall is the mnemonic that helped me to pass a viva: Please Don't Vaseline Nellie's Hair. The *V*, I suppose, stood for one vein or another and *Nellie* for a nerve the name of which, at present, I cannot recall.

I preferred the physiology lectures. Professor MacDowell entertained us. 'We have three instincts,' he would say, 'three instincts, gentlemen. One could call them the three *F*s: fear, food and reproduction.' It seemed Professor MacDowell would sometimes be consulted by patients concerned about their hearts. But that year, for reasons of wartime economy, the lifts at King's were not working and the Professor's office was high, high up, close to the roof. Thus the heart patients had to climb all those endless stone steps.

'I don't have to examine them when they reach my door,' he said. 'If they make it that proves their hearts are sound; if not, then it's just a question of writing out the death certificate.'

In the early summer of 1944 I took my anatomy and physiology examinations. I passed them and so at last entered Westminster Hospital where I could wear a white coat with a stethoscope sticking out of its pocket. It was the time of the doodlebugs and suddenly there was I in the Casualty Department, hopelessly at a loss, while some stricken woman, lacerated to pieces by flying glass, was lifted from a stretcher in great pain and just kept on saying over and over, 'Oh God, oh dear, oh God, oh dear, oh dear, oh dear, oh God.'

I wonder how many medical students during the war had a sense of guilt. I had sometimes. My brother Wilfred was in the army in India, and my brother Leo in the RAF in Egypt. My cousin Sydney had been killed at Dunkirk. All my old friends, other than medical students, were in the services except those few who had already died '*pro patria*'. In some ways one's vague sense of guilt in being allowed to complete one's studies was mitigated by working unnecessarily long hours in Casualty, assisting the harassed doctors even if it was only by putting in stitches and bandaging, by tapping hydroceles, or giving gas and oxygen anaesthetics.

One afternoon, escaping from Casualty, I attended Psychiatric Outpatients. Wilfred in a letter had suggested, 'Make yourself

known to Dr Ewing whom I know quite well.' But that after-
noon another psychiatrist was taking Outpatients. He had a strong
Viennese accent, a most reassuring thing in a psychiatrist, and he
seemed pleased to see me. In fact he was enthusiastic. 'You can take
Outpatients yourself,' he beamed. 'You've come just in time.' Star-
tled, I explained that I had only been at Westminster Hospital three
weeks or so and did not feel capable of taking on any Outpatients,
never mind psychiatric ones. 'I haf to be somevere at three,' he said.
'It is good. And don't vorry, you know how to take a case history, yes?
Zen take a case history and zen tell them to return next week ven I vill
see them myself.' Even as I was objecting he was racing for the door
shouting, 'Nurse! Nurse!'

So, wearing a white coat, I sat behind a desk like a real doctor and
the nurse sent in the first patient for me to see. My very own first
patient. I knew how to take a case history. Only a week earlier I had
been taught that in Casualty. First you had to put down *Complaining
of*, and then you asked the patient, 'What are you complaining of?'
and the patient would say, 'I have a pain here in my left chest, doctor,
that comes on after exercise.' And so you would write that down
opposite *Complaining of*. It was quite simple really. Then there were
other headings such as *Past History*, *Present History* and so on. Easy as
winking. Except my first patient complained of his wife. 'She gets up
in the middle of the night,' he told me, 'because she reckons she
hears voices. Then she walks up and down, walks up and down for
hours and hours. I can't stand it.' After listening to his grumbles,
inspired I said, 'Now I want you to bring your wife here next week
and then we'll sort things out.' To my horror he replied, 'But she's
outside, doctor. She's come along with me.' It was evident that I had
to see her so, swallowing, I nodded and said, 'Then I'll see her right
away. Would you mind waiting outside?'

His wife baffled me. She complained of her husband. 'He says he
hears voices and gets up in the middle of the night and walks up and
down remorselessly for hours. I can't bear it,' she said.

I did not know which one was crazy, who was hallucinating, which
one was telling the truth. On her case-history sheet I wrote 'com-
plaining of her husband's strange insomnia' and on his case-history
sheet I wrote 'complaining of his wife's strange insomnia'. And the
following week I never came back when they came back and I
avoided that Viennese doctor ever after. The great thing was they
both had called me 'doctor'. Neither of them called me 'sonny'.

In the autumn I joined my first medical firm and attended ward rounds. A dozen white-coated students on the firm would accompany the white-coated consultant physician, his white-coated registrar, his white-coated house physician, into the ward where sister and nurses fussed next to the beds of those patients who were to be examined and demonstrated to us. The consultant would walk two inches above the parquet floors unaided while the rest of us laughed at his quips, fawned, nodded wonderfully at his aphorisms. 'One finger in the throat and one in the rectum makes a good diagnostician,' the consultant said, quoting Sir William Osler, and some of us remembered another saying of Osler's which was, 'Look wise, say nothing, and grunt.' I often had to grunt when cross-examined on ward rounds.

Occasionally I would identify too much with the patient. I remember frequently worrying as we withdrew to the corner of the ward to discuss Mr Brown's symptoms that he, over there, half supine in bed, staring at us, would overhear low voices muttering 'malignant' or 'progressive'. However kind, consultants were not invariably tactful.

Indeed, on one occasion, as we stood around the bed of a patient whose history had been related to us in detail, I was asked to hazard a diagnosis. 'A duodenal ulcer,' I suggested. The patient smiled at me benignly. The consultant shook his head. 'No, Mr Green hasn't a duodenal ulcer. He has a chronic gastritis. You need to have some intelligence to have a duodenal ulcer, don't you, Mr Green?' Mr Green laughed – perhaps it was the laughter of contained aggression, I don't know. But he laughed and the students laughed a second later, so did the house physician, and the registrar, and the consultant most of all. 'Yes,' said the consultant, patting Mr Green's shoulders as if he were a good boy. 'Ha ha ha. You're lucky. You're too stupid to have an ulcer.' As we walked towards the next patient I looked back. Mr Green's head lay on the pillow. His eyes were closed.

A few weeks later, one afternoon while the firm waited for that same consultant who for some reason that day had been delayed, his registrar decided to teach us a singularly important principle of medicine. He asked a nurse to fetch him a sample of urine. He then talked to us about diabetes mellitus. '*Diabetes*,' he said, 'is a Greek name; but the Romans noticed that bees liked the urine of diabetics so they added the word *mellitus* which means sweet as honey. Well, as you know, you may find sugar in the urine of a diabetic.' By now the nurse had returned with a sample of urine which the registrar promptly held up like a trophy. We stared at that straw-coloured

fluid as if we had never seen such a thing before. The registrar then
startled us. He dipped a finger boldly into the urine then licked that
finger with the tip of his tongue. As if tasting wine he opened and
closed his lips rapidly. Could he perhaps detect a faint taste of sugar?
The sample was passed on to us for an opinion. We all dipped a
finger into the fluid, all of us foolishly licked that finger. 'Now,' said
the registrar grinning, 'you have learnt the first principle of diagno-
sis. I mean the power of observation.' We were baffled. We stood
near the sluice room outside the ward and in the distance, some
anonymous patient was explosively coughing. 'You see,' the registrar
continued triumphantly, 'I dipped my *middle* finger into the urine but
licked my *index* finger – not like you chaps.'

Apart from ward rounds, I also attended lectures. I do not know
now, objectively, whether they were tedious and badly presented, or
whether it was simply that I was a poor listener. But Dr Ernie Lloyd's
introductory lecture I found memorable. I did not know then that he
delivered this same lecture in the same way every year. Ernie could
have been a stage Welshman. He looked more like Lloyd George
than Lloyd George did, and certainly he was just as histrionic.

He began in his sing-song accent, 'Today I shall talk to you about
the heart, the old heart. It beats, do you see, seventy, duw, eighty
times a minute; minute in, minute out; hour in, hour out; week in,
week out; month in, month out; year in, year out. The old heart.' And
as his incantation continued he used his hands like a conductor as if
we, his audience, were a silent orchestra. I hear his voice still: 'And
the sound, oh the sound of a mitral murmur, it is like, oh aye, it is like
. . . the wind; the wind rustlin' gently through the corn [Long pause]
Po-etic, isn't it, boys?' At Outpatients, I learned many things from
him – also 'facts' that later I was to discover were quite wrong – for
instance, that pulmonary tuberculosis never affected the right
middle lobe. Well, I also learnt that there never was a 'never' in
medicine.

There were many other Welshmen besides Ernie Lloyd at West-
minster, not least C. Price Thomas, a brilliant chest surgeon (who
was to operate on King George VI) and who, having visited the USA
before the Second World War, exchanged his Welsh accent for a
strange Yankee one. Drawling, he would address each student as
'professor'. Touching his glasses he would ask some timid student,
'Why do you think that, professor?' Many of the students themselves
were Welsh. On one notable occasion so many of the cricket XI were
from Wales that when we went out to field our captain gave us his

orders in Welsh. The opposing side called us Welshminster.

In 1945 I joined my first surgical firm. It was always a question of doing things for the first time: first time to take blood from a vein, first lumbar puncture, first major operation, first postmortem, first childbirth, first death of a patient one had attended in the ward. Only repetition can lead to confidence so all these first times were a strain. No wonder so many medical students are frivolous. They are seldom mature enough to cope with so much ineluctable human sadness and sickness. What can young men and women do but make jokes, laugh and respond by some form of activism – in one mood horseplay, in another by trying to comfort and give help to those in the sick wards they so timidly linger in?

The most radical surgeon at Westminster Hospital was Sir Stanford Cade. How many times did I, along with other students on the firm, hear him conclude a graphic description of a patient's disease with the decision, 'This is inoperable.' And then, after a pause, 'I will operate.' One student on the firm at that time was 'Charlie' Westbury who was to become Sir Stanford's most brilliant pupil. Today Charlie gives those same ward rounds at Westminster Hospital and he too has become a radical surgeon, one universally respected.

Recently I met Charlie again. He startled me. He said that he had read a poem of mine called 'The Case' and wished to take issue with the suggestion advanced in the poem – that doctors too often see patients not as rounded human beings but simply as cases. (My poem was about a physician who knew the electrocardiograph of a patient but not the patient's name.)

'You see,' Charlie continued, 'if I saw some of my patients as rounded human beings and not as cases, because of the distressful nature of the surgery I have to undertake – sometimes in severely ill, pathetic children – I wouldn't be able to function. Give me so many inches of anonymous skin under the lights in an operating theatre and then I can use my skill; but if I were in a street and someone was knocked down then I'd find it difficult to cope.'

So much then for the so-called extroverted, tough personality of surgeons. Charlie was sensitive as a student and he is sensitive now. All the same, I do not think he found his student days, with their blatant confrontations with suffering, such a testing time as I did. The medical student learns more than the art and practice of medicine. He learns something about himself – and this is so whether he studies at Westminster Hospital, the Welsh National School of Medicine or Timbuctoo.

For my part, I found myself more and more given to reactive though purposeful daydreaming. For instance, I would be in the postmortem room and as the pathologist was trying to teach us morbid truths about diseased tissues I would not hear what he said as I kept thinking how the mesenteric colours inside the exposed abdomen resembled those of a cathedral window; or at Outpatients or on a ward round I would find myself trying to write a poem in my head. Mr MacNab, on one ward round, woke me up, I remember. The rest of the firm were all staring at me. Evidently I had been asked a question. They waited. Mr MacNab waited. 'Your name is Abse,' he said sarcastically. 'This is Wednesday afternoon, this is the Westminster Hospital, Christmas is coming and it is 1946.'

In fact the consultants at Westminster were amazingly patient with me. Earlier, in June 1946, my first book of poems was accepted for publication by Hutchinson so perhaps they expected a budding poet to be somewhat disarrayed.

I was more than disarrayed. For the next eight months I hardly attended Westminster Hospital and in the summer of 1947 I returned to Cardiff where I pronounced to my brothers that I no longer wished to become a doctor, I wanted to become a writer. I had a book coming out, some of my stuff was being published in periodicals, I had also written a play. 'You can't give up medicine,' Leo said angrily. 'Father has made many sacrifices so that you can study in London.' Wilfred agreed and added forcefully, 'It will be better for you – I tell you as a psychiatrist – to finish something that you've begun. If you don't it will mark you for the rest of your life. Besides, if you knuckle down you could qualify in a year. Then you could do what you like. Become a freelance writer if that's what you want – *after you've qualified.*'

It took me over a year to qualify but I am glad that after a further six months' absence from medical school I eventually took their advice. When I did return to the wards again, continuously, seriously, I must have been intensely self-righteous and smug. For I had decided that one must act purely, selflessly! In order to do so, I argued, one must live like a patient recovering from a serious illness. One must always be grateful – for a grateful man is more likely to bear gifts to others. I would take the skull out of the wardrobe to help me in my meditations. I discovered, then, with exalted melancholy, that the skull ceased to be an anatomical artifact but truly a skull and reminder of my own destiny. It became a threat, a sacred object that could help me extend my consciousness. I wanted to achieve lucidity and to act only with awareness. For some months a number of patients at

Westminster Hospital had to endure my over-enthusiastic acts of kindness.

Two years later, when I, a doctor, returned to Cardiff to take on a general practice locum for my Uncle Max, I was not only aware of my own inadequacies but also the inadequacies of my medical education. I no longer stared at the skull and indeed rarely thought of the skull beneath the flesh. Worse, I understood the truth and shame

> Of motives late revealed, and the awareness
> Of things ill done and done to others' harm
> Which once I took for exercise of virtue.
> Then fool's approval stings and honour stains.

But such introspection was time-consuming and, perhaps, self-indulgent. A voice on the phone was saying plaintively, 'Doctor, please, doctor.'

My Father's Red Indian

Look at a good map of South Wales and you'll see Ogmore-by-Sea plainly marked. It is halfway between Swansea and Cardiff, on the coast, of course, facing the small hills of Somerset that I can now observe hazily, fifteen miles away, across the grey, twitching, Saturday evening sea of the Bristol Channel. Not quite a village, not quite a resort, it is a place where sheep outnumber seagulls, where seagulls outnumber dogs, where dogs outnumber its human denizens.

My father loved Ogmore. He regularly drove the car down the A48 so that he could fish where the river, trying to rid itself of all the Welsh rain from the inland mountains, pours itself ceaselessly into the sea. 'I'll catch a salmon bass today,' my father would say optimistically in those far, long-ago days before the war when I was a small boy flying low over that Ogmore beach with my arms out-stretched, or kicking a pebble into the rocks and shouting 'Goal!' or just playing with my yo-yo and whispering, 'Knock, knock, who's there?' while the sea wind replied threateningly, 'Me, the bogeyman, me, Adolf Hitler, and I'll make you and little Audrey cry and cry and cry.'

I love Ogmore as much as my father did. That's why, since I've been in South Wales a week now, staying with my mother, I drove out here on my own today. I like the open acres of sheep-cropped turf that spread upwards from the rocks to the bluish ribbon road where the post office is and the petrol pump and the small Sea View Hotel. I like the green ferns, the gorse in yolk-yellow flower that smells of Barmouth biscuits, and the old grey stone walls flecked with mustard lichen. I like the tons and tons of sweet air, and the extra air between the fleeing clouds and the blue. I like the dramatic, slow, chemically coloured sunsets – unpaintable, unbeatable – and those lights of Porthcawl across the bay that in an hour or so will suddenly appear, so many shivering distant dots as darkness deepens. I like even those scattered bungalows over there that seer the slopes of Ogmore-by-

Sea, hideous as they are with their tidy lawns and hydrangea bushes and their neat, little, surrounding red-brick walls. Bungalows called Sea Breeze or Cap Dai or Balmoral or Cartref.

Just after tea I overheard a lady, a stranger to me, who lived in one of the bungalows, say in the post office, 'Jack Evans, 'e ought to be put away, I'm tellin' you, stark ravin', stark ravin', duw.'

Jack Evans, I thought, I wonder if it's the same Jack Evans? He would be an old man now.

A common enough name in Wales. I did not like to question this lady who wore a green scarf tied about her head and who said nothing more about Jack Evans. 'Ta-ta,' she called as she closed the door that made a bell briefly, sadly, tinkle.

'*South Wales Echo*, please,' I said, and carrying the newspaper I walked down towards the sea, towards a dog barking.

After the war, when I was a student, my father continued regularly to visit Ogmore-by-Sea. But the river had become polluted, the Bristol Channel more of a sewer, and he caught no more salmon bass, no more of those little flat dabs either, that my mother liked so much. Even the skate, with their horrible human lips, had vanished. Nothing lived in that sea except an occasional conger eel and the urine-coloured seaweed. Still my father stood there with his rod, all day uselessly until sunset when his silent silhouette listened to the crashing, deranged rhythms of the sea.

'Stark ravin', stark ravin',' the woman had said in the post office. And didn't my mother think Dad stark ravin' as he stood in his footprints throwing a line of hooks and raw pink ragworms into the barren waves?

'Might as well fish in the dirty bathwater upstairs,' my mother grumbled.

'But I'm not the only one,' father growled one day defensively. 'Since two weeks now another fella comes to fish near me. We'll catch something one of these days.'

'Who's this other crazy fisherman?' my mother asked.

'Name of Jack Evans,' my father replied. Then he hesitated and with his left thumb and index finger pulled at his lower lip. He was obviously going to announce something important. But he mumbled something. I didn't hear what he said that made my mother laugh. She laughed, stopped, laughed again, and choking cheerfully gasped, 'That's a good one, ha ha.'

My father, uneasy because of her response, ignored me when I asked, 'What did you say, Dad?'

My mother, chuckling, tried to wipe tears from her eyes. 'Your father says, ha ha ha, that this Jack Evans is ha ha ha ha ha ha, oh dear, oh dear.'

'What?' I asked, irritated.

'Ha ha ha,' my mother continued, 'a *Red Indian*, ha ha ha.'

'He is too,' shouted my father, angry now. 'For heaven's sake, stop laughing. His mother was an American Indian, his father Welsh. What's funny about that?'

My father picked up a newspaper but didn't put on his glasses. He just stared at the paper and said, 'He's a Welsh Red Indian. When his mother died Jack was sixteen so his father brought him back to Bridgend which is where the Evans family comes from.'

'We're Welsh Jews,' I said to my mother. 'So why should we laugh at Welsh Indians?'

'You and your old fishing stories,' my mother said dismissively and disappeared into the kitchen.

My father put down the newspapers. 'He's a very interesting man is Jack Evans,' my father said, pensively, quietly.

Next time my father went fishing by the river mouth at Ogmore maybe I would go with him and meet Jack Evans, interesting Welsh Red Indian. My father drove the twenty-odd miles to Ogmore most weekends but somehow I never found time to go with him. There was a film to see, a party to go to, or I just wasted time playing poker in the students' union. So I did not meet Jack Evans. My father, though, became more and more expert in the culture and history of the American Indian.

'Oh aye,' said my father. 'We do 'ave some very hinteresting conversations, me and Jack.'

'No fish, though,' I said.

'Had a definite bite yesterday,' said my father.

My father was not a religious man, not a philosophical man either, but standing there, by the side of the sea with Jack Evans, both men silent for the most part I should think, they must have thought thoughts, dreamed dreams that all men do who confront the man-absent seascape for hours and hours. My father never spoke a word of praise about the altering light in the water and the changing skies but he did occasionally stammer out some of his new-found Jack Evans knowledge, and when he did so my mother gazed at him with unaccustomed, suspicious eyes as if he were unwell, or as if he had brought home, uncharacteristically, a bunch of flowers.

'D'ye know,' he told us, 'the American Indians are a bit like Jews? They 'ave no priest between man and his Creator, see.'

'No mediator, no intercessor?' I asked.

'Exactly,' my father continued. 'And like Jews, would you believe it, they don't kneel to pray. They stand up erect, aye.'

'So what?' my mother said, disturbed.

'They don't try and convert people either – like Jews, see. An' they have a sort of barmitzvah, a sort of confirmation, when they're thirteen.'

'I don't like Jack Evans,' my mother suddenly declared as if she had decided he was a savage. 'What does he want?'

But I was curious to learn more about the Red Indian confirmation ceremony and so I asked my father to tell us more about it. It seemed, according to Jack Evans anyway, that after a purifying vapour bath the thirteen-year-old Red Indian would climb the highest point in the vicinity. Wishing to stand before God in all humility the youth would strip and stand naked and motionless and silent on tip of hill, or top of mountain, exposed to the wind and the sun. For two days and one night, for two sunrises and two sunsets, the naked boy would stand erect watching all the stars coming out and all the stars disappearing.

'Good night,' said my mother. 'What an ordeal for a young boy.'

We sat in the room, none of us speaking for a while. Then my mother said, 'I bet that Jack Evans could do with a vapour bath. Bet he smells and could do with some Lifebuoy soap under his armpits.'

My father looked up, pained. 'I'd like to meet Jack Evans,' I said quietly. 'I'll come to Ogmore with you next weekend, Dad.'

'All right,' my father said. 'I've told 'im you write poetry. He was very interested to hear that. Soft in the head I told him you were. But I 'spec' he'll be glad to meet you.'

'Fishing by there in Ogmore, both of them,' my mother said. 'Blockheads.'

The next weekend I sat in the back of my father's Morris Minor next to his fishing tackle, next to the worm bait in an old tobacco tin. My mother, at the last moment, decided to come too. 'Just for the ride,' she explained. Like me, though, I'm sure she was curious to meet my father's own Red Indian. On the other hand, my mother always did, still does, delight in travelling in a car. Always she sat next to the driver's seat, the window on her side open a little, however chill a wind screeched in to freeze the other back-seat, protesting passengers.

'Just an inch,' she would plead. And content to be driven, to rest from her house chores, ten miles outside the town she'd sit there regal, giving my father directions or humming happily the gone music-hall songs that have faded into nostalgia.

As we came down Crack Hill to leave the A48 for Ogmore her hum became louder and soon words, wrong words, replaced the hum. 'I know she loves me, because she says so, because she says so, she is the Lily of Caerphilly, she is the Lily – Watch the sheep,' she suddenly shouted. The hedges and green fields raced backwards and there, ahead of us in the bending road, forty yellow eyes stared at us. Afterwards, when father accelerated again, my mother asked in a voice too loud, 'He doesn't wear feathers an' things, does he?'

'For heaven's sake,' my father said. 'Don't be tactless. Don't ask him damn soft things like that.'

'Good night,' my mother replied. 'I won't speak to the man at all.'

She pulled out some Mintos from her handbag, gave me one and unwrapped another to push it into my father's mouth as he stared steadily ahead at the road. Through the window now the landscape had changed. Down there in the valley, beyond turf and farms, the river snaked its way this side of the high sand dunes and then, abruptly, as we climbed an incline the open sea fanned out, the dazzle on the sea, the creamy edge of it all visible below us as it curved elliptically on the beach from the promontory of Porthcawl all the way round Happy Valley towards Ogmore and the mouth of the river. Such a deception that sea. So beautiful to look upon but so empty of fish. Even the seagulls of Ogmore looked thin, famished, not like those who feasted on these shores before the war.

'Can't see anyone fishing down there,' I said to my father.

'Tide's coming in,' he replied. 'Jack'll be by presently.'

Jack Evans seemed in no hurry. My father fished alone and my mother and I waited until we became tired of waiting. We went for a turfy walk and when we returned we found my father on his own still, casting his line into the incoming sea. We decided to go for tea in the Sea View Hotel and we left my father the flask and sandwiches. When we came back again, still Jack Evans was absent. There was just the derelict wind and out there a distant coal tramp steamer edging its way on the silver dazzle towards Cardiff.

'Brr,' my mother said. 'It's an arctic wind. We'll wait in the car. Don't be long.'

We did not meet Jack Evans that day and the next weekend it was

raining monotonously. Besides I wanted to see Henry Fonda in a film
called *Strange Incident*.

'Duw, you want to see a cowboy film,' my father mocked me,
'when you could come with me an' meet a real live Red Indian.'

'It's raining, Dad,' I said.

'He'll be down there this week, sure as eggs,' my father said.

So father drove that Saturday to Ogmore alone and that night
when he returned he gave me a note. ' 'Ere,' he said. 'Jack Evans 'as
written this out for you. He said sorry to 'ave missed you last week.
But you might like this Red Indian poem of his. Read it out loud to
your mother. It's short, go on.'

I opened up the piece of paper. I have never seen such big
handwriting – bigger than a child's. *You up there*, I read to myself and
then I read it out loud for my mother sat there inquisitively. 'It's
about a falling star,' I said.

> 'You up there
> you who sewed to the black garment
> of endless night
> all those shining button-stars
> how your big fingers
> must have been cold.
>
> For the buttons do not hold
> some are loose
> some fall off.
> Look how one drops now
> down and in towards us
> and out of sight.'

My mother nodded. 'Very nice,' she said. My father seemed trium-
phant. 'Even I understand that, son – it's about a shooting star – now
why can't you write clear stuff like that instead of those *modern* poems
you produce?'

'That's how Red Indians think,' my mother interrupted him.
'They don't understand about shooting stars. I mean they don't know
the scientific explanation. They think God's fingers were just numb
with cold. Fancy. Good night.'

I stared down at the handwriting. Nobody genuinely wrote like
that, I thought. And then it occurred to me: Jack Evans didn't exist.
My father had made him up. Why not? Some people wrote novels,
others plays, or worked at poems like me. So why shouldn't my father
have invented a character? And yet? How would my father have got

hold of that poem or all those facts about Red Indian religion? My
father was no scholar. Somebody with erudition had talked to him
. . . so why not Jack Evans? All the same I looked at my father
suspiciously.

'I'll come with you to Ogmore again one of these days,' I said.

I did too. About once a month I accompanied my father on his
fishing trips. But I never met Jack Evans.

'Funny,' said my father, 'how he never makes it when you or your
mother come.'

'He's got Red Indian second sight,' I muttered.

I remember it was 21 June, the longest day of the year, when I
ambled into Cardiff Central Library and saw in the spacious refer-
ence room my own father studiously reading a book – something he
never did at home. At once I guessed the book was about American
Indian culture. Now I was certain he had invented Jack Evans, that
his recently acquired knowledge about American Indian history and
religion and poetry had been culled from books – not from any real,
gossiping individual. My father sat, the other side of the room, at a
long black table, bent over a book, unaware that his son was watching
him. And I felt guilty standing there, finding out his secret. I felt
furtive and quickly left the reference room lest he should look up.

My own father . . . crazy! Fooling us like that. As I ran down the
steps of the library, disturbed, I do not know why I wanted to cry. My
own father whom I loved, who was a bit eccentric, yes – but I'd
thought not this crazy – living in a fantasy world, having a fantasy
companion fishing with him in the sea that contained no fish. Hell, I
thought, good grief! I decided not to say anything to my mother.

That night after a silent supper my father brought a piece of paper
out of his pocket. 'I went to the library today,' he announced. 'I
wanted to find a Red Indian poem for Jack. They were very 'elpful.
The girl in the library let me 'ave a look at a book called *Literature of
the American Indian*. Very hinteresting. I found this in it. It's an
Eskimo poem, really. I'm not sure whether it's the same thing as a
Red Indian one.'

He handed me the piece of paper and I felt relieved. I wanted to
laugh. So my father hadn't made up Jack Evans. Now I felt ashamed
that I had ever thought he had. I stared at my father's handwriting
that was simple but small, mercifully small.

'Read it out, son,' said my mother.

'It's called "The Song of the Bad Boy",' I said.

My father stared at me bright-eyed, his mouth a little open. My

mother smoothed back her hair. They were waiting so I read it out
loud, 'The Song of the Bad Boy'.

> 'I am going to run away from home, *hayah*
> In a great big boat, *hayah*
> To hunt for a sweet little girl, *hayah*
> I shall get her some beads, *hayah*
> The kind that look like boiled ones, *hayah*
> Then after a while, *hayah*
> I shall come back home, *hayah*
> I shall call all my relations together, *hayah*
> And I shall give them all a thrashing, *hayah*
> I shall marry two girls at once, *hayah*
> One of the sweet little darlings, *hayah*
> I shall dress in spotted seal-skins, *hayah*
> And the other dear little pet, *hayah*
> Shall wear skins of the hooded seal only, *hayah*.'

My mother laughed when I finished and said, 'The little demon.'
And my father said, 'What does *hayah* mean?' I didn't know. Did it
mean anything? Did it mean Hooray?

'You can ask Jack Evans!' said my mother.

He never did though. Jack Evans never turned up in Ogmore
again. Regularly my father went fishing, regularly he stood near the
river's mouth on his own. First he assumed that Jack Evans was ill.
He did not know exactly where he lived. In Bridgend, probably. In
some ways, my father admitted, Jack Evans was a mystery man. 'An' I
can't look him up in any damned phone book,' Dad said. 'There are
so many Evanses about.'

Gradually, catching nothing except seaweed week after week, and
having no companion, my father became discouraged. Only in the
best blue weather would he drive the car to Ogmore and even then he
would rarely go fishing. His chest already had begun to play him up.
He would sit in the car and cough and cough, gasping for breath,
while my mother muttered anxiously, 'Good night, I do wish you'd
give up smoking.'

The next year he did give up smoking. He gave up everything. The
one Sunday we did go to Ogmore he did not even take his fishing
tackle with him. He sat for hours silently, then almost shouted, 'They
spoilt it, they ruined it. Oh the fools, the fools!' And he stared
morosely at the polluted sea.

The years have not made me forget the timbre of his voice, nor the
righteousness of his anger. I strolled over the turfy hillocks above the

rocks and stared at the wronged sea. I remembered my mother, now an old lady in her Cardiff flat, still saying, 'Good night,' and I continued walking towards the sea and the sunset. I wondered if there would be any fishermen this Saturday evening down by the mouth of the river. Because of the woman with the green scarf in the post office I half expected Jack Evans to be fishing there – an ancient grey-haired man not quite right in the head, standing where my father stood, wearing Wellingtons like my father did, as the smallest waves collapsed near his feet. 'Stark ravin', stark ravin'.'

I quickened my pace as the strong sea wind moistened my eyes. There was not going to be much of a sunset. A few seagulls floated like paper towards the flat rocks on my left. Soon I would be beyond the small sand dunes on my right and the grey wall and the last bungalows. Then the river mouth would be visible. Indeed, three minutes later I saw the river below me and, in the distance, one solitary man holding a bending rod. I wanted to run. I scrambled over the rocks, shuffled over pebbles until my feet became silent on sand. As I approached the fisherman, I saw that he was, alas, quite young and I felt stupid as I walked towards him, still carrying my *South Wales Echo*.

He had seen me and I veered away a little but the stranger called, 'Got the football results?'

I glanced momentarily at the newspaper in my hand. 'No,' I said. 'I got this paper earlier. Too early.'

The fisherman nodded and I asked, hesitating, 'Any fish in these seas?'

Perhaps the wind carried my words the wrong way for he replied, 'Costs 'ell of a lot these days, mun. The price of bait, duw, shocking.'

'Do you ever catch fish here?' I asked again, louder.

'They caught a cod down by there near the flat rocks last week,' he replied. 'I'm 'oping for a salmon bass meself.'

He probably lived in Ogmore-by-Sea. Perhaps he would know about the Jack Evans 'who ought to be put away'.

'Jack Evans?' he replied. 'No.'

I nodded and was about to turn back when he surprised me with, 'You don't mean Mac Evans by any chance?'

I wanted to laugh. I was looking for a Welsh Red Indian not a Welsh Scotsman!

'No, no,' said my new-found fisherman friend. '*Max* Evans, mun. We just call him Mac for short.'

'Is Mac . . . Max Evans a bit . . . er . . . crazy?'

His hands tightened on his rod so that his knuckles whitened and he laughed. Suddenly he stopped laughing. 'By Christ,' he said. And solemn, he paused again as if to tell me of some disaster. 'You should see Mac on a motorbike,' he continued.

I grinned, half turned and raised my hand. He smiled back. I walked away up the crunching pebbles, over the rocks, onto the turf. Way at the top, on the road, the lamp posts jerked on and Ogmore-by-Sea immediately became darker. Lights came on too in the post office and the Sea View Hotel, and as I walked up the slope the moon in the sky became more and more bright.

Pages from a Princeton Journal

August 1973

Other people scheme about money; other people count the pennies; other people tot up the profit and the loss. And I am pure. Have not members of my family, mother, father, brothers, sister, brother-in-law, told me since I was in my twenties, *You are an innocent when it comes to money. You're a poet, you know nothing about money.* I've always liked that assessment. Alas, though, I am not so innocent. I do think about money. I tot up the profit and the loss. I despoil the purity of the imagination with money thoughts. Secretly, when no one is looking, I sometimes read the *Sunday Times* Business Section. And now, I hope to have dollars by accepting the Princeton job.

We have four seats in the Pan Am Jumbo plane due out of Heathrow on Joan's birthday, 11 September, at 3.30 p.m. I booked the seats three months ago in order to obtain cheap fares. You see, I plan ahead. I think about money.

Have you taken out insurance?
How do you mean?
Flying. You should take out insurance.
My life even isn't insured.
You are irrational.

September 1973

Please, please sir, let me have that visa. I am rehearsing speeches, alternately fawning and gruff, as we prepare to leave the house. The telephone rings. It is, surprisingly, James Kinlay, the features editor of the *Sunday Express*. He does not know of my predicament, my desperation. His voice is smiling.

Just to tell you the article is fine and to wish you Godspeed in America.
How very nice of you to call.

Hesitating, I mentioned to him my problems about the form I should have had but haven't, about the visa that I need but have not got. I tell him I am on the way to the American Embassy now.

If you don't get that visa let me know. Maybe the Express can help.

Surely he did not mean anything by that? No. Of course not. It was his way of signing off, rather like 'your obedient servant' when you're neither obedient nor a servant. It's always a problem to put down the receiver gracefully.

It is a warm day, muggy for September in London. I discover the American Embassy to be overcrowded, bulging with the bright shirts of tourists. A few mephitic policemen also hover because of the possibility of IRA bombs. A 'serpentine' queue ascends the stairway to final officialdom. Others, at the bottom, are milling about purposefully not yet having even joined the queue. This is going to be a *long* wait. As I hesitate, sighing, at ground level, wondering how to join the queue, I hear from the top of the staircase, from higher than Kafka, an American calling my name. I cannot believe it. How does he know that I am here? Joan looks at me.

Is Dr Abse here, please?

K. is yet to be called. I cherish my own astonishment. Joan's voice, squeaky, responds, *Yes*. I nod and also call, *Yes*. All those victims undulating up the stairs turn their heads. *Yes*, I call again.

Two men, in suits, descend the stairs passing the inert, hopeless, queueing 'refugees'. They are looking at us. They are coming towards us. They nod reassuringly. They extend their hands smiling. We shake hands and they introduce themselves. It bodes good though I do not know who they are despite their willingness to tell me their names. They evidently want us to follow them and, trustfully, we do. We are led 'backstage' through several doors and one of the men quits to fetch a Mr X and we hear, in the distance, the murmur of dry voices. I do not understand. I can tell Joan does not understand. But it is evident that the man who has cordially remained with us knows my problem. He tells me he is the press attaché and that Peter rang him up. I am about to inquire Peter who? However he is asking me if I have any correspondence from Princeton University and any proof that they have signed Form DSP-66 (which has not arrived because of the vagaries of the post). I search in my briefcase for letters and cables. He reads them swiftly. He speaks to me conspiratorially about Mr X. I turn my head and notice on the wall a portrait of President Nixon.

Who is Peter? Who is X? I can see Joan is also perplexed. At last,

Mr X, a tall, stooping, saturnine man, approaches and listens attentively to the press attaché. I am distracted by Mr X's tic. As the press attaché speaks urgently to him his eyes blink rapidly every ten seconds and simultaneously his eyebrows jump up his forehead.

Gradually I begin to understand what has happened. It seems that the press attaché had been telephoned by a Mr Peter Vane, the foreign editor of the *Sunday Express*. Vane, whom I've never met, evidently has been forceful on my behalf. I warm to Vane. I like Vane. What a nice man Vane is. The press attaché continues to whisper. Mr X's eyes continue to blink, eyebrows jumping.

It is a question of Form DSP-66. Dr Abse has the original letter which officially invited him to be the Visiting Writer at Princeton University with the salary stated therein. He has here, you see, a cable that DSP-66 was sent to him from Princeton on August 31st.

August 31st? That was a week ago.

Can you help him?

It is necessary, I'm afraid, to have the DSP-66.

Have you any suggestions?

Mr X stares again at the cable. He stares at the letter. He stares once more at the cable. He blinks. His eyebrows jump but the words on the cable do not change. He tells me that if I should receive tomorrow (Saturday) or Monday morning the DSP-66 I could come and see him direct and then he would issue me a visa immediately. There would be no question of me having to queue up, nor would there be a moment's delay in my receiving a visa. *But I have to have DSP-66.*

We are booked to leave Tuesday. Me, Joan, my younger daughter, Susanna, and my son, David. I took a charter flight, cheap fares, which is only valid if we fly at the time and date given. I would have to buy four new fares at full price to New York if I do not catch the plane on Tuesday. That will cost me hundreds of pounds. Moreover, I have rented my house beginning on Tuesday so that I shall have to move out and stay in an hotel until I can leave. And I can't leave, it seems, because Form DSP-66 has gone astray and it will take one more week, at least, before receiving another one appropriately signed. Today is Friday. Tomorrow the Embassy is closed. I am being met in New York on Tuesday – I –

Sorry, I can't be more helpful.

In the press attaché's office I ring up Mr Peter Vane to thank him anyway for trying on my behalf – and to thank James Kinlay for speaking to Peter Vane. Mr Vane calls me Dannie. I slip in a Peter.

But they still won't give you the visa, Dannie.
Not without Form DSP-66, Peter, which has to be filled in at Princeton.
And you need that form by Monday?
Yes.
Listen, could you phone Princeton, ask them to take another DSP-66 to our New York office?
Maybe. Princeton is only some fifty miles from New York.
If so, Dannie, I'll get our New York office to put it on the next plane out. I'll arrange for a messenger here to meet that plane at Heathrow and take it to your home in Golders Green. How's that?

I am staggered by this offer. I telephone Mrs Lewis, the secretary of the Creative Arts Programme in Princeton. A transatlantic call. I feel important. I am bossy. I am masterful. I insist that the form is taken at once to the New York offices of the *Sunday Express*.

I shall take it myself.
Thank you, Mrs Lewis.

I put the phone down. My eyebrows jump. Saturday morning no American letters in the post. But late Saturday afternoon, a motor-bike stops outside our house. A man in a helmet – surely Hermes, no less – opens the gate and walks up the pathway. I open the door. He hands me an envelope which contains DSP-66.

Thank you.

Hermes works for the *Sunday Express* and has a Cockney accent. *All right, guv,* he says.

September 1973

Last Tuesday we took the Pam Am Jumbo plane to Kennedy Airport. Later, on arriving at the house in Pine Street (Princeton) that we had rented sight unseen, we were alarmed to find it already occupied. They descended on us as soon as we entered the kitchen. They were conspicuously visible as a black mass on Susanna's bare leg. David too was severely bitten, and so, pursued, we hurriedly abandoned the house, all of us scratching, cursing.

Fleas!
I've never seen so many fleas.

We took ourselves to the Nassau Inn hoping for shelter, comfort, baths, showers, beds. We were exhausted anyway. The Nassau Inn was posh, plush, air-conditioned, free of fleas, wonderful. But we had come in the back way. To reach the foyer we walked down a thickly carpeted corridor. The carpet so thick I felt I had ataxia. We proceeded past an open conference door. I dropped the cases for a moment and peered in. A determined man stood on a raised platform and aggressively asked the large audience facing him (they had their backs to us), *Any questions?* Nobody replied. In that awkward hush I aggressively shouted out. *Yes. How do you get rid of fleas?* We stayed just long enough to witness the backs of heads becoming profiles.

Later I recited to Joan:

> *It sucked me first and now sucks thee*
> *And in this flea our two bloods mingled be.*

Princeton is very handsome. Imitation Oxford colleges have been set together, strategically placed, in a square mile of park. This is the campus. And it is bordered by a Hampstead-like street of shops. Beyond this pleasant shopping road unfold affluent Hampstead Garden Suburb-like houses and mansions. There do not seem to be any working-class dwellings.

At dusk the campus is particularly attractive. The lamp-posts glow softly along pathways that negotiate the colleges, the squirrel-haunted trees, the sculptures by Moore, Picasso, Lipschitz. Students move purposefully towards assignments. So do lone dogs. The windows are lit up with soft yellows and are full of shadows. Already they are older by centuries as the sky slowly reveals night and all its stars.

Among my colleagues in the Creative Arts Programme are Edmund Keeley, whose translation of Seferis and Cavafy I have long admired, and Theodore (Ted) Weiss, the well-known American poet and editor of *Quarterly Review of Literature*.

My students, whom I meet on Tuesdays and Wednesdays, also seem very nice, very polite, intelligent, and not a little gifted. One of them, though, is more blunt. He tackles me on my own. He wants to ask me something but I can see he is unusually hesitant. I am curious to know what he wishes to know. He ums, he ahs, he pulls his nose with his fingers. Eventually he blurts out, *I hope you don't mind me asking you . . .*

What?

Well . . .

What?

How did they – pardon me – how did they come to invite you to Princeton University?

How do you mean?

Um.
Mmmm?
Well, they asked Anthony Burgess – that's understandable . . .
Mmmm?
He's famous. But you?
No, no. I'm not famous.
It may be better for us.
Why?
I'm not sure Anthony Burgess gave much time to students. I mean, if you're famous perhaps you haven't time to spend on students.

October 1973

We saw Chekhov's *The Seagull* at the McCarter Theatre. Poor production. Had Chekhov been alive to see it he would have suffered a haemoptysis during the last two acts.

Why do you always wear black?
I am in mourning for my life.

How hard for actors to utter lines that have become too celebrated. Phrases seem comical that should lean into melancholy. In a letter to a friend, I had earlier told Susanna, Chekhov, in his self-deprecating manner, described *The Seagull* as 'a comedy with three female parts, six male parts, four acts, a landscape (a view of the lake), much talk about literature and five tons of love'. We had just seen Nina returned and distraught, Treplef had shot himself, the actors were taking their bow, and above the applause Susanna, sincerely baffled, whispered, 'And he called that a *comedy*?'

During the rehearsal of the first St Petersburg production (which was a disaster), I can imagine Chekhov's full mouth opening, his Russian eyebrows steady, as he interrupted the actors with 'the chief thing, my dear fellow, is to play it simply, without theatricality. Just very simply.' What better advice can a dramatist give to any actor in one of his plays?

A visit to New York. On the way to the Holland Tunnel we saw the Statue of Liberty. I first saw the statue from the air. Was it seven years ago? I was flying in a turbo-prop to Washington from La Guardia airport. From my window, just as we slowly climbed higher, I watched the speedy shadow of the plane on the water below aiming for a green object. The plane's shadow resembled a cross and for a moment, perfectly, the Statue of Liberty was crucified.

Since then the noise in New York has become louder. Soon we were to hear the scream of the police car. Prospero, it is evident, on Manhattan Island has lost his powers and Ariel is absent for the air is unacceptable. In a back doorway, down a New York side street, I saw Caliban giving himself a fix. Meanwhile the Statue of Liberty is still the same colour as a dollar.

Joe Frank kindly invited me to the Gauss seminars given by Allen Tate. Because of laryngitis Tate's autobiographical talks were given in a weird, scratched whisper. He is thinner than I had remembered, his face skull-like. Only those sitting in the front two rows could hear him. From time to time he would put out his tongue as is his habit after making a wry joke. But since his humorous remarks could not be heard hardly any laughter resulted. The silent audience at the back merely witnessed that occasional grimace of his in which he opened his mouth and protruded his tongue so that this gesture became monstrously visual, grotesque.

I recall his visit to our house in Golders Green. Michael Hamburger joined us, his car having broken down nearby. Michael came into the living room moaning, 'I need to phone the AA at once.' In America the AA is called the triple A so, for several minutes, there was a delicious misunderstanding. Allen Tate, most solicitous, thought Michael needed to be in immediate touch with Alcoholics Anonymous.

American icecream may be better than ours – Howard Johnson's Butter Pecan, for instance. Their trees may be more various, taller, more spectacularly autumnal and colourful than ours. But the American TV and radio are pathetic compared with the BBC.

News of the Arab–Israeli war has been utterly trivialized, the news items themselves frustratingly brief, and there is no commentary in depth. Everything is presented in a restless hurry so that those repetitive advertisements for furniture stores (Hey Jerry, what's the story?) for washing powders (He's the bold one) for spaghetti sauces (Dat's Italian) can take their pride of place. The more grave the news the more offensive the ads. When the Israelis counterattacked and seemed about to crush the Egyptian army (before American–Soviet intervention), 'Mike' Keeley remarked how the Egyptians resembled Cavafy's 'Trojans':

> Our efforts are those of men prone to disaster,
> our efforts are like those of the Trojans.
> We just begin to get somewhere,
> begin to gather a little strength,
> grow almost bold and hopeful,
> when something always comes up to stop us.
> Achilles leaps out of the trench in front of us
> and terrifies us with his violent shouting.
> Our efforts are like those of the Trojans.
> We think we'll change our luck
> by being resolute and brave,
> so we move outside ready to fight.
> But when the great crisis comes,
> our boldness and resolution vanish,
> our spirit falters, collapses,
> and we scurry around the walls
> trying to save ourselves by running away . . .

I find it difficult to feel sympathy for these Trojans though, who have friends in the Kremlin and fat cousins who control the oilfields. Besides, each time Israel is at war I am involuntarily anxious and surprised by my own involvement as I listen to each and every news item on TV or radio. It is as if my own life was endangered. Only later, when the threat has dissipated, when Israel seems once more relatively secure, can I listen sorrowfully to the dirge high on the walls or note the vultures sailing over. I become a Jew the moment I hear the word *Israel* spoken by one not Jewish.

November 1973

When Philip Larkin (whom I have never met) writes to me about the Poetry Book Society possible choices and recommendations (we happen to be co-judges this year) he prefaces his letters with 'Dear Abse'. Years ago, teachers, headmasters addressed me so – more recently, knighted publishers or air vice-marshals. Philip Larkin's letters are friendly enough but I do not like being called by my bald surname. So I write back hopefully to Hull with a 'Dear Philip Larkin' and sign myself 'Dannie Abse'. I do not like to reply Dear Philip or Dear Larkin or – as if he were a professional pre-war cricketer – Dear Larkin P. – and I cannot sign myself off with a Dannie and a tap dance.

During my recent poetry-reading tour in Ohio several professors in the different English departments have sympathetically remarked on my absence from Philip Larkin's Oxford anthology. Their honeyed words of outrage on my behalf forced me to recover a lost embarrassed smile. 'Yes,' I murmured on each occasion, boring myself, 'Philip Larkin is a good poet but his anthology is something of a disappointment.' Gradually my embarrassed loser's smile would fade as the professor diplomatically changed the direction of the conversation. I knew that smile of mine. Anyone can see it on my face when I'm playing chess and my opponent says, 'Checkmate.'

Saturday morning David and I watched Princeton play Yale at soccer. The sun shone without any warmth whatsoever and the air laden with gaseous ice made me feel the age in my mouth and the femurs in my thighs. The temperature was far below freezing point as, shivering, we shouted forlornly and without enthusiasm every half-hour, 'Prince-ton, Prince-ton.'

At half-time we were shocked to observe the other spectators produce from fur coats, briefcases, hampers, not flasks of hot coffee but cans of beer and coca-cola to which they added *ice cubes*!

Americans appear to be more religious than the British. The roomy churches are well attended on Sundays. On weekdays, processions suddenly startle routine streets with the banging of big drums and men wearing placards that announce 'GOD LOVES AMERICA'. In bus station terminals from Oregon to Ohio, from Ohio to New Jersey, middle-class youngsters loiter ready to buttonhole any unholy passengers with holy bibles. The white God himself has definite peak-hour spots through his accredited surrogates on TV and radio. The Seventh Day Adventists are more Seventh Day than in England, the Jews more Jewish, the Methodists more Methodist.

December 1973

On the train to Providence, Rhode Island, Ted Weiss seemed inordinately depressed. We were to read together at Brown University and Ted, who now must be in his mid-fifties, spoke of his own poetry mournfully, of his doubts about its quality. He even complained that he was not known as amongst the first of his generation. *Unless you are hailed as among the first of your generation*, he argued, *unless you are famous in the way that Lowell is or Berryman was, is it worth the game?* And I, just saying the obvious, *Well, there's no choice, Ted.*

He stared out at the New England landscape that unreeled backwards to New York and at sudden glimpses of sheet water brimming with the winter light. He tried to cheer himself up. He spoke of Bill Carlos Williams, of how Bill not long before his death had stayed with him and of how this old doctor also had expressed uncertainties about his work. *He was a frail old man*, Ted explained, *he had recently suffered another stroke and I tried to reassure him about the solid amount of work he had left behind him. But he asked me, Ah but is it poetry, Ted? On the other hand, Robert Frost stayed with Renée and me, too, and Frost had no doubts. He was vigorous. He relished his own poetry, his own accomplishments, he savoured them. . . .*

Later, when Ted read at Brown University it was with unadulterated confidence. His own poems cheered him up better than I could.

The temporary thaw this morning made time audible. Silent snow and ice are made not only of water but of time frozen, imprisoned time. Today its noise was released – drip, drip, drip, drip – the sound of the melting seconds of one month ago.

January 1974

Those roundabouts of lit cocktail parties when I first attended them last autumn reminded me of the leisurely evenings of an RAF officer abroad. Only the voices, in crowded, elegant rooms, drawled American and the near and background conversations proved to be obsessively about Watergate – not that last round of golf with Robin.

Since then the rich maple leaves have haemorrhaged from the trees. Now the frail sunlight causes the ice on the bare branches to resemble sticky glycerine. The parties still revolve, the faces the same, the American feet in English suede shoes still indent the same expensive carpets, but no one mentions Watergate and Nixon now. Not once have I heard anyone discuss Vietnapalm since I arrived in the USA.

In Britain, as the *New York Times* recently suggested, the news placards are forever announcing shocks: FARES SHOCK, STERLING SHOCK, MINERS SHOCK. All these acute shocks however do not leave us anaesthetized. Rather it is the Americans who seem seriously shocked: no further revelations of governmental criminality can surprise them. For the moment, anyway, they are numb with tawdry truths of Watergate, tax evasions, lies, bugging, burglary.

The mannered artificiality of the East Coast academic lifestyle sometimes makes me want to laugh. It is sometimes comically expressed in their literary journalism. Consider the near nineteenth-century verbosity of today's front-page notice of Joseph Brodsky's poems in the *New York Times Book Review*. It begins: 'Poetry is an immodest art. The poet may be modest imagining that the times pass him by, ignoring his pain, regarding his delicate intermediation of time and eternity as irrelevant to the large enterprise of social architecture and historical reconstruction, but the poet knows a secret which only egregious self-destructiveness obscures, that the great poem sings a succinct universe, comprises the whole myth of man's life and death.'

The tone of this kind of rhetoric becomes hilarious when it breaks down into sheer robust honesty as it does in the current issue of the *American Poetry Review* when Bernard Mathieu wonderfully abandons rhetorical decorum: 'Blaise Cendrars,' he writes, 'once found out that the poet Rainer Maria Rilke, who was then Rodin's correspondence secretary in Paris, had ditched a young girl friend after unscrupulously dallying with her and had caused her great heartbreak. Cendrars knew the girl very well, so he took the trouble to look up Rilke at the *Closerie des Lilas* and beat the shit out of him.'

The telephone call that awakens us from blank sleep as we're told the worst news (that a person one loves is seriously ill, or dying, or dead) is one, I imagine, we all fear.

Joan woke me up. I had not heard the early-morning phone ring. Joan's voice quivered. *My mother's had a stroke.* For a little while the transatlantic call that summoned Joan to England, to Lancashire, left us each in our own head.

The morning after Joan had gone, I walked down freezing, snow-locked Nassau Street and, like an omen, heard the bell tolling from the church. It seemed too apt: the bell tolling, the hearse and the few cars lined up on the church drive. A small group, most facing the same direction, stood between the church door and the black long car. They were motionless and the bell tolled. For me they were strangers mourning a stranger. And if one of them had looked up then, and smiled, how odd that would have been. But they stayed solemn, uncertain in that interval, and I thought of my mother-in-law as I raised my face towards the church's high tower where the great bell was swinging.

When I spoke on the phone to England on the Thursday Joan's voice was small. Mary had died that night.

What are shadows? Darkness cut into shapes.

I phoned Joan again today – she will be away another two weeks. And I have to go to Florida on the 29th.

Postscript

When I returned from the poetry reading tour in the Deep South, apart from the work at the University, and a production of a play of mine (*The Dogs of Pavlov*) in New York, I began to write some poems again and had less time and no wish to continue this journal.
So I'm afraid it just petered out.

An Old Friend

Summer

After my academic year in the USA I returned to the old routines. I would work at the clinic in London and some weekends, with my wife Joan, I'd drive down to Ogmore-by-Sea to our house, Green Hollows. Now and then, en route, we would pick up my aged mother from her Cathedral Road flat in Cardiff so that she could stay the weekend with us; and sometimes one of my daughters, Keren or Susanna, or my son David, with or without their friends, would accompany us. Then Green Hollows would be loud and crowded; otherwise it seemed spacious and quiet.

That June evening when Wyn Phillips first called on us only my wife, my mother and I were there. I had been in Cardiff to record a 'Dial a Poem' earlier and, back at Ogmore, I told my mother that if she wished to hear me read it, all she had to do was dial a certain Cardiff number. She stood in the hall, the telephone receiver next to her ear, while I dialled the numerals for her. 'I haven't heard you read your poetry for twenty years,' she complained. I leaned towards her and the telephone receiver to ensure that the correct dialling tone sounded. I heard a click, a woman briefly introducing me and then my own voice reading a poem. My mother (in 1975 she was eighty-five years old) stood very still, listening, concentrating. Then she bellowed into the phone, 'Speak up, son.'

Later, while Joan prepared the evening meal I took mother out into the garden. It was still warm enough for her to sit in a deckchair on the terrace and turn her face towards the far sea where people lingered on the beaches and a few – specks from this distance – braved the new darkness in the arriving waves.

Meanwhile, because the grass was overgrown, I pushed the mower laboriously forward, then with greater ease pulled the machine towards me. Every few minutes the spray of green stuff and daisies ceased, for the blades would choke, the wheels lock. Where I had been working, the lawn was a lighter green than elsewhere. I had managed to make the mower function more continuously when I happened to gaze up towards the terrace. My mother had struggled to rise from the deckchair, her stockings were wrinkled and she looked beyond me in apparent dismay. I turned to see a stranger coming towards me. Because of the metal whirring of the lawn mower I had not heard the wooden gate's click or footsteps munching the gravel drive.

'Wyn Phillips,' the stranger introduced himself. 'You remember, we were at school together. At St Illtyd's.'

I remembered a Wyn Phillips – when boys we had both played for St Illtyd's cricket team: but this cadaverously thin individual resembled no youth I had known. Besides, Wyn Phillips and I must have been roughly the same age whereas this man was old.

'Wyn Phillips?' I hesitated.

'I've lived in the Far East for years but now I've a bungalow down the road. I've had to retire, you see, because of my health.'

His voice was soft, unassertive. He spoke as if in enemy territory. With the years, physically, it would seem, there had been less a development than a shocking metamorphosis.

'Gosh,' he said, with sudden warmth, 'do you remember, Dan, the time you and I managed to sink that rowing boat in Roath Park lake? We'd drunk too much. We became U-boat commanders!'

I had no recollection of such an incident. My mother continued to stand up, staring at Wyn Phillips with a peculiar, anxious intensity. I edged towards the terrace. 'This is an old friend of mine,' I said to my mother. 'Wyn Phillips, whom I haven't seen for years.'

'You've left the gate open,' said my mother, scolding our visitor. 'You'll let the sheep in.'

'Of course,' said Wyn, smiling at the old lady and turning towards the gate. 'The sheep in Ogmore get in everywhere.'

'They'd eat the nice flowers here,' my mother said. 'The devils.'

Our garden, which spread out in front of Green Hollows – mostly to one side of the short drive and below the terrace – thanks to Joan's industry looked handsome. I would not have minded the sheep attacking the grass but not those white and red roses, the peonies, the blue anchusa – or even the bruised purple-red valerian that, weed-like, sprang up everywhere and which we called by the local name, devil's dung.

After he closed the gate no flowers captured Wyn Phillips's

attention. He stood beneath a tree, sighing, 'Good heavens, good heavens.'

I pulled a leaf from one of the branches and passed it to my unaccountably agitated visitor. 'It smells like a dispensary,' I said.

'Do you know the name of this tree?' he asked.

'No,' I said. 'I've often wondered.'

He lifted the leaf to his nostrils, unsmiling. He sniffed it again and again as if it were important that he should identify its medicinal odour, his eyes closed as if he were at a concert and listening to profound music. He opened his eyes, troubled. 'I've smelt that smell before,' he pronounced, 'but I can't recall where. I'll keep this.' He put the leaf in his pocket. 'I have a friend who used to work at Kew Gardens. When he comes to Ogmore next I'll get him to identify it. I'm sure it's a rare tree for this country. An Oriental tree.'

'My daughter-in-law's wonderful with the garden,' my mother beamed.

I examined our tree with fresh interest. 'Not every man has an Oriental tree in his garden,' I said.

'I can do better than that,' Wyn Phillips countered. 'I have an Asian wife. You must meet her.'

'When I was a girl,' said my mother pointlessly, 'and I lived in Bridgend, we used to come to Ogmore in a pony and trap.'

Autumn and Winter

In subsequent visits to Ogmore-by-Sea I did not see much of our neighbour Wyn Phillips, though his bungalow was only a few minutes' walk downhill towards the river mouth. I was busy: our children and their friends had joined us; or I had to visit my mother in Cardiff; or I had an article to write, a book to review, a deadline to meet; or a football match to go to. Besides, Wyn Phillips and I had different interests. Old he may have looked, but he had a mind like a questing adolescent: he delighted in talking about abstractions, about the Meaning of Life and Death. Perhaps it was because he had been so ill. It seemed he had suffered a polyarteritis which, the doctors had told him, 'had fortunately become arrested'.

Once he solemnly remarked to me in the Craig – the nearest pub to Green Hollows – trying to initiate a soulful debate, 'I think you know yourself, Dan. But I don't. I don't know who I am.' And this before he had even sipped at his first pint of beer! Wyn was not given to making small talk or being light about things. And despite my occasional probings he hardly referred to his life in the Far East or even to his wife, though he did reveal that she liked reading poetry. 'Malay poetry,' he added.

I am not certain that he pursued such earnest existentialist questions with other people so remorselessly. I sensed that because I was a doctor and wrote poetry he half believed I knew the secret of things, was all-wise. Talking to Wyn, because of his overestimation of me, I often felt inadequate.

One late morning, during the Christmas period, Wyn Phillips telephoned. 'Come over for a pre-lunch drink,' he urged me. 'I have important news for you.'

'Joan's in Bridgend, shopping,' I said.

'Leave a note for her – ask her to join us later.'

I left Joan a note. *At Wyn Phillips for a drink. He invites you to join us. 12.18 p.m. Love, D.* Then I ventured into the cold, misty day, passing my Oriental tree, now leafless, of course. As I proceeded down Craig-yr-eos Road I heard the foghorns sounding from Nash Point. I could not see where sea and sky joined because of the smudging mist. When I reached the turf and turned towards the estuary I kept to the path next to the stone wall until the new-built houses and bungalows loomed into sight. Here the sound of the sea seemed louder, a continuous background noise.

These new structures had been built on sand. Farther up, where we were, it was rock, solid rock. The meaning of the Welsh word *craig* was *rock*. Craig-yr-eos Road – 'Rock-of-the-nightingale'. How many decades, on their unstable base, would these new homes last? Yet what a view they all had on a clear day, despite the tarmac that had been laid down for cars to park on; despite too the coastguard's low stone building with its red flag which even in this mist looked like a public urinal commanded by a communist. Beyond the river mouth, now, I could see indistinctly the sand dunes – the second highest in Europe.

When I was a boy those sand dunes had been requisitioned for an army shooting range. Now, though – probably even in this weather – all kinds of isolated, strange people walked their hidden ways, or jogged through them. Joan and I sometimes went walking there in the milder seasons. And we had been startled by young men running through in single file, utterly silent because of the soft sand, between the narrow valleys of the dunes. It was like meeting joggers in a desert.

In the Phillipses' front room I heard again the distant foghorns sorrowfully hooting. 'It's an eerie sound,' Mrs Phillips remarked. Soon after, she scuttled away saying she had lunch to prepare and left me holding a glass of sherry. At once, Wyn launched into a Big Theme: 'So many things are changing here in Wales,' he declared. 'A man is what he is partly because of his surroundings, right? But they're putting up new buildings, tearing down old ones, building new bridges, new roads, so that the old familiar places become bloody well unrecognizable.'

'You can say that about Ogmore,' I said.

'When things alter so much,' said Wyn with sincerity, 'don't we feel assaulted deep within us? We become anxious. That explains nationalism.'

'How do you mean?'

'Don't we need to redefine ourselves since so much is crumbling away, or being added to without our permission? For a start, it forces us to define our nationality. I have to say, for a start, that I'm Welsh.'

I must have looked at the bottom of my glass – for Wyn, as if prompted, brought over the bottle of sherry. 'Well, I'm learning Welsh as a matter of fact. Still, I didn't bring you over to tell you that. It's news I have about your tree.'

His friend from Kew Gardens had stayed with them in Ogmore, and they had walked over to Green Hollows.

'It's a Korean tree,' Wyn said triumphantly. 'An *Evodia danieli*. From Korea.'

'*Danieli*,' I said. 'That sounds apt.'

'I told you it was a rare Oriental tree,' said Wyn. 'Here, let's drink to it.'

But then he began to cough and cough and cough so that he could hardly catch his breath. His wife came in, worried. He sat down on the sofa, wheezing and gasping, while I took the glass from his hand and said gently, 'You'll be all right, Wyn. Breathe in and out, slowly. That's right.'

Spring

On Sunday my youngsters luxuriated in having a lie-in. So did my mother that particular morning. The sweet Ogmore air of May must have knocked them out. Joan came in from the garden asking, 'Would you mind going up to the farm to get me a dozen eggs?'

The Powell farm was but a mile's walk – it straddled the road this side of Southerndown. I put the *Observer* to one side and elected to go the indirect way, along the turf near the seashore, then to climb upwards, steeply, to the high road. At the bottom of Craig-yr-eos Road, though, instead of going towards Southerndown I turned towards the river mouth. I decided to call on Wyn Phillips briefly, just to say hello, just to see if he was okay. Other friends, earlier that month and in April, had visited Green Hollows. I had boasted as, one by one, they passed under the *Evodia danieli*, 'This is a rare tree, do you know? From Korea. Have a whiff of one of its leaves.' And each, in turn, had looked thoughtful, suitably impressed.

But Wyn had not been into our garden this spring, since the leaves had budded. Suddenly I felt a sense of dread, a feeling of utter emptiness, purposelessness, blackness, depression. My mother would have remarked, 'Someone walked over your grave.' And I wondered whether I would find Wyn critically ill. A minute later there he was, as if summoned, coming towards me looking so much fitter than he had appeared to be in the winter.

'Yes,' he said, 'I'm fine. I've put on weight.'

'I'm just off to the Powell farm for eggs.'

'You're going the wrong way.'

He offered to accompany me on my errand. Despite the uninterrupted sunlight there were so few people about that they all greeted us with a 'Good morning, lovely morning.' A few people walked their dogs doggedly, a few on the rocks fished for fish patiently, and we stopped from time to time to gaze across to the seagulls flying level with the cliffs of Southerndown or to observe nearer, below us, for we were higher now, the reflected sun on the wrinkled, silver-paper sea.

Before we climbed towards the farm, Wyn turned forward a few yards to the edge of the cliff as if he had spotted something extraordinary. 'My God,' he said, putting his hand on my arm, 'they're screwing.'

I looked down obliquely between the rocks. Far below, on an apron of pebbles, a young man and woman copulated. Both were clothed above the waist, both bare below it. It occurred to me that they would have been more comfortable in the sand dunes, hidden by the sharp rush and marram grass. I turned away.

Wyn said loudly, 'Hang on. It's interesting!' They would not have heard him because of the sighing sea.

'C'mon, Wyn,' I said.

But he continued to watch them unashamedly while I began to

climb slowly towards the farm. 'It's a Sunday morning service,' he called to me.

He caught me up soon after, saying accusingly, 'You're a puritan.'

'You're a voyeur,' I responded, irritated.

Wyn Phillips suddenly became enraged. I did not mean to quarrel with him. He had observed in Green Hollows that we owned some binoculars. Right? Why? I told him truthfully that they had been a gift from my sister years ago, that I rarely used them. But I had used them? Yes, I had used them. And why had I used them? To look at the coast of Somerset, at Tusker Rock, at the ships out at sea sometimes when I was bored. Or towards the promontory of Porthcawl or Happy Valley beyond the dunes. Or to catch a seagull in motion, or to . . . 'And what if you saw two neighbours copulating, you'd put the binoculars down, would you, you'd put them down if you were on your own and no one knew that you, peeping Dan, were watching, right?'

'Don't be childish, Wyn,' I said.

He stood still, a little out of breath. 'It's too much for me to climb up to the farm,' he said quietly. 'I'm going back.'

'Wait for me,' I said. 'I won't be a tick. Sit here for a bit.'

'No. I'm going back.'

I nodded. He started to move down between the fresh yellow-flowered gorse towards the cliffs again, then halted to call vehemently, 'You should know yourself. You don't know yourself. I was wrong about you.'

Summer

The summer of the drought. The reservoirs empty. I was unable to leave sweltering London. One Saturday in early July, working in the library, I thought with resentment, 'How ridiculous not to be at Ogmore in weather like this.' Before I quit the reference room I noticed a book on the open shelves called *Living Trees of the World*.

Soon I was reading, under '*Evodia*', 'The most familiar kinds have large deciduous pinnate aromatic leaves, broad clusters and dry fruit capsules which open to reveal glossy black seeds.' I paused. Aromatic the leaves of our tree were, yes, but it had never developed fruit capsules. In Korea, no doubt, it would have done, but in Wales the tree declined. I read on: '*Evodia danieli* . . . of Korea and northern China, about twenty-five feet tall.' Ours reached to only half that size. A young, still-growing *Evodia danieli* perhaps? Or stunted, because not growing in its natural habitat? I quit the library.

At the end of the month we did manage to snatch one weekend in Ogmore. The whole family joined us. We bathed in the sea that was as warm as the Mediterranean. There had even been fires in the bracken: large patches black as tar were surrounded by scorched ferns and gorse. Once, after a swim, after coming through the wooden gate I looked up intently at our *Evodia danieli* and spotted green capsules. 'Look,' I said excitedly to Joan, 'this non-Welsh weather has made our tree sprout fruit.' It had never done so before. I pulled down a couple of green capsules. 'Open them up,' I continued, 'and we'll see the glossy black seeds.'

Joan could not open it with her fingers. 'I don't think it *is* a fruit,' she said. 'It's like a nut, an unripe nut.'

'Our Korean tree's gone nuts,' said our son David.

'A nut?' I said, surprised.

'Sunstroke,' said David.

In the kitchen David cut across it with a knife. Hearing voices, my mother who had been asleep joined us, stood near David, watching him. 'Gosh, he's a clever boy,' my mother said, happily.

Cut, it resembled a cross section of a very small brain.

'It's a walnut,' Joan said. 'It's not an *Evodia danieli*, it's a walnut tree.'

'I've always liked walnuts,' my mother declared. 'When you were so high, son, remember how on my birthday you bought me some nutcrackers from Woolworths? In those days every item was six-pence.'

My own son was laughing – the uninhibited laughter of a seven-teen-year-old. How absurd! Wyn's friend, that expert, had got it wrong. 'Maybe it's an Oriental walnut tree, Dad,' David said, as if to console me.

'This is definitely a walnut,' Joan said, thinking prose.

'Who told you it wasn't a walnut tree?' my mother asked me.

I told her. She had met Wyn Phillips a year ago. 'Remember, mother?'

She did not remember. 'Is he a Yiddisher boy?' she asked.

During August, American friends stayed with us – Mack Rosenthal and his wife Vicky. Bank holiday weekend, we drove to Ogmore. In the car Mack told us how he was writing another critical book – on

Yeats, among others. As we approached the Severn Bridge Mack railed against the 'non-poetic' treatment of Yeats by so many learned academics.

'I don't want to read another essay on Yeats,' I said truthfully.

Mack did not hear me. He was in full flight! 'Hibernophiliac critics, Maud-Gonneomaniac critics, critics who plunge into the chthonic mysteries, critics who begin books entitled *Yeats* by quoting Dr Johnson and conclude by quoting Dr Buber, critics . . .'

'Where are we now?' interrupted Vicky as I slowed, preparing to pay the toll to cross the Severn Bridge.

A Welsh poet had pointed out that the toll money was craftily collected on the *English* side of the bridge.

'The Welsh ground down again,' I informed the Rosenthals.

'Will we be in Wales when we cross the bridge?' Vicky asked.

I looked forward to showing Ogmore off to Mack and Vicky – 'that gong-tormented sea', the altering light on the estuary, the stepping stones across the river near the ruins of Ogmore Castle.

'Have you friends in Ogmore?' asked Vicky.

'Not close friends,' I said.

'There's Wyn Phillips,' said Joan.

'Wyn has no sense of humour. I wonder what he'll say about the walnuts.'

When we arrived at Ogmore we gladly tumbled out of the dry warmth of the car. The Rosenthals, perfect guests, made suitable noises about the splendour of the sea views.

'How about an icecream?' I suggested.

At Hardee's store they sold Thayer's icecream, the best in Britain in my opinion. 'It's creamy,' I boasted, as if I manufactured the stuff myself. 'As good as American icecream. You can only get it in South Wales.'

'Wow,' said Mack. 'I like icecream in all its depth and variety. It is often uncomplicated in appearance but its taste may promote under-lying reaches of associations. I say all this, of course, icily.'

'I'd sure like to taste a Welsh icecream,' said Vicky, a little worried in case Mack was offending me.

'Life without icecream,' continued Mack, 'would, I believe, be very much less worth living.'

'Oh, c'mon, Mack,' Vicky said louder. 'I really would like an ice-cream.'

I set out for Hardee's while the others sorted themselves out after the journey and unpacked. But I did not bring any icecream back to

Green Hollows that afternoon. I had no sooner closed our front wooden gate than Mrs Phillips appeared down the narrow Craig-yr-eos Road. I smiled. 'How's Wyn?' I asked.

She smiled and paused. 'He's dead,' she replied. She continued to smile so that for a moment I thought that I had misheard her. 'He died a month ago,' she said.

'When I saw him in May,' I said stupidly, 'he looked so much better. He'd put on weight.'

'The steroids,' Mrs Phillips explained.

I struggled to discover appropriate words. Mrs Phillips stood there disconcertingly smiling. Her husband had died a month ago, so perhaps she had no more public crying to do. 'Wyn left a letter for you,' she said. 'Will you come down with me now?'

'Of course.'

Why had she not posted it to me? And what had Wyn written about to me? I remembered our last meeting: how I had climbed to the Powell farm for eggs while he called out, scandalously condemning me, 'You don't know yourself.'

'It's hard to believe Wyn's gone,' Mrs Phillips said, her mirthless smile no longer enduring.

A mile or two out to sea, black Tusker rock was visible and, beyond it, a coal tug slowly moved eastward towards Cardiff, small, caught in no binoculars. The turf above the rocks was strangely discoloured – straw-coloured because of the long absence of rain. We turned there and soon the squat, desolate coastguard's building came into view. Uncharacteristically, the car park was full. I had never seen it so crowded, sunlight glinting on rooftop after rooftop.

'I'm so very sorry,' I said quietly.

When we reached her bungalow the sign startled me: 'FOR SALE' and curtly beneath it: 'PRIVATE CALLERS FORBIDDEN'.

'Where will you move to?' I asked.

'I'll go back to Singapore,' she said. 'My relations . . . I don't know why we came here in the first place. Wyn had no real roots here.'

When she gave me the envelope (quite a large envelope) I did not know whether to open it there and then. But Mrs Phillips seemed to have no curiosity about the letter and moved a little towards the door so that, rightly or wrongly, I imagined she wished me to go. We shook hands silently.

As I climbed Craig-yr-eos Road I opened the envelope. There was no letter inside it. Only a dried leaf with an unmistakable aromatic odour. The leaf which Wyn had thought to be an *Evodia danieli* – I had not had the opportunity to tell him about the walnuts – was brittle, friable. It was probably the leaf Wyn had put in his pocket a year earlier. I walked on to Green Hollows wondering, holding the leaf carefully in one hand, the envelope in the other.

Success

This piece was commissioned originally by *Punch* for a series called 'Success'

At that charity affair, I sat on the platform with Bernard Kops, Frank Norman and Arnold Wesker. We had answered questions about moon probes, Mao Tse-tung, a TV programme called *The Man from Uncle*, Centre 42, the French athlete Michel Jazy (who had recently run a mile in 3 minutes 53.6 seconds flat) and the Viet Cong. Then someone asked, 'Would each member of the panel comment on what it's like to be a success?' My colleagues did not seem to be inhibited by any sense of false modesty: one after one their perorations each lasted long enough for even a slowcoach Roger Bannister to have run *his* mile. At last it was my turn.

'I pass,' I said, quite pleased with my contrasting brevity. After all, wasn't it improper, somehow, for a poet to pronounce that he was successful? 'It is not seemly to be famous,' Boris Pasternak had written:

> It is not seemly to be famous
> Celebrity does not exalt;
> There is no need to hoard your writings
> And to preserve them in a vault.

Alas, my Pasternak-like reticence, my puritanical response, pleased no one. Embarrassed, the chairman hurried towards the next question and the audience, I tardily began to sense, was thinking what the hell, especially what the hell was I doing, sitting up there with famous Mr Kops, notorious Mr Norman, internationally exalted Mr Wesker, not even trying to answer *brilliant* questions. No one thought, what a nice fellow, what a nice, *modest* fellow, what a nice, modest, *successful* fellow that Dannie Abse is. I had nonchalantly uttered, 'I pass,' and they, neither being Pasternak readers nor poker players, had taken me at face value, had missed my amusing irony, had interpreted my abbreviated response to mean, 'I'm a failure, sorry chaps.' Yes, I lost that round. I missed out.

Now, fifteen years or so later, I have been awarded a second chance: the editor of *Punch*, no less, a journal that once published the ever-lively, punchy work of Thomas Hood, has asked me to recount my experience of Success as a Poet. I have it here in writing. This time I yield to such pressure – and without difficulty, for I have a natural tendency to boast. I have always boasted – except for that one charity brains trust lapse. I think it must be a genetic consequence for it's in the family. When I happen to meet my two elder brothers – Wilfred, a psychoanalyst of repute, and Leo, the well-known MP who wears my cast-offs – we frequently vie with each other to pronounce on our recent successes.

'Did you read my paper on the theory and rationale of electro-convulsive therapy?' asks Wilfred, thumbs in braces.

I haven't even time to mutter, 'Snappy title,' for Leo cunningly darts in with, 'Did you hear about my *important* speech in the House of Commons last week?' Evidently his speech had floored 'em.

'Did you read *my* poem in the TLS on Friday?' I counter, coyly suggesting it was a knockout. We are all winning, we are all talking at once, we are impossible.

On occasional public platforms I have discovered that, if in a tight spot, I am given to quoting. It is easier, after all, to quote someone else than to think for oneself. (You can quote me on that.) So, now, I begin my answer to Mr Coren's kind invitation to boast with, 'I know my play is a success, the question is . . . will the audience be one?' I offer this quotation because some people may believe that its author, Oscar Wilde, was at the time merely trying to be entertaining and that he did not profoundly mean what he said. For there is, in popular currency, an idea that writers – be they dramatists, poets, novelists – are never wholly satisfied with what they have written, that after a decent cooling interval, they perceive their work to be not entirely successful; moreover, that the very blemishes now visible to them continue to be wonderfully active: they prompt them to start again on a new play, new poem, new novel, to chase after the rainbow's end in their obsessional search for a form of perfection.

A number of serious writers themselves evidently subscribe to this notion. Did not Paul Valery declare, 'A poem is never completed, it's only abandoned'? In my own experience, though, Valery's statement is not true. A poem abandoned is one that has failed. Any good poem of reasonable length is complete: no word can be added to it, no word can be subtracted from it. Indeed I feel certain (some will believe I am deluded) that I have written such poems, successful poems which are more intelligent than I am, more witty than I am, more lyrical than I am, feel more than I do, are wiser than I am. Despite this certainty, my ambition is still to write the next poem and then the one after that.

That the work, rather than the author of it, be successful, need it be said, is what matters most. For instance, I see many contemporary poets held in high regard, celebrated, but how many of them will prove to own a real, enduring talent? History, over and over again, reveals that the temporary success of a poet and the permanent success of his work do not necessarily coincide.

Not that success, in the worldly sense, is unimportant. Even Gerard Manley Hopkins, for once forgoing the habit of Jesuit renunciation, remarked, 'I say deliberately and before God I would have . . . all true poets remember that fame, the being known, though one of the most dangerous things to man, is nevertheless the true and appointed air, element, and setting of genius and its works.' For my part, without some degree of success I would wonder whether my need to write poems was somehow a symptom of an ill-defined neurosis. I mean, to be a poet without any acknowledgement when young may matter little: 'One day . . .' the young aspirant can say to himself optimistically; but to reach the middle of middle age or beyond and still to have no success, still to find difficulty in having poems published as many do, still to feel utterly neglected as many do, must make the ageing aspirant wonder whether he is engaged in a neurotic activity. Remembrances of the neglect of certain poets, such as Manley Hopkins, during their lifetimes can serve at best as a transient palliative. Thoughts such as these once prompted me to write:

> Love, read this though it has little meaning
> for, by reading this, you give me meaning.

When I was a student, in 1946, my first book of poems was accepted by Hutchinson and I received £50 advance. Later they printed 500 copies. For my second book Hutchinson, perceiving they had been over-generous, gave me £25 advance and still published 500 copies. Since then I have been fortunate, things have improved greatly, so that now, in middle age, I do not have to feel I am in some way neurotic in writing poetry. Hutchinson confidently allow a first print run of over 5000 copies. That, of course, does not make my poems successful, and to some that quantity may seem derisively small. 'How many?' said Yevtushenko, and did not stay for an answer.

That one can be 'successful' as a poet in Britain and still not be famous, because of the public's limited interest in poetry, is a valuable advantage. Sometimes, not often, it happens that a stranger accosts me saying, 'Aren't you . . . the poet?' Such recognition – it depends where, when, how and who – may or may not give me pleasure; but how exposed and vulnerable and awful to be truly famous – as Yevtushenko is in Soviet Russia. For the famous generally expect to be recognized all the time – in street, in train, in restaurant. Indeed, some become displeased when any recognition is withheld. I recall how an uncle of mine was drinking in an Italian hotel bar with a seemingly pleasant stranger. Eventually, my uncle asked, 'What, sir, do you do for a living?'

The Italian smiled. 'I'm Gigli,' he replied.

My uncle looked puzzled, as if there had been some language difficulty. 'What do you do for a living?' he repeated more slowly.

Now unsmiling, the stranger said, 'I'm Gigli, I'm Gigli.'

After a slight pause my uncle put down his glass and insisted again, 'Yes, but what do you do for a living?'

Outraged, Signor Gigli, muttering and spluttering, bolted for the door.

Even such success that I have had brings with it certain drawbacks. Through the post arrive unsolicited and unwelcome poems. 'My son, I'm sure, is very gifted,' a proud father writes. 'I have no knowledge of poetry myself but I should be glad of an expert's opinion.' The poems prove to be tediously long and display not a minim of talent. But I know father and son want undiluted praise not criticism, and that neither are likely to be possessed by Manley Hopkins's spirit of renunciation and heroic acceptance. So I spend half a morning composing a tactful letter which in the end I tear up as much in rage with myself as with the father and son. In the same post, I discover an invitation. 'I know your mother's cousin's son's wife,' writes somebody. 'Could you come to Basildon in January to address the literary society I hope to form? You will be our first speaker. I fear, alas, I can offer you no fee.' I am halfway replying to this devastating invitation when the telephone rings. I pick up the receiver and hear a foreign voice ask, 'Zat Dr Abs, ze poet?'

I cough. 'Abse,' I say.

'No, I want Dr Abs, ze poet.'

I clear my throat again. 'Speaking,' I say, resigned.

It seems my caller has a friend with a common medical problem and he continues, 'I want a poet to treat him since he's so sensitive. You're the only poet I've ever heard of who's also a medical doctor, yes?'

I give him the names of several others quickly.

My moans and groans then, as you see, are trivial. They are the quotidian complaints of a poet living in Philistia where the political establishment, fortunately, does not take poetry too seriously. There are no poets in Britain, happily, in jail for being subversive – though I dare say some ought to be for their lack of talent! I only have to think of the fate of so many notable European poets, subjected to grim political pressures, to realize how lucky one is to be a poet working in a tolerant, liberal ambience. I am thinking of Mayakovsky committing suicide, Lorca murdered, Mandelstam arrested and destroyed, Hernandez dying in a Franco prison, Celan in a Nazi concentration camp, Pasternak in disgrace, Brecht exiled, Czeslaw Milosz exiled, Joseph Brodsky exiled – I've named but a few.

There are small advantages in being a poet in Britain other than the large one of being unmolested by coercive authorities. Cecil Day Lewis recounted how he was moved by a literate guard from a third-class carriage to a first-class one. That guard, evidently, felt that poets should be rewarded somehow since no one doles them out luncheon vouchers.

No guard has ever smilingly directed me into a first-class carriage but not long ago I learnt of the advantage of being a poet in my home town. While in Cardiff one day I found that I needed to 'spend a penny'. I was near Roath Park Recreation Ground where I used to play football when a boy. I recalled a green-painted public urinal at the eastern end of the fields. I walked towards the distance optimistically. There it was, presumably as smelly and fly-blown as ever. Arriving, I discovered a notice: 'LADIES'. I walked around it but there was no 'GENTLEMEN'. However, nearby stood one of those permanent temporary structures that proved to be a branch library. I assumed I would find a haven there.

The man stamping the books looked up when I whispered to him, conspiratorially, 'Excuse me, is there a gents here?'

'No, not for the public,' he replied, also whispering. 'But poets, Mr Abse, can use our private lav. First right, through that door, then second left.'

I have benefited in other ways too. I have been offered free tickets to football matches in South Wales and to Test matches at Lords.

Through poetry readings I have been invited to places abroad that otherwise would have remained inert for me, exotic names on a map; also to surprisingly attractive places in Britain that otherwise I would have missed. Because of my reputation as a poet not only have I travelled in the realms of gold and many goodly states and kingdoms seen but with Roy Plomley I have visited that Saturday evening 'desert island'. I don't particularly want to boast about this but I have even been to Basildon and, yes, to 23–27 Tudor Street to sit for lunch and to swank wittily (move over, Chaucer) at the Punch Round Table. Yet even now, as I ponder on 'success', I cannot help but uneasily remember how Chekhov responded when asked to consider the same question. 'What's the criterion?' he wondered. 'You'd need to be God to distinguish success from failure unerringly. I'm off to a dance.'

Failure

> The stage is a scaffold on which the playwright is executed.
> *Chekhov* (LETTERS)

I

On my thirteenth birthday one of my mother's best friends – the one who laughed more often and louder than any person in Wales and whom I had to call Aunt May not Laughing Gas – gave me a thick, heavy, blue-bound volume of plays by G. B. Shaw. Since it contained 1220 pages (I own the book still and its leaves have not spotted or turned brown) it was considerably more substantial than the William and P. G. Wodehouse books that had, until then, been intermittently engaging me. Suspiciously, I opened this thick-as-a-bible volume at its preface, which oddly turned out to be 'A Warning from the Author'. I was accustomed to such brief admonitions as could be found in GWR carriages, which had 'Penalty for Pulling Communication Cord £5'; but G. B. Shaw's authoritarian warning ambled on for a page and a half to conclude:

> When you once get accustomed to my habit of mind, which I was
> born with and cannot help, you will not find me such bad company.
> But please do not think you can take in the work of my long lifetime
> at one reading. You must make it your practice to read all my works at
> least twice over every year for ten years or so. That is why this edition
> is so substantially bound for you.

I had no intention of reading the edition once. To tell the truth, I had never heard of G. B. Shaw who seemed somewhat conceited from his introductory remarks and, besides, his 'Warning' was not all that well written. Mr Graber, my English master at school, had told us that to begin a sentence with *But* and to use such words as *get* showed a weakness of style.

However, before I was thirteen and a half, measles visited me and since I was bored during my convalescence, I opened again the pages of my unwanted present. Not many people, I suspect, come to read Bernard Shaw because of a virus. First I turned to *Widowers' Houses*, then to *The Philanderer*, then to *Mrs Warren's Profession*. I became addicted. Over a period of months, though now healthy, I read all Shaw's plays. I liked them enough to investigate the work of other dramatists. Indeed for a time, berserk, I read only plays.

I had been once to the theatre. That had been three years earlier when the big boys from Marlborough Road Primary School were conscripted to see a matinée performance of *The Merchant of Venice* with Donald Wolfit as Shylock. All of us had been impressed by how far Mr Wolfit could spit. Philip Griffiths decided if we could spit like that it would be worth sitting at the back of a Western Welsh bus and having a go at the driver's neck. It would be worth paying the inevitable £5 fine, bloody worth it. 'My gob's as good as Donald Wolfit's your honour. . . . I couldn't resist it your honour.' 'Quiet, boy. £5 fine or jail.'

I had told both my elder brothers – Wilfred and Leo – of Wolfit's prowess in projecting sputum convexly after the departing Antonio. Wilfred, not listening, said reflexly, 'Well done,' but Leo was fired by my information. Suddenly he *was* Shylock. 'Fair sir,' he was saying, his seventeen-year-old eyes rolling as he hunchbacked himself, 'you spit on me on Wednesday last; you spurned me such a day; another time you called me dog; and for these courtesies I'll lend you thus much moneys.' Leo stared like a madman, arranged a nasty noise in his throat, ignored Wilfred's 'Now watch it,' and deposited a heavy round of spit onto the grate of the coal fire where it momentarily sizzled like sausages. Leo was already quite an actor, for all orators are surely actors?

By the time I was thirteen and a half my brother had become entirely professional, as befitted a future Member of Parliament. Leo, twenty years of age, would stand on a soapbox in Llandaff Fields – the local Hyde Park Corner – and denounce with righteous passion the unemployment in the Welsh valleys, the paradox of slums and cripples in a world of colours. He always sounded wonderfully spontaneous but I knew that like an actor he would carefully rehearse his fresh-languaged speeches. He would lock the door of his bedroom and then his voice would rise and fall remarkably. 'It is given to man,' I could hear him roar. He was very good.

Along with Wilfred he became my temporary hero. 'When you shut yourself in like that, Leo,' I asked him with sincere interest, 'do you practise your speeches before a mirror?' I didn't get a reply. It was like asking a poet whether he used a rhyming dictionary.

'What do you think of Bernard Shaw?' I cross-examined my knowledgeable brothers.

'*Saint Joan*'s good,' Wilfred said.

'Shaw? A castrated monkey,' Leo said dismissively.

I remembered my brothers' considered judgements of Shaw. Two years later Leo told me about Eugene O'Neill. There was an O'Neill play at the Prince of Wales Theatre called *Desire under the Elms*. 'Now that's got more guts, is much more visceral than Bernard Shaw,' Leo proclaimed. I had never heard the word *visceral* before. I liked the word. I repeated it to myself.

I went with my friend, Sidney Isaacs, to see the O'Neill play. On the way, in the lurching tramcar, I confidently informed Sidney that *Desire under the Elms* would be better than any play of G. B. Shaw's.

'I thought you admired Bernard Shaw,' said my friend.

'Not so much as I used to. Shaw's plays don't wear well, you know, except perhaps for *Saint Joan*.'

'Have you seen *Saint Joan*?'

I ignored that. 'The trouble is,' I continued, 'Shaw has got no balls. . . . He's a eunuch. But O'Neill, now, he's really gutsy . . . er . . . visceral.'

From the corner of my eye I could see that Sidney, who had become strangely quiet, was staring at me with a new, inadvertent admiration. Perhaps he felt that I should be one of those fancy, bitch theatre critics who pronounce in the Sunday papers after they have sat, free-ticketed, proud and pampered, in a gangway seat, row G.

We enjoyed *Desire under the Elms* from the gods, so much so that we began occasionally to frequent the Prince of Wales Theatre instead of the Olympia Cinema, the Park Hall, the Empire. We saw *Young Woodley*, *Little Women* and beheld Donald Wolfit again, this time as King Lear:

> Come, let's away to prison;
> We two alone will sing like birds i' the cage:
> When thou dost ask me blessing, I'll kneel down
> And ask of thee forgiveness; and we'll live,
> And pray and sing and tell old tales, and laugh
> At gilded butterflies, and hear poor rogues
> Talk of court news; and we'll talk with them too,
> Who loses, and who wins; who's in, who's out;
> And take upon's the mystery of things,

As if we were God's spies; and we'll wear out
In a wall'd prison, packs and sets of great ones
That ebb and flow by the moon.

Ill-produced *King Lear* may have been, ill-acted for the most part too, but the language of England soared and I soared with it. I sat in the high gods of the Prince of Wales Theatre and I heard the active words of Shakespeare as I had never heard them before and I was exhilarated in a way I could hardly explain or define. Somehow, young as I was, silly as I was, I felt most wonderfully altered and refined. More than that; when, later, I licked the back of my own hand and brought it to my nostrils, like old King Lear himself, I could smell the smell of mortality.

2

When I was a medical student in London I had a book of poems accepted, which encouraged me to try and earn some money – for my patient landlady's sake as much as my own – by occasional freelance writing. Later, because of an inept poetry-drama I had written called *Fire in Heaven* I was invited to become a sporadic critic for a fortnightly theatre magazine. I boasted of this part-time appointment when I returned home to Cardiff for Christmas. 'Stop wasting your time,' my father advised me, 'and get on with studying medicine.'

The magazine was not important enough to be offered *first-night* free tickets by theatre managements and I was not important enough to cover the main plays in the West End. This the editor did himself. So on second-night performances of plays, frequently new plays, and frequently staged it seemed to me in the vicinity of Notting Hill Gate (I was forever taking a 31 bus) I took my seat in row G among a sparse audience – how sparse depended on how many friends the actors had, the size of the cast and whether or not the author was alive and well and living in Notting Hill Gate. No matter; before the house lights came down and the curtain went up, there I sat with my swanky chest stuck out, an invisible sceptre in my left hand and my two eyes narrowed, ready to write my best worst.

Since that stint as second-string, second-night theatre critic, I have never envied those columnists, however important, who year in, year out have to provide hebdomadal copy. What a job for an adult! Even when the production is of a justly admired classic – a Greek play, a Shakespeare, a Chekhov – some self-infatuated director, probably called Peter since most directors are so named, will decide the script needs pepping up a bit. To ensure Peter's production will make its mark, *Lysistrata* is given an all-male cast, dwarfs only are allowed to appear in *Julius Caesar* and *The Cherry Orchard* is set in industrial Newark, New Jersey. Hazlitt, referring to the egomania of so-called creative people, tells us in *Table Talk* of a friend of his who discovered a very fine Canaletto in a state of curious disfigurement, the upper part of the sky having been smeared over and fantastically variegated with English clouds. On inquiring to whom it belonged and whether something had not been done to it, Hazlitt's friend was informed 'that a gentleman, a great artist in the neighbourhood, had retouched some parts of it.' That great artist of the neighbourhood, I suggest, could well have been christened Peter.

Mary McCarthy once cast a cold eye on current drama for the American magazine *Partisan Review*. Readers of that magazine, being serious people, did not really want to visit the New York theatre. She, by giving all plays truthful, some would say acidulous notices, confirmed their prejudices. After reading her in *Partisan Review* they were able to mutter comfortably, 'I guessed that play wouldn't be worth seeing.' She did those *Partisan Review* readers a wonderful service. By giving them no fashionable reason to attend this or that play Mary McCarthy saved them an immense amount of trouble, time, and money. She was a public benefactor.

The theatre magazine that I wrote for, alas, had quite a different readership: men and women keen to see plays week after week, month after month, year after year. They did not want to be put off by negative copy. I did not do too well. I was too sincere. The editor did not suggest I should be more temperate but when I managed to remain awake through the whole of a play called *The Same Sky* by Yvonne Mitchell at the Lyric Theatre, Hammersmith, I softened my critique. At that moment I understood the furtive circumstances, the occasional guilt-tinged feeling of every journalist in the world who has to supply overlooked copy.

Some imagine writers to be encouraged by other writers' impoverished creations. Bad poems, they believe, allow an aspiring poet to think, 'I can do better than that'; bad plays, similarly, tempt a potential dramatist to try his hand at the game. This notion is wrong. Rather it is those rare poems that thrill, those rare plays that enchant which prove to be seminal. Academic critics, some of them anyway, seem somewhat puzzled that any living writer has enough arrogance not to be crushed by tradition, by the unsurpassable works of those artists who have preceded him. But of course writing has nothing to do with arrogance or humility. Simply, there are needs to be gratified and besides 'there is no competition'.

I soon gave up pretending to be a theatre critic and over the next decade enjoyed certain plays I visited as a paying customer, among them Ibsen's *The Wild Duck*, Pirandello's *As You Desire Me*, Eugene O'Neill's *The Iceman Cometh* and Tennessee Williams's *The Glass Menagerie*. Those plays stage-struck me sufficiently to think that one day I might try again to write a play. Should not a poet, I secretly asked myself, be able to contribute something uncommon to the theatre?

Not poetry-drama – I did not deeply admire the then fashionable plays of T. S. Eliot, Christopher Fry, Ronald Duncan. There was such a thing, though, as *poetic* drama. It was not just a question of diction. *The Tempest* was more of a poetic drama than *Macbeth*; Pirandello's plays closer to poetry than those of Eliot. Nor was it a question of raising the language at appropriate moments: there were too many plays where the language suddenly became moonlit and the audience treated to a patch of artificial poetry. 'Poetic drama must be written by dramatic poets,' wrote Alan S. Downer. 'If the truism is chiastic, truth yet lies in the figure.' Poetic drama, not poetry-drama – that was the crucial point. And was poetic realist drama, I wondered, possible – or was it a contradiction in terms?

In 1958, I adapted a poem of mine for radio, dramatized it – a poem called 'The Meeting'. It was broadcast on the Welsh Home Service. My father listened to it and groaned. Perhaps he was right. It would be better to write a play proper with more distinctive characters – a stage play. I would try and write it as Poetic drama.

'It'll fail,' my father said. 'That's not what people want. You'd do better to write for TV. Terrible rubbish they put on. Even you might have a chance there.'

I finished my play and called it *House of Cowards*. By then poetry-drama was discredited in the British theatre, T. S. Eliot and Christopher Fry no longer fashionable. Nobody would notice the difference between the designation *poetry-drama* and *poetic drama* so I did not give it any tag at all. In the summer of 1960, my play – my first real play as far as I was concerned – would be produced at the Questors Theatre in Ealing and directed by John McGrath.

I asked my father if he would care to come to London and see it.

'You say the Questors Theatre is amateur?' he asked.

'It's the premier amateur theatre in Britain,' I explained.

'Duw, an *amateur* theatre,' my father said sadly. 'That won't bring the butter home, son.'

3

Though performed at the Questors, *House of Cowards* won the Charles Henry Foyle Award for 1960. 'The Foyle Award,' I explained to my father, trying to impress him, 'is for the best play produced outside the West End. It's the first time an amateur theatre has been given that award.'

'Amateur dramatics, that doesn't count,' my father said, unimpressed.

'£100 goes with the award too,' I added.

'You'd do better in the football pools,' Dad said with scorn.

It was a game, of course, that my father and I were playing. He invited me to report to him my self-directed gossip and then he, in turn, liked to tease me. I knew that and he knew that. In any case, I was encouraged by winning the Foyle award and I got myself a theatre agent, Peggy Ramsay, who had, and has, the just reputation of being one of the best in Britain. In her office she said to me imperially, 'Dr Abse, you come in here today a duck. One day you'll leave this office a swan.'

It seemed that Bernard Miles would stage *House of Cowards* at the Mermaid Theatre but that possibility became more and more remote and ceased to exist altogether when Donald Albery bought an option on the play. I was summoned to a theatre in St Martin's Lane where I hoped my play would be put on when *Oliver Twist*, its present occupant, finished its run. I was shown into an office in the theatre to meet the lady who initiated, or at least carried out, Mr Albery's theatrical enterprises.

I had never been in such a room. The walls consisted of four huge mirrors, ceiling to floor. As we conversed, the lady never looked at me directly once. She addressed me through the mirror on the right or the mirror on the left and I could not tell whether she was looking at one of my reflections or at one of her own. In turn, I addressed her profile. Finally I quit this mirrored room, leaving her and her multiple reflections all artificially smiling in that decor of extreme narcissism.

Oliver Twist with Ron Moody was a great success. A box-office smash. My option ran out, was renewed, ran out again, and with *Oliver Twist* asking for more, going great guns, Donald Albery, or the

Lady of the Mirrors, lost interest. Eventually at last, *House of Cowards*
was accepted for its first professional production. Warren Jenkins of
the Welsh Theatre Company wanted to stage it in Cardiff during
January 1963.

'In Cardiff?' I said to Margaret Ramsay, surprised. 'That's my
home town.'

It seemed Warren Jenkins had quit TV to be the director of the
new Welsh Theatre Company under the aegis of the Welsh Arts
Council. For their first season he would direct successively Tennes-
see Williams's *Period of Adjustment*, my new play *House of Cowards* and
Molière's *Tartuffe*. The company had great high hopes that it would
evolve into the Welsh National Theatre with, eventually, its own
building.

'Meanwhile they are centred at the Prince of Wales Theatre,'
Margaret Ramsay explained. 'Perhaps you know it?'

The winter of 1963 proved to be the coldest and most malignant in
Britain for centuries. Because of seemingly perdurable arctic condi-
tions, cars under snow remained stranded in the city streets like, so
many ruined igloos. The icy conditions hardly encouraged people to
venture out at night. They found it difficult enough to get home from
their workplaces. As a result, the cast of the new Welsh Theatre
Company presented *The Glass Menagerie* to an almost empty theatre
auditorium.

'They wouldn't come this weather if it were Pontypridd Williams
not Tennessee Williams,' I said to Warren Jenkins.

I hoped the weather would change before *House of Cowards* was
staged. It can't go on and on like this much longer, I consoled myself;
but it did so, on and on and on, snow falling on snow, turning each
new morning into a blank new page across which howled a wind
surely arranged by a BBC overenthusiastic sound-effects man.
Worse, the heating system in the Prince of Wales Theatre partially
failed. It became colder inside the theatre than outside. I sat wrapped
up in an eiderdown watching the so-called dress rehearsal. How
different this theatre had been when I was a boy!

My father because of his chest condition – he was to die of it the
following year – did not leave the house, curious though he was about
my play. He sat hunched over the coal fire, waiting for me each night
in order to ask in his best, ex-cinema-proprietor voice, 'Better house
tonight, son?' And I would shake my head. Thanks to Peggy Ramsay
one management did come down from London – Bob Swash – and
Warren Jenkins tried to paper the theatre by giving away free tickets

to warm-blooded university students and nurses. No use, they would not come. Bob Swash could smell the smell of failure. 'Every play has its destiny,' Margaret Ramsay told me, resigned. Later, I felt my destiny had to be with another drama agent.

I could blame the weather, I know that, for the failure of *House of Cowards* in Cardiff; but that was not the whole story. Seeing the play in production allowed me to see its blemishes more clearly: I had overstated things, too often gone over the top. It needed pruning, it needed more than pruning. If it had had another production I would have wanted to make a number of important alterations in the text; but it never has had a further professional airing.

In his essay 'Poetry and Drama', T. S. Eliot wrote of the 'desire to write something which will be free of the defects of one's last work', and how that desire acts as 'a very powerful and useful incentive' to write another play. Such incentives have prompted me, once every five years or so, to try again. Indeed, frankly I am proud of one or two plays I have written – not least one called *Pythagoras*, first produced at Birmingham Repertory Theatre by Peter Farago in 1976. I have been lucky in that all of my plays have been produced; unlucky in that not one of them has established my reputation as a dramatist. And yet luck has probably little to do with it. 'I must complain the cards are ill-shuffled till I have a good hand,' Swift said.

My brother Leo, who has often loyally come to an opening of a play of mine, once brutally whispered to me – while the audience was clapping the actors at the final curtain with enthusiasm and I was feeling somewhat elated, complacently pleased with myself – 'You should stick to poems.' A seagull flying in the thrilling liberty of the blue sky shuddered as an arrow hit it. Later, with little enough of praise and too much censure – for I wanted from my brother only unadulterated admiration – he hinted that my plays needed to be so crafted that they provided the audience with a less strenuous emotional experience. I did not care for such opposition. How stupid of Leo: how stupid, myopic, feeble-minded, dastardly, insensate, asinine. What effrontery! What insolence! What a dunce! 'Go on, Leo,' I said, 'I can take criticism.'

Was he right, I wonder? Perhaps I should have allowed my plays more continuous, inner gaiety, 'gaiety transforming all that dread'; or, at least, more proliferating pretty blossom to disguise the under-lying nettle. I hear my schoolboy ghost say to me now, rather late, 'Too nakedly visceral, mun. Five pounds fine.'

Notes Mainly at the Clinic

The routine X-ray showed horizontal, linear condensations adjacent to both hemidiaphragms. I wondered if my patient had ever been exposed to any asbestos dust.

'No, but my father worked at Hebden Mill.'

'In West Yorkshire?'

'Yes.'

'You lived nearby, near the mill?'

'Quite near, as a boy, yes.'

When I questioned him further I learnt that his father, on returning home from the mill, had the habit of brushing down his coat jacket. No doubt, infinitely small fibres of crocidolite (blue asbestos) had, as a result, been sprinkled into the air and the young boy had then innocently breathed them in.

The work at the clinic has always been repetitious; these days it is worse – there are fewer patients, longer gaps of not doing anything during the day. I hardly see any people suffering from pulmonary tuberculosis, which used to be such a common scourge. Sometimes I worry whether I shall be made redundant (an increasing possibility); and sometimes I feel, puritan that I am, a little guilty that I'm not working hard enough. Guilty, I mean, of occasionally doing nothing, guilty of waiting like a prisoner for the clock to turn and turn again, guilty of being almost dead for an hour, guilty of postponements on rainy days, of things not done, things not said. A reprieve would be to pronounce to someone, anyone, positively, 'You are ill,' or 'You are cured.' That would prove that I was alive. . . .

This morning I had to report on some hundreds of routine chest X-rays. One after one I looked at them. I found no abnormality whatsoever: the lung fields invariably clear, the heart sizes and shapes all within their normal limits. At one point, bored, I began to wish I would see something other than normality – some sarcoid infiltration, an aortic aneurysm, a pneumothorax or, better still, a mysterious shadow, one I had never seen before, one perhaps never reported on ever, illustrated in no textbook. Then, like a stern headmaster, I reproved myself: I didn't want any of these anonymous people whose X-rays I was scrutinizing to be ill, did I? I did not want to summon one pale patient to my room and say, 'I'm sorry but . . .'

Of course not. I carried the X-rays, along with my report, to the clerk in the outer office and said, 'Rejoice, all these patients are healthy.'

The power, within us, of denial. M. S. six years ago had a lung removed because of a bronchial cancer. He now comes to see me only for a reassuring annual check-up. I do not know if he ever truly has understood the nature of his disease. When I first read his case notes I discovered that, while his relatives had been told the truth, he himself was informed that he had 'a lung abscess with complications'. He had had post-operative radiotherapy and saw me regularly for clinical examination and routine chest X-ray. I never saw any reason to discuss with him the original diagnosis. He never raised the matter himself.

In my experience, such an avoidance of an intolerable diagnostic truth is common. The doctor does not have to tell it out loud and plain, is hardly ever challenged with genuine force to do so. The patient will talk about his old symptoms, his old operation, his old wife, the old football team he supports, but he will rarely say, 'Doctor, that diagnosis of a lung abscess was just a lot of old codswallop. I'm not an idiot to be fobbed off with that patently fictional diagnosis. If it had merely been a lung abscess why did I have radiotherapy, why are you seeing me so regularly, why are you palpating my liver *now* with such care?'

Today, before palpating M. S.'s liver, I happened to glance at his fingers. Two fingers of his right hand were clearly nicotine-stained. Why, he had given up smoking cigarettes when he had had the operation. Now, absurdly, had he started again?

'Look, doctor,' M. S. said. 'I know you've given up smoking yourself. You told me so years ago. But it's easy for you – you're looking at X-rays like mine all the time.'

M. S. had undergone major chest surgery, must have had terrible anxieties, must have secretly wondered, if only at dead of night, about his former disease; but now, here he was, saying to me, 'It's easy for you, doctor.'

On one hand the power of denial, on the other the power of suggestion. A number of my patients need to give up smoking because they have been exposed to blue asbestos – there is a synergistic effect with the inhalation of tobacco smoke and blue asbestos fibres. I mentioned this to one of my colleagues, Dr Margaret MacDonald, who has begun to practise acupuncture with what seems to be total enthusiasm. I thought perhaps acupuncture might help those who had difficulty in kicking the habit, through the power of suggestion.

'That is not how acupuncture works,' Margaret insisted.

The continued existence of acupuncture in a 'modern' state like China has sanctioned doctors like Margaret MacDonald, as well as quacks, to practise this form of treatment in the West. In the last decade or so newspapers and popular periodicals have given acupuncture much free publicity; there have been medical journalists who have tried to give acupuncture a scientific gloss. In Britain, and no doubt elsewhere, there exist acupuncture clinics where men in clinical white coats, resembling the glamorous doctor heroes of television medical romances – though frequently they are not, in fact, qualified doctors – stick needles into hopeful patients. Most of the patients leave the clinic (the decor of one I visited resembled a cross between a lush private nursing home and a Chinese restaurant) with the symptoms they had when they entered. All leave with less money in their wallets or handbags.

It is significant that one acupuncture doctor interviewed in the *Sunday Times* declared that he preferred to treat 'chronic ailments which have defeated Western medicine: for instance, migraines and other types of headaches; duodenal and stomach ulcers; indigestive disorders; lumbago, fibrositis, sciatica, neuralgia; acne and other skin troubles; asthma, hay fever; high blood pressure; depressions and anxiety states' – all symptoms or ailments known to be related to stress or other psychological disturbance. The doctor would probably obtain the same results, providing he believed in the efficacy of it all, by sticking the needles into himself while his patients watched him. However, the acupuncturist could well respond, 'Do orthodox physicians prescribing placebos, tonics and vitamins obtain better results with those patients suffering the same intractable conditions?'

Of course, the power of suggestion can be packaged in a capsule or concentrated at the point of a needle. Or, for that matter, in any object which has for the patient certain potent associations. Some years ago I was asked to give a gas and oxygen anaesthetic for a minor operation – a removal of an infected toenail. My colleague had nearly finished scrubbing up so I placed the mask over my patient's mouth and nose ready to administer the gas and oxygen anaesthetic. 'It will be over soon,' I had reassured the patient – and so it would have been but, at the last moment, the theatre door opened. An intruder's mouth opened and closed noiselessly in oral gesture. Then shuf-flings, whisperings, eyes meaningful behind masks. I gathered my colleague needed to answer, immediately, outside, an urgent tele-phone call. He temporarily quit the theatre and so I removed the mask from the patient's face. I was about to explain everything as best I could to the inconvenienced patient, to apologize to him for the delay, but he lay there with eyes closed, his head as still as a statue's. He had had no anaesthetic whatsoever. He had breathed in only ordinary air through the mask yet he had swooned. For a half-minute the mask had been over his face and he presumably thought he was breathing in the gas. Accordingly he had fallen into a profound sleep – as profound as Adam's – and I suspect that in that trance he could have had not only his toenail removed but a rib as well. My patient was roused only by strenuous shouting and shaking!

So much for the reports concerning operations undertaken in China with patients 'anaesthetized' by acupuncture needles.

On Friday I hoped to leave the clinic early. I intended to spend the weekend in Wales with my aged mother. Alas, that day, we had a relief radiographer and he proved to be slow and incompetent. Many of the X-rays turned out to be underdeveloped or overdeveloped, under-penetrated or over-penetrated, fogged or partially fogged. Patient after patient had to be returned to the X-ray Department for a repeat X-ray.

At last, it seemed there were no more X-rays to be read and I prepared to catch the later train from Paddington. I was at the door when the telephone rang. 'One more X-ray,' the inept radiographer announced. 'Dr Wicks would like a report as soon as possible. The X-ray'll be ready in a jiffy.'

I settled myself in the chair again to study the current *British Medical Journal*. I waited. And I waited such a long time that I guessed the radiographer had messed up the X-ray once more. I read another article in the BMJ. I looked at my watch. If the X-ray was not ready soon I would miss yet another train from Paddington. Somewhat irritably I hastened to the X-ray Department where I at once encountered the radiographer. 'It's ready, doctor,' he announced cheerfully before I could utter a scolding word.

On the screen, in the dark room, hung the long overdue X-ray. I hoped it would not be fogged or in any other way spoilt, would not need to be repeated. The radiographer touched the switch and the screen lit up brilliantly. Astonished I saw that the patient's chest was tilted at an absurd angle of forty-five degrees – left shoulder up, right shoulder down. What a genius of a radiographer, I thought. However, I could read the X-ray and there was nothing wrong with the man's chest. I could pass it as normal despite it being utterly skewwhiff. I have never seen anything like it.

'I have to congratulate you,' I said to the radiographer with heavy sarcasm, 'that this X-ray . . .'

'The patient's behind you, doctor,' the radiographer interrupted me.

I turned towards the open darkroom door where I could see, beyond, a man sitting in the adjoining X-ray room. At once I approached him, followed by the radiographer.

'Your X-ray is normal,' I reassured the patient, 'though the radiographer here has somehow contrived to tilt your X-ray in such a way that it makes you look as if you're a cripple.'

The patient stared at me uncomprehendingly. No doubt the radiographer, ticked off indirectly in this way, smouldered morosely behind me.

'Can I go?' asked the patient.

'Of course,' I said, smiling.

The man rose from the chair most awkwardly. To my horror I discovered he had only one leg. I observed him limping pronouncedly over the brown linoleum towards the corridor outside the X-ray Department. I turned towards the radiographer who leaned against the wall, his face a study of sweet, sickly triumph.

The lady wished to interview me for a woman's magazine, *Good Housekeeping*. She was a novelist, Carolyn Scott. So one lunch hour last year, I walked from the clinic to Soho Square to meet her near the statue of King Charles II. Later, over lunch, she conducted the interview, which progressed predictably until she suddenly asked, 'What moves you to tears, Dr Abse?' It was a very bare question. I thought of my very aged mother in South Wales whose powers were failing alarmingly so that now she did not know what day of the week it was. However, I did not speak of my mother. I did not know Carolyn Scott so I spoke rather in general terms – as I can now see for the interview has been finally published. I remarked, 'I am moved by the inevitability of certain things, how people we know and love grow senile, how certain diseases cannot be cured – by the fact that Antigone is condemned, must die, and nothing can change that. There are people, perhaps more mature than me, who are resigned to these things, but inwardly, deep down, I don't think I can be resigned.'

Carolyn Scott's response to this disarrayed me. 'Perhaps I shouldn't tell you,' she confessed softly, 'but I have an incurable disease. Its progress is . . . inevitable.' Of course, that confession was not published in *Good Housekeeping* nor did Carolyn Scott report our dialogue that followed it. For my part I noticed for the first time how thin she was, cachetic, and how there was an unhealthy, translucent pallor to her skin. I guessed she had a cancer, was taking anti-mitotic drugs. I had to say something and I am no Spinoza. Clumsily, hesitantly, I talked about how some managed to confront a seemingly fatal illness and, in so doing, I leaned on the truthful crutch of a medical cliché: 'There is never such a thing as "never" in medicine.' I know and she knew that 1 in 10,000 cancers do recover spontaneously. Alas, I read in *Good Housekeeping* that Carolyn Scott died before the interview was published.

Early next year, 1 February 1982, I am to be made redundant. As part of a quarter-of-a-million-pound saving there has to be 'contraction and rationalization'. So, as they say in the football world, I am for an early bath.

It will be strange to vacate this consulting room. I have been lucky, until now, in my medical career. I originally took up chest work because of a sweet accident. When I was conscripted into the RAF for National Service and was sent, with a number of other young doctors, to Moreton-in-Marsh for one month's induction (square-bashing) in May 1951, I resented being separated from Joan Mercer (my future wife) who lived (with me) in Belsize Square, London. So when, one evening in the mess bar, I heard that the RAF Mass

Radiography Section was based in Cleveland Street, *in London*, I became very interested, suddenly, in mass radiography. After all, Cleveland Street was near Goodge Street station, a short tube ride on the Northern Line. Moreover it was halfway between the BBC and my publisher, Hutchinson!

Towards the end of our induction period a form was circulated to us all in which we were invited to put down our geographical and professional preferences regarding future postings. Though it was rumoured that little attention was paid to our responses, on the form I firmly entered 'HOME COUNTIES' and 'VERY KEEN ON MASS RADIOGRAPHY'. The idea of mass radiography had never crossed my mind until that bar conversation but I figured that while my colleagues would ask for 'GENERAL PRACTICE' or 'SURGERY' or 'DERMATOLOGY' or some other speciality they had some engagement with because of this or that house job, not one of them, no one at all, would elect for 'MASS RADIOGRAPHY'. Probably, in the whole history of the RAF medical services, no neophyte ever had.

I was posted to HQ Mass Radiography, Cleveland Street, in London for a further month's training. Then, to my horror, I was to join the mobile X-ray unit in Northern Ireland! However, soon after, I was returned to HQ to become an assistant to the squadron leader in charge of all radiography units. The squadron leader had a PC, i.e. a permanent commission. I liked him; he was an easygoing fellow who frequently absented himself from his office without explanation. Too easygoing, the RAF thought, for a year later, because of certain incidents about which I am still not clear, he was court-martialled and I found myself promoted to Squadron Leader in charge of five doctors, five units, the central chest clinic, etc. So began my chest experience.

And when I left the RAF I was offered the job here, a job limited to office hours and of a diagnostic nature only, a repetitious job, one frequently boring, but one that has given me time to write and to pursue a more general academic interest in medicine. Besides, as a doctor practising within the strict confines of my own small speciality, I have been quite good! I do not want an early bath.

My patient, G., was ostentatiously polite. I had the feeling that he would hurry to open a door for me; but now it was time for him to quit, to open the door for himself. Instead he hesitated, then said, 'I wonder if I might ask you a personal question, Dr Abse?'

'Of course.'

'Have you a son called Albert?'

'No,' I said. 'My son's called Jesse David.'

He then mysteriously withdrew a piece of paper from a pocket of his suit.

'This poem of yours is very very meaningful to me and my wife, Dr Abse,' he said.

Surprised, I glanced at the paper, at an early poem of mine, one that I had written when a medical student. It was called 'Albert' – I still liked it well enough though I would hardly expect that particular poem to be very special for anyone:

> Albert loved dogs mostly though this was absurd
> for they always slouched away when he touched their fur,
> but once, perching on his shoulder, alighted a bird,
>
> a bird alive as fire and magical as that day
> when clear-eyed Héloïse met Peter Abelard.
> Though cats followed him the bird never flew away.
>
> And dogs pursued the cats which hunted the bird.
> Albert loved dogs deeply but was jealously hurt
> that they pursued him merely because of the bird,
>
> the bird alive as fire and magical as that day.
> So one morning he rose and murdered the bird.
> But then the cats vanished and the dogs went away.
>
> Albert hated dogs after – though this was absurd.

I handed the paper back to G. 'It's the only poem I've ever written derived from a dream,' I said. 'I dreamed years ago of someone with a bird on his shoulder followed by cats, followed by dogs. . . .'

G. nodded. He rose from his chair. 'You see,' he said at last, 'I have a son called Albert. He's six now. A year ago he murdered our canary.'

Despite Albert's father, few of my patients are aware that I write poetry. I am always surprised when they do know – as I was last week when one of them brought in my new book, *Way Out in the Centre*, to be signed. He had read a review of it in one of the Sunday newspapers and, as I signed it, asked me how I felt about reviewers and reviews. It so happened the notice he had read had been a

generous one so I was able to respond benignly, though I added
Conrad's dictum about how an author should go to a book review
only with a ruler.

In truth, it takes some five years to put a book of poems together so
it is almost as irritating to be praised in a few lines as it is to be
dismissed curtly. Of course, what every poet wants is a huge space
devoted to him alone by a reviewer he can respect who writes
knowledgeably and sensibly, i.e. enthusiastically, about his new
book. It was either a poet, or God himself, who wrote that graffito on
a wall near Belsize Road in Swiss Cottage: 'LOVE ONLY ME'.

In fact there are some journals where poets unaccountably, or
accountably, may be ignored completely – I mean in publications
accustomed to notice new poetry books – in my case, for some reasons
that I, wholesomely paranoid after midnight, think I understand, in
two literary magazines, *Stand* and *Agenda*. On the whole, though, I
am with Chekhov when he declared (to Gorky):

> Critics are like gadflies which stop a horse ploughing. The horse
> strains, muscles tensed like double-bass strings. Meanwhile there's a
> wretched gadfly tickling and buzzing on his crupper, so he has to
> twitch his skin and flick his tail. But what's all the buzzing about? The
> gadfly hardly knows. It just feels restless and wants to proclaim its
> existence while asserting its ability to buzz away on any subject in the
> world. For twenty-five years I've been reading criticisms of my
> stories. But I don't remember one helpful hint; nor have I heard one
> word of good advice. The only critic to impress me was Skabichevsky
> who once wrote that I'd die in a ditch, drunk.

Most medical authorities may acknowledge a multifactorial cause of
cancer. Nor would they necessarily mock W. H. Auden's poem 'Miss
Gee'.

> Nobody knows what the cause is
>   Though some pretend they do;
> It's like some hidden assassin
>   waiting to strike at you.
>
> Childless women get it,
>   And men when they retire;
> It's as if there had to be some outlet
>   For their foiled creative fire.

Even the occasional surgeon postulates a mysterious relationship between tumour formation and loss of emotional equilibrium. Thus D. Lang Stevenson in his paper, 'Evolution and the Neurobiogenesis of Neoplasia' writes:

> There is evidence to suggest that brain states signifying profound alarm and despondency, particularly in a medium of ageing hormones, are connected with tumour formation and that this indeed may be one of the common causes of human cancer. The time measurement between the event, bereavement of a close contemporary for instance, and the appearance of the tumour has been found constant enough to be statistically significant.

The radiotherapist Professor G. B. Mitchell has also testified on the relationship between bereavement and cancer:

> Not infrequently, one observes the recurrence of a malignant tumour which has been healed for many years, perhaps ten years, sometimes much longer, after surgery or radiotherapy or both. . . . It appears as if tumour cells had lain dormant and then, after many years, started to grow. Such a recurrence often seems to have been precipitated by an emotional upheaval such as follows the death of a husband, wife, or child.

But perhaps the most startling theory about the aetiology of cancer comes from the Department of Psychiatry at Jefferson Medical College in Philadelphia. Psychiatrists there suggest that a patient may suffer cancer *as an alternative to going mad*.

In the Manchester hospital they had arranged a concert for patients and staff. Peter Senior asked me to read some poems of mine that touched on medical themes. I declined. I did not think it wise to read a poem, say, about a brain operation to patients who may be worrying about such surgery! Alas, most of the medically coloured poems that I have written tend to be somewhat grim.

'The Smile Was', insisted Peter Senior. 'That poem celebrates childbirth. It's a very affirmative poem.'

'Yes, but it's quite long,' I said.

Years ago, when a student, I had attended a hundred births. What had struck me then was how the mother invariably smiled when she heard the newborn baby cry out. Not an ordinary smile but one secretive, gentle, ineffable. I became accustomed to wait for that smile and I was never disappointed. Whether the baby had been longed for or not, was legitimate or not, that strange unambiguous smile would appear to transform the mother's recently struggling face into one calm, momentarily beautiful. In the wards I had been taken aback by the ambivalence of patients' responses but the smile of the new mother, it seemed to me then, when she heard her baby crying for the first time, was utterly pure, unadulterated.

In the mid-sixties I wrote a poem about that particular smile and Peter Senior now prevailed upon me to read it. Before I had finished the first section I became aware of gasps, whisperings and sighings to the left of me. As I glanced wonderingly to the audience on the left I read on:

> That agreeable radiant smile
> no man can smile it
> no man can paint it
> as it develops without fail
> after the gross, physical, knotted,
> granular, bloody endeavour.
>   Such a pure spirituality from all that!
> It occupies the face
> and commands it

I became aware of dozens of women intensely glowering at me. Why? I was halfway through the poem when it occurred to me that those sitting in rows of chairs to my left were women – only women. Christ, I thought, they're all probably from the gynaecological wards, all probably have had, or are about to have, their pregnancies terminated. And here I was, here I had to continue celebrating the benediction and mystery of childbirth, the mother's pure smile:

> Never,
> not for one single death
> can I forget we die with the dead,
> and the world dies with us;
> yet
> in one, lonely,
> small child's birth
> all the tall dead rise
> to break the crust of the imperative earth.

The youthful often indulge in rescue fantasies. In their daydreams, the beautiful, the good, the helpless, are frequently saved from harm by an heroic protagonist who remarkably resembles the dreamer.

Walter Mitty owns many faces – not a few of them are sixteen years old. When I was a schoolboy in Cardiff I came out of the Olympia Cinema one late Saturday afternoon having seen a film about the great Paul Ehrlich, the father of modern chemotherapy. I felt uplifted by the film, which featured Paul Muni, glad that one day I would be a doctor. Such a noble profession!

It was half past five and my eyes did not blink as I crossed St Mary's Street, an imaginary stethoscope in my pocket. Before the traffic lights changed their coloured signals, I had saved an old lady from asphyxiating, administered first aid to the mayor shot by Tiger Bay gangsters, and operated on Adolf Hitler – without success.

It has been suggested that rescue fantasies merely represent, symbolically, unconscious desires to save our own mothers from the cruel embraces of the men they married. So that old lady I had saved in my youthful daydream had been none other than my mother in disguise! Now, older by far, once again in Cardiff, but not in daydream, I had to attend, hesitatingly, the old lady who was my mother. My rescue attempts, as son and doctor, were hopelessly ineffectual. Her new bridegroom would not be denied.

My mother taught me my name, my father taught me the time.

Exit

As my colleague prepares the syringe
(the drip flees its hour glass)
I feel the depression of Saul,
my mother's right hand grasping still,
her left hand suspiciously still,
and think – Shadow on the wall,
Nothing on the floor – of your
random, katabolic ways:

merciful sometimes, precise, but often
wild as delirium, or like a surgeon
with cataracts grievously unkind
as you are now, as you visit
this old lady – one beloved by me –
as you blunder and exit, moth-blind,
mistaking even the light
on mirrors for open windows;

and as my colleague prepares the syringe
I remember another butchering –
a botched suicide in a circumspect
bedsitting room, a barely
discernible fake of a girl-corpse,
a marmoreal stillness perfect
except for the closed
plum-skin eyelids trembling;

and as my colleague prepares the syringe
I picture also a victim of war
near a road, a peasant left for dead,
conscious, black-tongued, long-agonized,
able to lift, as my mother can now,
at intervals her troubled head.
And as my colleague drives the needle in
I want to know the meaning of this:

why the dark thalamus finally
can't be shut down when we sleep
with swift economy? Of that king
and his queen – David and Bathsheba –
the old parable is plain:
out of so much suffering
came forth the other child,
the wise child, the Solomon;

but what will spring from this
unredeemed, needless degradation,
this concentration camp for one?
My colleague forces the plunger down,
squeezes the temgesic out,
the fluid that will numb and stun.
'Shadow on the wall . . .' I call, 'Nothing
on the floor . . . Patron of the Arts!'

And as my colleague extracts the needle
from her vein, the temgesic acts
till the bruised exit's negotiated.
Then how victoriously
you hold the left passive hand
of the dummy in the bed
while I continue uselessly
to hold the other.

What a patient declares, as an afterthought, just before leaving the consulting room, often turns out to be most important. J. S. was at the door when he hesitated. 'I know you're a chest man,' he said, 'so I suppose there's no point in raising the problem of my feet with you.' I waited. Sheepishly, he explained, 'I've hellishly itchy feet, doctor. Especially at night, I have to scratch them like hell.' Could I help him perhaps? Refer him to a skin specialist?

Our interview extended. Soon I learnt how much J. S. was troubled because of his domestic situation. His wife, he maintained, was getting at him ceaselessly, his son was a delinquent, and he confessed there was another lady abroad who much occupied his thoughts.

'No wonder you're getting itchy feet,' I said.

J. S. seemed baffled by my comment. *He* could not see the relationship between his almost acknowledged desire to get away from home and the state of his feet which he scratched so ferociously each night.

'Calamine lotion can be very soothing,' I said, 'but if I were you I'd ponder on the connection between your itchy feet and your domestic plight.'

He left pondering! And I sat back wondering whether my amateur psychiatrics had done him and his marriage harm or good.

I had remarked on the wireless that I felt myself to be 'a dilettante doctor and a professional poet'. Not a very wise remark, certainly not one that would impress patients. Joke though it may have been, and lightly spoken, yet I thought it had truth in it. For medicine has been for me, in some respects, a hobby that has been well paid, whereas poetry has been a central activity paid poorly. I have worn a white coat so many hours a week and then, with relief, I have discarded it so that on enchanted or/and precarious occasions I could don a purple one. Or so it used to be. But over the years the white coat has gathered to itself a purple glint in some lights and the purple has assumed some white patches.

I used to like Chekhov's response when he was advised 'not to hunt after two hares'. He wrote in a letter:

> I feel more confident and more satisfied with myself when I reflect that I have two professions and not one. Medicine is my lawful wife and literature is my mistress. When I get tired of one I spend the

night with the other. Though it's disorderly, it's not dull, and besides, neither of them loses anything from my infidelity.

I could assent to that reflection and savour it because, like those who write poetry seriously, whose ambition it is to write the next poem and then the one after, I did not feel that I was a poet except for a few hours, say six times a year, when I had completed a poem to my own satisfaction. Yes, I could persuade myself, I'm no more a poet between poems than I am a doctor when not at this clinic.

But now that I think about it more deeply I am not convinced of its truth. At one time, when I sat behind my desk listening to some soft-spoken individual saying, 'It worries me, doctor,' perhaps I did play, in some measure, a given role, a part in a play even though if blood flowed it would be real; but with the years a man becomes the part he has been cast in until he can hardly be anything else.

'Look! There goes Dr Amazing. See how he leaves the clinic no longer a doctor.' That's not true, someone has fallen down in the street and where a little crowd gathers he has to step forward; he arrives home and one of his daughters has a high fever so he must write a prescription; the telephone clamours in the hall and after-wards he has to travel 160 miles to urge other doctors to do this, to do that, because his aged mother is dying. It is no use: though the white coat seems to be discarded he laughs the laugh of a doctor, he cries the tears of a doctor, he dreams, at night, the dreams of a doctor. Or the dreams of a poet. Or both simultaneously. As a matter of fact, he always wears that purple coat, too – though it only becomes visible some six times a year.

Because of the pre-Christmas snow blizzard last night only one of the seven expected patients turned up. I look out of the window. Snow is falling; it seems to fall in slow motion over north Soho; it must be falling all over Britain. My patients are unlikely to come now, not even C. who has always been so keen to continue with his annual chest surveillance.

Five years ago he sat in that chair there, facing me, the X-ray screens behind my head blazing, his X-rays visible on them. I had to tell him that he had a small shadow on the left lung which could well prove to be active tuberculosis. I had half turned to the screens, to his X-rays which showed the soft shadow, the non-homogeneous loss of translucency in the left upper zone and apex. 'Nothing essentially to be anxious about,' I had tried to reassure him, 'but further investigations are needed in hospital.'

The drama of his face and then his voice fatalistic, saying, 'I see,' so that once again I affirmed that if, indeed, it did prove to be active tuberculosis then that condition, nowadays, was most amenable to treatment.

'There are drugs,' I had said, 'even more modern than streptomycin which are very effective against tubercle bacilli.'

Most patients when told there is something wrong with their X-rays – even those without any symptoms, without any possible premonition of such a verdict – remain acutely calm. They do not tend to show too much of their emotional map to me, a mere sympathetic stranger. To be sure there are, have been exceptions: men and women who will not read the lines allotted to them in that well-shaped, well-mannered play written by an Englishman called Anonymous. Some of these exceptional patients have confronted me aggressively as if the disease I had discovered in their lungs was all my fault. Then I have felt like the messenger of ancient days who carried bad news to a king. Others have gently opened themselves to me: in such moments of anxiety, apertures have appeared in their personalities so that their profound selves have been briefly revealed. Why not? Though it makes it more difficult for the doctor – he has to write a fresh script, he has to give something more of himself, and this all takes time – everything profound abhors a mask.

Over Christmas I have been rereading the *Collected Poems* of Sylvia Plath which have recently been published. The notion that poets must suffer in order to write well, be deranged as Sylvia Plath was, has a long tradition. There are those who continue to see in the Philoctetes legend of the wound and the bow the predicament of the poet who, while owning special gifts (the magic bow), is alienated from his fellow men by his suffering psyche (the stinking wound).

The lives and writings of a number of modern American poets, in particular, have been illustrative of the Philoctetes predicament. It has been pointed out how even that apparently impersonal major poem of the twentieth century, 'The Waste Land', was written while T. S. Eliot recovered in Switzerland from a nervous breakdown. In a lecture at Harvard University many years after the poem was published, T. S. Eliot, afflicted with modesty, admitted to a half-truth:

> Various critics have done me the honour to interpret the poem ('The Waste Land') in terms of criticism of the contemporary world, have considered it, indeed, as an important bit of social criticism. To me it was only the relief of a personal and wholly insignificant grouse against life; it is just a piece of rhythmical grumbling.

Of course 'The Waste Land' is much more than that. In any event, some more recent prominent American poets – Robert Lowell, Anne Sexton, Sylvia Plath – have been altogether less reticent than T. S. Eliot about their personal mental suffering. On occasions, they have boasted of their breakdowns and suicide attempts as warriors might of their war wounds; and these very boastings, it must be said, helped to crank the machinery of a fame-making mythology.

This same machinery continued to be active in Sylvia Plath's case after her death, after her 'successful' suicide in 1963.

Yet, leaving all the sentimentality and all the theatrical hooha aside, it is translucently evident that her talent was extraordinary, that her work, though limited by neurotic elements in her nature, was vibrant and arresting partly because of those same elements.

Al Alvarez was probably right when he maintained, 'The real poems began in 1960 after the birth of her daughter Frieda. It is as though the child were a proof of her identity, as though it liberated her into her real self. I think this guess is borne out by the fact that her most creative period followed the birth of her son two years later.' There are intimations in Sylvia Plath's work that her sense of her own identity was far from secure. Perhaps she felt most herself when she was at work on a poem. In that early, fine poem 'Black Rook in Rainy Weather', she talks of the 'rare random descent' of the inspirational angel who allows her to 'patch together a content of sorts', to gain – and this is the point I'm trying to make here – 'a brief respite from fear/of total neutrality'.

There is no doubt that she felt herself, on one level, to be possessed by the malevolent ghost of her once beloved father. 'I am,' she wrote in 'The Bee Meeting', 'the magician's girl who does not flinch.' She conceived herself to be a passive victim manipulated by a magician's power or a Hiroshima victim or a kind of Jew who survived a concentration camp. As a 'victim' she made her own inward devastation a mirror of recent history.

Many of her late poems have an oneiric quality. It is not surprising that they should be so, given the time of night when they were written. 'These new poems of mine have one thing in common,' she wrote. 'They were all written at about four in the morning – that still

blue, almost eternal hour before cockcrow, before the baby's cry.'
They were also written apparently when she felt herself to be, once
more, a victim – lonely, separated from her husband and, because of
her mental make-up, clearly desperate. She was a prey to over-
whelming separation anxieties. She had been separated from her
father when she was a small girl – by dying he had abandoned her, an
act she had not felt as being inadvertent.

In *The Savage God* A. Alvarez wrote:

> As the months went by her poetry became progressively more
> extreme . . . the last weeks each trivial event became the occasion for
> poetry: a cut finger, a fever, a bruise.

But to go a little deeper, it is obvious that these 'trivial' events had
enormous significance for her. They represented her deepest feel-
ings and her most central resentment. She wrote a poem called
'Contusion'. She felt bruised spiritually. She wrote a poem about a
cut finger called 'Cut' – and that's how she felt herself to be, her
whole being, cut. Cut and bruised and wounded.

Besides, the cutting of her thumb ('the top quite gone', she wrote,
'except for a sort of hinge of skin') no doubt nourished her feelings of
separation. The separation of a bit of her own body was resonant with
her long-held, submerged separation anxiety. Of course, all this may
be a wild guess and there will be some who will think it not proper to
hazard guesses of this kind. Nevertheless, the nature of her late
poems is such that one is tempted to look at her poetry as medical
evidence of a state of mind. For her desperation is so clearly touching
and so painful even when encapsulated in genuinely wrought poems
which do more than express a private terror.

Dr H. often sends his patients for a chest X-ray. Any patient
complaining of pain in the chest, any aching muscle, any cough, any
tickle or soreness in the trachea, any pimple on the skin of the chest
and he rushes that patient to our X-ray Department as if it were an
emergency. I happened to be in the X-ray Department when a tall
healthy-looking lock forward, if ever I saw one, presented himself.
The radiographer handed me the form signed by Dr H. asking for a
chest X-ray because . . . I read it again astonished . . . because of
impotence. I cannot imagine what Dr H. thought might be discovered
by X-raying this patient's chest.

I'm not quite sure how I feel about Dr H. He is a man ill at ease with himself. I sense that sometimes he is disgusted by his own ineptitude, that though aware of his own ignorance about medical matters he does nothing to remedy the ignorance – rather like the doctor in Chekhov's *Three Sisters*, Chebutykin. It is Dr H.'s acute awareness of his ignorance, surely, that makes him so cautious, why he sends so many of his patients for a second opinion, or for special investigations, however inappropriate. I suppose, sometimes, this or that specialist does discover some abnormality. Then Dr H. feels justified, and will be able, without qualm, to refer his next thousand patients for X-ray or barium meal or electrocardiograph or electroencephalogram.

I should like to meet Dr H. when he's off guard, out of the armour of his white coat, when he's drunk perhaps, without disguise. I suspect then he would resemble Chebutykin even more: 'Damn them all . . . the lot of them! They think I can treat any illness because I'm a doctor, but I know nothing, absolutely nothing. I've forgotten everything I used to know. I remember nothing, positively nothing. . . . The devil take them! Last Wednesday I attended a woman at Zasyp. She died and it was my fault. Yes. . . . I used to know a thing or two twenty-five years ago but now I don't remember anything. Not a thing!'

How frightening to consider those hordes of doctors practising who happen to be ignorant, incompetent – or eyes glinting like scalpels dangerously because of their own personality problems. Yet so many doctors bumble through even if their patients don't.

I wonder if Bill M. is still legally treating people? When I was a student he was the prize duffer of the medical school. Though he studied assiduously and seemed to have no other compelling interests to distract him, he failed his finals, in season, a dozen times. Soon after my twenty-first birthday I had my only operation, a tonsillectomy. I remember being wheeled, euphoric with omnipon, into the operating theatre. I looked up, two-eyed, objectively, in the spirit of science, to see who of my colleagues would be giving me the intravenous injection of pentothal that would turn the switch off from the current of the sun, knock me out. Among those standing there I, perturbed, saw Bill M. masked, gowned, gloved, and ready. That awesome vision sobered me. Gone, suddenly, the unreasonable complacency of omnipon. I managed to cry out despairingly, famously, 'Not . . . you . . . Bill.' Then darkness and silence of snow descended.

The administrative people are making arrangements for another doctor to use my consulting room next month when I shall be 'unemployed'. Some official – from the Ministry of Works, I think – came in to look at *my* desk, *my* carpet, *my* curtains. At least, I have felt that they were mine since I have inhabited this office so long. The man was polite enough but when he quit I felt I had been burgled.

There are many people, I am one such, who are basically rooted, who experience much anomie when their life situation changes or even when there are actual journeys to be undertaken and lived through. When I sojourned elsewhere, as I did in 1973–74 in the USA, I felt that real life only continued in London or South Wales! Well, part of me is me because of the introsumption of familiar landscapes, seascapes, objects, possessions, books, records and, yes, even the curtains, carpet and desk of *my* office. When things are removed, or I am removed from them, there is a small, a very small assault on whoever it is that I am. Of course, I am not *so* insecure that I cannot endure it, but I do sense the holes in the air, I do see the patchy oblongs on the walls where the paintings have come down and I do feel, then, temporarily diminished because of such absences.

To be sure it is absurd to feel diminished by such things. More serious is it when those whose lives are so entangled with our own disappear forever from this earth. No man is an Island, entire of itselfe. How just, those walking, emaciated statues of Giacometti becoming thinner and thinner as they walk towards FIN. Did he not sculpture the metaphor, any man's death diminishes me?

Once more the uncertain light: snow, ice and freezing fog, as before Christmas, but in addition a rail strike so again most of my patients cancelled their appointments at the clinic. Having little to do, I chatted for some time with a colleague, Dr B. (who is Polish) about the merciless, created events in that place on the map called Poland where all the successive traffic signals in the cities are at amber. Somewhere else, a closed, official car hurtling through slush; empty streets.

Later, at midday, I walked over to the local library to pick up some books, returning through unpopulated Soho Square: the wooden park benches abandoned, the paths mostly obliterated by the snow and, absolute over the grass, a huge white fitted carpet. The pigeons, baffled, wheeled on a roundabout as if a fair-rifle had cracked. The statue of King Charles II did not cough; he was clear of snow except

for his feet. Snow on King Charles's feet. Cold feet. And up there –
meaningless, damp, a sky the colour of meths through which I could
see its grey lining. Winter entered my mind like a memory and with it,
momentarily, despite their absence, the compromising misery of the
down-and-outs who usually dangle their shadows listlessly in this
square.

A voice in my head, not mine, whispered, 'Be grateful, be grateful.'

Last day – and yet not last day; and no great farewells either because I
have now been offered occasional sessional work here later in the
year. Anyway it was the last day in this consulting room which I have
now occupied for over a score of years. How many times have I
looked through the south windows, over the patched rooftops of
London, towards Centre Point? Or through the north windows with
their view of the Post Office Tower? There are so many unlikely
things one can become sentimental about!

I thought the day at the clinic would end on a cheerful note, a
rousing finale, for the last patient proved to be completely healthy.
Four years ago he had had a nasty-looking X-ray: bilateral extensive
mottling in both lungs, a sarcoidosis which could have left some
crippling residual scarring. So he had been prescribed steroids,
which acted magically; the mottling vanished and when the steroids
were stopped did not reappear. Nor did he suffer any side effects
from the steroid treatment. His present X-ray showed again the lung
fields to be clear with no hilar lymphadenopathy or any other sarcoid
manifestation. He left my office smiling. And, after writing up his
notes, I was about to follow him but the radiographer requested me
to read one more chest X-ray, a routine one.

It belonged to an officer in the RAF who had reached the age of
fifty and who, therefore, was required to have a medical check-up,
including a chest X-ray. Because his X-ray showed a small opacity in
the left mid-zone I had it repeated. It was no artifact. The opacity was
clearly there; nor was it present on an earlier X-ray of his taken in
January 1977. I wondered: was it a tumour? If so, malignant or
benign?

'I don't think it is tuberculosis,' I told the radiographer. 'Could you
ask the officer to come up from the X-ray department to see me?'

He would need to be investigated in hospital. He might well have
to undergo a thoracotomy – having his chest opened – before the
diagnosis became certain.

I did not tell him this. I stated facts not guesses: that the shadow in the left lung could be old or new, could be almost five years old and thus a scar of little significance, or else it could be something of more recent origin. 'That we must find out,' I said.

'Can you tell me what it isn't?'

'No, I can't even do that,' I said truthfully, and then, blessed be all clichés, 'It's like looking at a black cat in a dark room. A light needs to be shone on it before it can be properly identified. That's why I want you to be investigated further.'

We talked some more. I learnt several other facts which could be relevant – that he did not smoke and, then, something that made me pause. It seemed, a few years back, he had suffered an epididymo-orchitis. After a slow, cautious, clinical examination I telephoned the doctor at the hospital chest unit and arranged for him to be admitted after this weekend was over. I tried to reassure my patient within limits and leaned again on the crutch of a cliché: 'Everything in medicine is guilty until proved innocent. So we have to make sure.' The flight lieutenant did not seem unduly perturbed. He shook hands with me and left for his RAF station.

Afterwards I wrote up my report and gathered a few personal papers from my desk before putting on my overcoat. When I put out the lights, I noticed more vividly the lit, peaceful oblongs in the Middlesex Hospital building across the street. I stood for a moment in the almost darkness, as I have done so many times before, listening to the distant traffic noise of London – a huge, harsh needle scratching continuously on a worn, a very worn record that turned clockwise and turned again.

> I have spoken so much lately
> of death and of treachery;
> better to have sung the forgotten
> other song of Solomon.
> Forgive me. I do not believe
> the rainbow was invisible
> till Noah saw it;
> nor was I refreshed
> by strange bread in the desert,
> spring water in the desert.

The two drab tablets of stone
were two drab tablets of stone,
yet, beloved, this is my heritage;
also music of Solomon's song
on psaltery and dulcimer,
that which is lost but not lost –
like the beautiful rod of Aaron,
the beautiful rod of Aaron
first with its blossom
then with its ripe almonds.

Part Two

Events Leading to the Birth of Solomon

I wanted to put the phone down. I had no wish to write a film script. The producer's representative was persistent. He read me some lines from the Bible which concluded, 'And David comforted Bathsheba his wife, and went into her, and lay with her; and she bore a son, and he called his name Solomon and the Lord loved him.' Wonderful, yes, but I had no ambition to work on a 'movie'. Would I, at least, have a drink with the producer himself, at his flat in Knightsbridge? I insisted there was no point. 'Come for a drink anyway. He'd like to meet you.' Finally, because on Friday night I had to visit the PEN headquarters (then at Glebe Place in Chelsea), I agreed to drop in beforehand for a drink at Knightsbridge.

I was surprised to discover, at his rather Presidential flat, six suited men waiting for me. The producer offered me a drink saying that he understood that I was a poet. Then he remarked that Jack Lee, the cameraman, had a brother who wrote verse. I had sipped a centimetre of my drink before the producer told me what he had in mind. I said, perhaps Laurie Lee might be interested? He seemed puzzled. Jack's brother, one of the men explained. The producer repeated what he had said before I interrupted him. I remarked again that I wasn't interested. He told me there would be much money involved. As courteously as possible I informed him (and the other five silent men who had been given free tickets for our dialogue) that I had no interest in writing any film script, not even the 'Love Story of David and Bathsheba'. Finally the producer, accepting defeat, asked me with sincere curiosity, 'Mr Abse, what sort of car do you run?'

That weekend I could not help thinking of The Events Leading to the Birth of Solomon. But surely from the 'movie' point of view that plot was already old hat? Years ago, I recalled, they had already cast Gregory Peck as David. I wondered, what did David really look like? The Bible tells us he was 'of a beautiful countenance and goodly to look at'. Perhaps a curious amalgam of Gregory Peck and the statue of Michelangelo? And what of Bathsheba? I reread the Old Testament story and marvelled at its economy of language:

> And it came to pass in an eveningtide, that David arose from off his bed, and walked upon the roof of the king's house; and from the roof he saw a woman washing herself; and the woman was very beautiful to look upon . . .

The Bible story haunts the reader because of its dignified directness and its compression. Still, what is omitted teases the inquisitive mind. King David, you remember, is the villain. He, struck by the beauty of Bathsheba, summons her to the palace while her soldier husband, Uriah, is away at the eastern front, and then without further ado gets to know her in the biblical sense.

Worse is to come. David's whole part in this story seems unutterably discreditable – but before we pursue the plot further let us consider certain matters that the Bible does not illuminate. For example, we do not know whether or not Bathsheba welcomed David's advances. Rembrandt tries to give us an answer in his great painting. He pictures Bathsheba as having an ambiguous reaction to David's summons. Her expression seems to reveal both a resigned sadness and a dreaming anticipatory pleasure. Certainly, it is quite credible that Bathsheba was not entirely blameless – though the Bible would not have it so. After all, David was a charismatic character: eloquent, a musician and poet, a man who had been an outlaw and who was now the king. Why shouldn't such royal charisma have switched her on?

The Bible, tastefully, does not describe the seduction scene. Our present culture demands a keyhole view. I can imagine the producer suggesting that David softened up a reluctant Bathsheba by playing her some canticles on the harp and singing her psalms. I could, Mr Producer, put that into verse:

> When the naked lady stooped to bathe
> in the gushing waters of a spring,
> the voyeur on the palace roof
> just happened to be the king.
>
> So she was summoned to the palace
> where the king displayed *his* charms.
> He stroked some riffs across the harp
> and sang her a couple of psalms.

If we wish to whitewash David a little (for some reason I do) I think it fair to wonder whether or not David was led on by the dewy lady.

For all we know, the king's intention, when he summoned Bathshe-
ba, was not firmly defined. Indeed, it seems unlikely that he was
totally committed to bed.

After all, David was no panting youth but a middle-aged man with
many wives and concubines. To put it bluntly, David had not even
heard Bathsheba speak. There is many a glamorous woman whose
squawky voice puts Satan behind an otherwise passionate sybarite.
Perhaps I can best pose my question in another quatrain of doggerel:

> Some say, 'Sweet victim in the palace,'
> Some say, 'Poor lady in his bed.'
> But whose teeth like milk were white,
> whose eyes like wine were red?

A true misogynist could go further. He might even suggest, pointing
perhaps not to Rembrandt's painting but to one by Rubens ('Bath-
sheba Receiving the Letter from King David'), that David was less a
voyeur than Bathsheba a conniving exhibitionist: that she deliberate-
ly bathed herself, sporting herself naked, in full view of the palace
hoping that David would take his customary evening walk on the
roof. I do not believe that, of course. I only mention it as David's
newfound crooked defence counsel.

I have to report that David has had more eminent and more
devious defence counsels than me. Many, many centuries ago, in the
Talmud Sanhedrin, Rabbi Johanan insisted that David was no
shabby voyeur. On the contrary, he suggested that Bathsheba was
modestly, privately, washing herself behind a screen while David was
on the palace roof. Then, suddenly, Satan appeared in the form of a
bird. David aimed an arrow at the winged creature, but missed. The
arrow continued its trajectory to tear open the fabric of the delicate
screen and, hey presto, revealed Bathsheba in all her desirable
nakedness.

(Would the producer buy that scene, I wonder?)

Truth to tell, my fellow defence counsels, those bygone rabbis,
seem to me counterproductive in their outrageous attempts to
whitewash hero David. Male chauvinists to a bearded man they
would make any woman jurist puke. They have suggested that there
were extenuating circumstances for David's adultery, that God
Himself was responsible so that He might say to other sinners, 'Go to
David and learn how to repent.' Alternatively Rabbi Rabba reckoned
David only sinned in order to acknowledge God's moral superiority
over him!

Let me be more realistic. What has happened so far is one more sad little incident of adultery. An event hardly to be admired but, given our twentieth-century conditioning, one that does not shock us. It might have been the end of the matter, that sordid but not apparently calamitous one-night episode, if later Bathsheba had not discovered that she was 'with child'. It is here that we move from the divorce court and accusations of 'alienation of affection' to the Old Bailey, to a case of murder.

For David arranged, finally, the death of Uriah, setting him 'in the forefront of the hottest battle'. Yet that was not David's original intention when he recalled Bathsheba's husband from the north-eastern front. Since Bathsheba was with child, soon all Jerusalem would know of the king's indiscretion. But by bringing Uriah back on leave from the Ammonite war the child to be born would be thought to have been fathered by Bathsheba's husband. There would be no paternity case. No blood test. Such a ruse was deplorable – but it was not murder. Unfortunately, when Uriah returned to Jerusalem, he would not, as the French would delicately put it, 'pay his wife a visit'.

> Scandal's bad for royal business
> the king must not father the child
> so he called the Hittite from the Front
> shook his hand like a voter and smiled.
>
> In his uniform rough as a cat's tongue
> suddenly the soldier suspiciously said,
> 'Hard are the stones of the Eastern Front
> but, sire, harder at home is my bed.'
>
> Flagons and goat meat were offered
> but the Hittite refused to go home;
> he sat outside the palace gates
> his eyes as dark as the tomb.
>
> The merchants came and departed,
> they turned from Uriah appalled,
> for the soldier sobbed in the stony heat
> and ignored his wife when she called.

What was the real motive for Uriah not going home to Bathsheba as requested? In the Bible the reason Uriah gives seems noble, romantic, even altruistic. His comrades lie on the stony, eastern desert. Therefore he has no right to enjoy his wife and his soft bed. Well, such soldiers there may be on this earth but not many of us have encountered them. Maybe he had other, non-articulated reasons. Is it not likely that Uriah had some inkling of why he had been recalled from the front? Is it not likely that he wondered why he, of all the soldiers, had been singled out to report to David in Jerusalem? Besides he had come to Jerusalem and through Jerusalem, and perhaps Jerusalem tongues wagged then as tongues in that city still wag today.

If so, it is evident that Uriah was a man grievously hurt, a proud man angry with his wife, a man moreover who, perhaps, suspected his wife's complicity – as I do. To be sure, it may be that Uriah suffered from some unhappy sexual pathology: a man who preferred a stone bed among men to a soft one with a woman. If so, we can suspect Bathsheba's complicity even more and understand it more, indeed forgive it more.

Dr Juan Bosch in his study of David finds no extenuating excuses for the king's behaviour. He writes:

> But his [David's] instruction to Joab, given because he wanted to steal another man's wife, can only be put down to arrant, predatory, self-indulgent vice.

Yet consider the scene imaginatively: Uriah loitering outside the palace gates, day and night, with his eyes as dark as the tomb. Consider how the king felt seeing him there, sitting there with his sacks, with his bundles, staring back at David, *saying nothing*. Uriah must have become for David more than a man. He must have become the embodiment of an accusation.

And what did Uriah want: Is it not possible that that poor mournful man, knowing what had happened, did not care to live? Let me revert to my doggerel:

> He sat with his sack, sat in the sun,
> sat under stars, and would not quit –
> scowled at the king accusingly
> till the king got fed up with it.

> 'Tell me, Uriah, what do you want.
> Gold or land? Speak and I'll comply.'
> Then two vultures creaked overhead
> to brighten the Hittite's eye.

> 'Death.' That's what he sought in the desert
> near some nameless stony track.
> And there two vultures ate the soldier
> with the dagger in his back.

I am not saying that David was not guilty. After all he arranged for Uriah to return to the front and be killed. I am suggesting, though, that Uriah conspired in his own death, that Dr Bosch's judgement on this matter is too simple, that the whole story is, in fact, more complex because we only know what the protagonists in the story said and did – not what their motivation was, not what they thought, nor what their psychological make-up happened to be.

Because of this fundamental ignorance it behoves us, it seems to me, not to think of this 3000-year-old story in terms of black and white. Besides, out of this union of David and Bathsheba, eventually, after the death of Uriah and the curse of the priest Nathan, after much pain, after the death of the first baby, after repentance, tenderness and love, came forth wisdom, for another child, Solomon, was born.

Or to put it another way, Mr Producer:

'Is there no justice after sunset?'
cried the voice of a raging priest.
So a small child was cursed in the palace
and the small sobs of the women increased.

So Bathsheba's baby sickened
as the king by the cotside prayed
while the insomniac mother stared
at the crack in the ceiling afraid.

Loud doors slammed in the palace,
wild voices cried, 'The child is dead.'
Then Bathsheba's teeth like milk were white,
then her eyes like wine were red.

That night the king climbed to her bedroom,
how gently he coaxed the bereaved,
and in their shared and naked suffering,
the wise child, love, was conceived.

When King Solomon Spoke Welsh

'That flatterer has aspirations to become a politician,' I heard my mother pronounce on some visitor to our home in Cardiff while she tied up my shoelaces. She spat out 'flatterer' scornfully, as if the very word had an evil taste to it like my father's brown cough medicine. Probably our visitor did not merit mother's condemnatory scorn – he was, perhaps, merely flirting with her too openly.

'You like flattery,' my father countered. 'You feed on it.'

'Nonsense,' mother said.

'You invite it,' father said.

'Nonsense,' mother said.

'Those who need flattery all the time,' my father opined, 'should banish from the house all mirrors and buy themselves a parrot.'

My mother ignored that. 'So plausible,' she said of our visitor. (No worse thing can be said of any politician.) 'And it's time,' she now addressed me, 'It's time a big boy like you learned to do up his own shoelaces.'

When I was a big boy and able to do up my own shoelaces – that is to say, some forty years later – I read Michael Burn's little known 'Welsh Love Letter'. Mr Burn, having lived in Wales, knows all about *hwyl*, and bears witness to how some Welshmen, on occasions, word-tipple to become blind sober:

> Were all the peaks of Gwynedd
> In one huge mountain piled,
> Cnicht on Moelwyn,
> Moel-y-gest, Moel Hebog,
> And Eryri on top,
> And all between us,
> I'd climb them climb them
> All!
> To reach you.
> O, how I love you!

Were all the streams of Gwynedd
In one great river joined,
Dwyfor, Dwyryd,
Glaslyn, Ogwen,
And Mawddach in flood,
And all between us,
I'd swim them swim them
All!
To reach you.
O, how I love you!

Were all the forts of Gwynedd
In one great fortress linked,
Caer and castle,
Cricieth, Harlech,
Conwy, Caernarfon,
And all in flames,
I'd jump them jump them
All!
To reach you.
O, how I love you!

See you Saturday,
If it's not raining.

It was through my family – parents, brothers and sister – I suppose, that I first came to feel that there must be something reprehensible in exaggerating the truth merely to please another person. Besides, I read those regular headlines in the *South Wales Football Echo* on Saturday nights about Cardiff City FC who languished, in those pre-war days, at the bottom of Division Three (South). Every week the team ran on to the Ninian Park field in their blue shirts while a brass band played 'Happy Days are Here Again'. Every week they lost; but every *third* week the *Football Echo* carried the same headline: 'CITY FLATTER ONLY TO DECEIVE'. I.e. the 'Bluebirds' scored first – then lost. (Or if they didn't actually score they might have hit a post.)

To *deceive*, that obviously was the purpose of flattery, that was why our visitor had annoyed my parents; and the *Football Echo*, too, knew what was what. Some years later I learnt the same lesson from reading those seventeenth-century English poets who wrote verses 'To Cynthia', or 'To Amarantha', or 'To Chloris'. Transparent flattery, I decided, by effete knights such as Sir Francis Kynaston or Sir Charles Sidley. They simply uttered their vapid blatherings about radiant eyes, snow-white breasts, coral lips, in order to deceive one or the other hesitating lady into their wicked beds.

Mind you, their smarmy mouthings seem decidedly saline compared with the full-blooded rhetoric of their Welsh contemporaries. Here's Huw Morus (1622–1709) for instance, a flatterer with a real professional mouth on him:

> Slip of loveliness, slim, seemly,
> freshly fashioned, modest maiden, star serene,
> sage and queenly, gracious, granting heart;
> paragon . . .

That's just the opening. By now surely he's captured the girl's attention. Surely she is listening to him with more than usual interest as he continues:

> foam of the sea,
> loveliest lily of the land,
> soft of hand, white-breasted, brisk, bright, flower-crested,
> who'd not be charmed where blood is warmed?
> Moon of my nature, it was you
> I viewed in my desire,
> because your brow is like the snow,
> able, notable, gifted, gay, flawless,
> laughing, skilful, peerless pearl of girls.

By now surely old Huw has taken the wide-eyed, open-mouthed girl's hand in his hand. Even if she should crudely utter, 'You talkin' to me, kid?' our Huw would blithely continue (in Gwyn Williams's translation):

> If from all lands girls came in bands
> and from a tree one could see
> that sweet society of all loveliest ones,
> the paragons of town and country,
> dazzling, shapely, stately, fair, I declare
> Moon of Wales, your loveliness prevails.
> Your praise and glory, peerless girl,
> now impel me to applaud
> your sweet looks, your subtle tongue,
> dawn-sweet dearest, purest, prettiest, many-beautied,
> unpolluted and reputed spotless rose . . .

We do not have to continue. We can guess the end of the script as together they walk into the sunset.

Yet come to think of it, flattery is more, was more than just a way to deceive another. Huw Morus wanted to be loved himself, didn't he? That was one reason why he laboured to turn a pretty phrase for the lady. And most people who flatter excessively, who have the habit of complimenting everybody, right, left and centre, do so because deep down, surely, they are frightened of being disliked. Look at all those pious people praying their prayers, singing their psalms, ceaselessly offering compliments to the Lord (Blessed be His name) as if the Lord (Blessed be His name) wanted such magnified continual praise. Listen: 'Thou art my rock and my fortress, the buckle and the horn of my salvation and my high tower,' etc. Or 'The judgements of the Lord are true and righteous, altogether more to be desired are they than gold, yea than much fine gold; sweeter also than honey and honeycomb,' etc. Yes, listen to them, restless and noisy as a hundred bluebottles on a cathedral windowpane. There they go in church, chapel, mosque and synagogue, flattering the Lord (Blessed be His name) because secretly they are scared that He (Blessed be His name) won't like them, worse will actively dislike them and then . . . *trouble*.

But let me return to the more secular considerations. (I too don't want to be disliked.) Why have I been rude to Sir Francis Kynaston and Sir Charles Sidley? Why have I been condemnatory of these seventeenth-century masters of the white lie? Am I, I ask myself, jealous of their ability to be so fluently insincere? I must confess that, boy and man, I have not been much good at flattery. I do not mean to congratulate myself on a beautiful defect. No, there is virtue in pleasing others with finely chosen, almost true, words. But confronted by an absolutely stunning lady, dressed in a pulverizingly low-cut dress, soft neck adorned with a chain of gold, I find that I can only splutter, 'You *are* looking well.' Often the lady seems surprised by that medical opinion. I know, though, that my doltish spluttering has more to do with my very early upbringing than with any later medical training.

On the other hand, I dare say that even if I had the wisdom of Solomon, even if I spoke with his kingly voice, breathed his kingly words into the delicate left ear of that desirable Cynthia, Amarantha, Chloris – 'Thy teeth are like a flock of sheep, Cynthia,' or 'Thy two breasts are like two young roes, Amarantha,' or 'The smell of thy garments is like the smell of Lebanon, Chloris . . .' – I would be robustly rebuffed, my royal flattery prompting laughter or annoyance rather than acting as an aphrodisiac.

Nor have I ever managed to receive the rare, exaggerated compliments that have come my way with grace – and this is not simply due to lack of practice. When I was a young man, less clapped-out than I am now in looks and in spirit, when I was, in Solomon's words, ready to be like to a roe or to a young hart, I went to a literary party in London where I met an American lady editor who had published some of my poems in her magazine. I had never before experienced an articulate American 'coming on strong'. Midge – for that was her name – did not have the gift for British understatement. Quite directly she, being, I presumed, somewhat astigmatic, described my own physiognomy with adjectives usually chosen to promote a forthcoming Metro-Goldwyn-Mayer movie. She out-Solomoned Solomon. And since she evidently thought I did not resemble Boris Karloff I stood there, shifting my weight from one foot to the other, until she concluded her hymn of praise. It was absolutely necessary to respond. Hesitantly, truthfully, I said, 'Well, I have a small sebaceous cyst in the lobe of my right ear.' It was then that I discovered the barely repressed ambivalence of all flattery, for she quickly cast upon me two cold eyes and said, 'How vulgar you are. Why don't you learn to say "thank you" like a woman?' She spoke, I later decided, with the wisdom of Solomon.

If I had been brought up differently, if flattery in my family had been commonplace, I would have been able to deal with Midge's compliments as if I were the Queen of Sheba. Alas, my elder brothers and sister never accepted the role of cheering wildly, indiscriminately, from the touchlines. To this day when I see them – perhaps after many months – they frequently become serious of aspect and I know at once that they are about to begin a peroration with, 'I have to tell you, Dannie . . .' Why do they have to tell me? They were all born with little hatchets in their hands; and of course they were all born in Wales. For the Welsh – I speak in generalizations – have an irritating habit of telling those near to them, or familiar to them, uninvited home truths.

Oh, we like to tell little lies to strangers, usually for their own sake. ('I'll come at once,' says Mr Jones the plumber over the telephone to desperate Mr Smith, newly arrived in the district and now up to his knees in fast-rising water. After all, Jones reasons, why should he depress Smith further by telling him the truth, that he can't call round for days?) It is another matter, though, when we address our own people – then, for their sake, we do not beat about the green bush. (Remember the copy of that old advertisement: 'Her Best

Friend Wouldn't Tell Her'. Well, her best friend was definitely not
Welsh.) Yes, we may display gaudy inventive gifts to strangers, tell
tall tales of spirits from the vasty deep, of walking sticks that fly, of
psychopomps who tiptoe down the back lanes at night, but when it
comes to talking to our very own, to Dai the spy or Gwyn the mouth,
then we become ourselves: we tell the truth, the whole truth and
nothing but the grim, devastating, unwanted, scandalous truth.

There is a legend that the Queen of Sheba came from far away,
from the city of Kitor, and that it took her three years to reach
Jerusalem. So what language did King Solomon and the Queen first
converse in? It was Benaiah who conducted the Queen to Solomon
as he sat in a house of glass to receive her. The lady, deceived by an
optical illusion, imagined Solomon was sitting in water so, stepping
towards him, she raised her garment to keep it dry. The king stared at
her bare legs and said, 'Thy beauty is the beauty of a woman, but thy
hair is masculine; hair is an ornament to a man, but it disfigures a
woman.' For three years, three long years, the lady had journeyed to
hear the wisdom of Solomon and there he was telling her in primal
Welsh this truth unvarnished by flattery. What other language would
he have chosen, being all-wise?

If anybody should doubt that what the English describe as tact the
Welsh call hypocrisy, then he should listen to the loud deliberations
of the judges at an eisteddfod – not so much the National Eisteddfod
but all the other local eisteddfodi that take place in Wales. The
judges, on such occasions, are merciless in their public comments;
they don't so much speak sentences as make incisions; and they do
this to the manner born without benefit of a Cambridge education. I
had forgotten how brutal eisteddfod judges could be until I became
one myself in Monmouthshire some years ago when Monmouth-
shire was still called by that name.

There are those who would deny the Welshness of the denizens of
that border county; they remark on how the eisteddfodi there are
conducted in English. But here's the good news from Gwent: the
choirs sing beautifully and the judges put the knife in with true Welsh
finesse. I remember being transported by the singing of the miners of
Blaenavon. No sooner had they finished, however, than my fellow
judges came tamping in, blood-stained javelins in hand, to accuse
that harmonious choir, at least harmonious to me, of giving them a
monstrous plural earache, an acute sustained otitis media. They
dispensed no Welsh flannel. But now I have a confession to make:
when my turn came to comment on the recitation of poems – it was in

this capacity that I had been invited to be a judge – I, alas, failed to leave the victim for dead. Even when Bobi Davies, arms flamboyant, hands epileptic, eyes a-rolling clockwise then anticlockwise, screamed a poem of Dylan Thomas execrably:

And death shall have no dominion.
Dead men naked they shall be one
With the man in the wind and the west moon . . .

I could not afterwards, face to face with that same nice Bobi, dispatch him without administering at least an ounce of flattery, a drop of sweet balm, a little bit of very local anaesthetic. In doing so, I fear I incurred the withering wrath, the contempt of my fellow judges. Had I not behaved worse than any hyphenated, condescending Welshman working for the British Foreign Office, even worse than the Prince of Wales?

And what about the vote of thanks afterwards, yes the vote of thanks to Ianto who had been honoured by being asked to organize the whole thing? For months he had planned, arranged for the miners from Blaenavon, the steelworkers from Ebbw Vale, to send their choirs; for the older schoolboys and schoolgirls to come in their busloads from valleys to the east and valleys to the west, and for the same busloads to return with their same complement, minus no one, east and west to the same, the very same village in the valley. Oh, what a dedicated man of organization must Ianto be, so selfless, so efficient, surely a general among men? Duw, what a eulogy he would surely receive by way of the vote of thanks.

It was two hours to midnight in the biggest cinema at Pontypool where all gathered to receive the prizes, to hear the speeches after the long day's eisteddfod was done. Every plushed seat was occupied, from the back of the balcony above to the front of the pit below. And the stage too was packed with dignitaries. But it was past midnight (or felt like it) before it was time for the vote of thanks for Ianto. Looking at the chained watch from his waistcoat pocket one of the home-grown elders on the stage, a most important man, the most important man – you could tell from his locks which were long and white like Lloyd George's – struggled to his feet to appropriate applause. '*Now*,' he uttered, making the very word *now* one of the most dramatic in the English language, '*Now*,' he said, 'I shall propose a vote of thanks to Ianto.'

He hesitated, obviously searching for laudatory adjectives to come to mind and in the brief silence that followed no one rustled a paper, no one coughed, no one cleared his throat. 'Well,' he continued, 'considering it was the first time Ianto organized it all, he didn't do too bad. Given the experience 'e's now 'ad, 'e'll do better next time. The few cock-ups evident, I hesitate to mention them, needn't be dwelt on . . .'

That home-grown elder, a born eisteddfod judge if ever there was one, then abused Ianto for some ten minutes about very minor slips of organization while all those around me nodded their heads in serious agreement. 'Nevertheless,' he concluded, 'I 'ope we shall honour Ianto again next year – that we will allow him the privilege of volunteering again.' He then sat down to another round of sincere applause.

Finally Ianto rose, blinked, waited for silence and then responded. 'Ladies and Gentlemen,' he said, 'I'm glad it worked out more or less. By way of excuse, all I've got to say is . . . I only got my teeth this afternoon.' Then he sat down, smiling, to even greater applause – it went on and on as if King Solomon had solved a riddle. (A man near me clapped so loud, so hard, so long that I could not decide whether he was one of Ianto's relations or Ianto's dentist.)

Some days later I received a thank-you letter from Ianto himself. 'Thank you, Mr Abse,' he wrote, 'for adjudicating. Yours sincerely, Ianto.' Flatterer, I thought; and I thought too of his smiling new false teeth that King Solomon would surely have described as being 'like a flock of sheep'.

Despite men like Ianto there are those who fear that the 'Welshness' of many of my compatriots is somehow being seriously drained away, that the old ways, the old religion, the old language, even in the interior of Wales, is being lost now that each house, farmhouse, cottage, sports a television aerial like a twentieth-century flag. For instance, where have the righteous orators gone, they ask, the word scriptural or political, intense and thrilling? Gone for the most part, they say, those gesturing figures in pulpit, or wild-eyed on soapbox, gone into the photographic plates of a Welsh social history book or into the remembering imaginations of poets.

'There is no present in Wales, only the past,' R. S. Thomas proclaimed sternly. It is not a new complaint. Edward Thomas, visiting Wales before the First World War, also uttered how Wales was the locus of the past. Phantoms, he said, followed phantoms in a phantom land – 'a gleam of spears, a murmur of arrows, a shout of victory, a fair face, a scream of torture, a song, the form of some conqueror and pursuer of English Kings'. And generations earlier, come to think of it, another poet, Matthew Arnold, visiting nineteenth-century Llandudno, remarked that Wales is 'where the past still lives, where every place has its tradition, every name its poetry and where the people, the genuine people, still know this past, this tradition, this poetry, and live with it and cling to it.'

Are the Welsh 'genuine' people so backward-glancing as these romantic poets, Arnold, Thomas and Thomas, suggest? The more a nation looks to its past the more, paradoxically, that past, that tradition arrives into the present vivid and alive. Besides, even when the old customs are sadly mislaid, when the Welsh language itself is lost indisputably, as it is in many regions of Wales, it does not signify that the people of Wales suddenly become Englishmen.

They are a perdurable people. They may gossip in English but they gossip as only the Welsh can; they light up the English language with an italic music even as they gossip. Listen to their lilting, biblical-toned, lost-tribe metaphors and comic hyperbole; how graphically they chat up strangers, tell shameless healing lies to them and, in the next breath, utter with relish terrible, wounding truths to their own. And still they continue innocently, so innocently, to mislead gullible tourists as they always have done since the first visiting dragon-slayer with his bloodhounds and crusading hunting horn was persuaded to mistake Bethesda near Bangor for Bethesda in Jerusalem.

Two weeks ago I happened to be standing outside the Wimpy Bar in Neath when a lady driver, comely and as black as the Queen of Sheba, stopped her Ford Escort to inquire the way to Llangadog. I could not help this stranger from the east (Birmingham, I think). But at once a minion gathered. I overheard directions recommended and indeed insisted on that I swear would never be found in any AA mapbook. Who knows where she is today, that Sheba in a Ford Escort? I see her sitting in the driving seat, peering past her wagging screen-wipers at the usual, slow, soft, persistent, old-fashioned Welsh rain which drenches the hedges, the trees, the narrow, curving, empty road in the early-evening country gloom of nowhere. Drive on, Sheba. I know over the next sodden, green hill – I have been there or I have dreamed about it – is a pub near a Shell garage called Solomon's Temple where, after the third or fourth or fifth pint, everybody, but everybody, speaks pidgin Welsh without pomp or sense like the wise King himself and all, past closing time, are flattered and all, for one illegitimate minute, are happy.

Words Words Words

'I'll expect you next Wednesday,' I had said. She never arrived. When I phoned her later, she said, 'Oh dear, a verbal misunderstanding. You should have said *this* Wednesday. By *next* Wednesday I assumed you meant the Wednesday of the following week.' After I put down the phone I recalled that rather poor joke about the three half-deaf passengers travelling through the West Midlands. As the train slowed, the first passenger asked, 'Is this Wednesbury?' 'No, Thursday,' the second passenger, Bill, replied. And the third passenger, Mel, continued, 'I could do with a drink too.'

But why did my friend misinterpret 'next Wednesday'? Unconsciously did she wish to postpone our date? After all, a slip of the tongue, Freud teaches us, may reveal a telling and unsuspected significance. So perhaps verbal misunderstanding too may suggest purposes, desires, the listener may not consciously acknowledge. Consider Mel, the third half-deaf man, who had said, 'I could do with a drink too.' Doubtless he was a lover of alcohol, if not an alcoholic! He did not want to hear Bill tell him the day of the week. Rather he wanted to hear the heart-rending cry of a fellow tippler.

Of course not all verbal misunderstandings result from unconscious longings or negations. One can settle a pillow or turn towards the window and echoing T. S. Eliot say, 'That is not it at all, that is not what I meant at all,' without narrowing one's eyes in a paranoid way. Eliot himself had cause to complain of innocent verbal misunderstandings of his work. One of Eliot's poems, 'Journey of the Magi', begins:

> A cold coming we had of it
> Just the worst time of the year
> For a journey, and such a long journey . . .

These lines were translated into German so that they signified:

We had a cold coming
Just at the worst time of the year
For a journey, and such a long journey . . .

It is unlikely that the translator wished to diminish Eliot, or that as he translated these lines he happened to suffer from a particularly heavy and distressing head cold. No, he was just ignorant.

And sometimes we have reason to be grateful for such ignorance. Unforgettable passages in the King James Bible prove my point. Marvellous constructions also arise from verbal misconceptions. Even the unicorn is probably a mistranslation from the Hebrew, and without that fabulous beast so many paintings would be blank, so many tapestries never begun, so many poems deleted. George Barker's assertion that unicorns don't exist because they have better things to do is but an amusing lovely slander. They do exist and we are richer for them, and all because of a verbal misapprehension.

Yet some purists believe it is better not to understand a language at all than to understand it imperfectly. To be sure, I can think of one occasion when I could have argued this brief. I had attended a writers' conference in Israel and afterwards was invited, along with an Israeli writer, to discuss the proceedings on radio. First I was to speak in English; then the Israeli writer would respond in Hebrew. 'Then, Mr Abse,' said the radio producer, 'you take up the thread and so on and so forth. I would like a first-class argument.' I pointed out that, alas, I wouldn't be able to understand one word the Israeli writer said for I had no Hebrew. The producer hesitated only for a moment. 'You're a poet,' he said, 'use your imagination.'

So I spoke for a minute, listened to a language I couldn't understand for a minute, then rebutted what I hoped the Israeli writer had said. We continued our argument for a quarter of an hour, and after the broadcast the producer embraced us both, 'Beautiful,' he shouted, 'beautiful.' No doubt our Hebrew–English dialogue was a symbolic political parable of some kind. Anyway, deaf men spoke to deaf men that Wednesday and we all went off for a drink.

2

'Even if you don't recall in detail Robert Southey's *Life of Nelson* (1813), you would have read, surely, Southey's poem "Madoc"? You remember: it's about Madog ab Owain Gwynedd, that legendary twelfth-century prince – the youngest son of Owain Gwynedd, King of North Wales.' Rather than admit a defeated, self-shaming 'no' many of us prevaricate when confronted with such a challenging and pulverizing monologue. We grunt an ambiguous, 'mmm' or maybe flex the head gently in a non-committal modest way, or brazenly essay a 'yes' in a stretched voice. All display of obscure erudition leaves us a little resentful. For our own ignorance is too rawly exposed, the superiority of our friend and adversary in conversation too openly affirmed.

We feel similarly towards those who 'have swallowed a dictionary', whose vocabulary is wide and idiosyncratic and whose expression of it fluent. An ostentation of vocabulary, spoken or written, arouses in us feelings of envy and of admiration. Look at *my* word-hoard, some writers – men more often than women – seem to insist as if they were pointing to their new white Rolls Royce or at their wife's diamond as big as the Ritz or, more directly, to their own exposed outsize genitals. And some of us, perhaps, are suitably crushed. But isn't that the intention, or at least the unconscious motive, of the lexical author? A man who deliberately uses words that others are likely to be ignorant of is committing a minor act of aggression, and in so doing would inform us of his power and superiority.

There are some writers I admire even though they constantly use uncommon words. In reading the late poems of Auden I have often had to extend my arm laterally for a dictionary to look up words such as 'nisus' and 'ensorcelling'. If writers do display a rich vocabulary, however irritated we may be by their verbal swank, this very richness does argue for them an authority which we are persuaded to acknowledge. Authors like Aldous Huxley and Arthur Koestler who have occasionally peppered their prose with scientific-jargon words – 'neoplasm' instead of 'cancer', or even 'dermis' instead of 'skin' – perhaps have done so in order to achieve, though spuriously, a *tone* of authority.

Verbal ostentation is not confined to writers. The ego-clamour of any dinner-party conversation is likely to be quelled by an insistent doctor's voice saying, 'I saw a patient today suffering from sub-acute bacterial endocarditis.' A doctor, whatever his deficiencies in common knowledge, though he may never have heard of Auden, Huxley or Koestler, can by casually talking about say 'coccidioidomycosis', or 'sub-acute combined degeneration of the cord', reduce others with far more eclectic scholarship to a position of transient inferiority. The doctor–patient relationship is based on such a balance. If doctor and patient acknowledge each other as equals the patient would not recover so quickly and the doctor would become ill!

Because of this assumption, or rather presumption of superiority, the doctor in addressing a patient will simplify his word-hoard in a most transparent way. Observe how he strides into Casualty and all the patients on the benches become silent except for the blind man who is saying, 'I 'ope if 'e gives me stitches, 'e'll numb it first, nurse.' Now our white-coated hero descends a step to address the first patient, who happens to be a Nobel prizewinner, with a breezy, 'Not to worry,' and 'Just a little prick,' and 'How's the waterworks?' He will not even ask for *urine*. To demand *piss* is too indelicate. So he says to the patient, who because he is a patient has become temporarily illiterate, 'I'd like a sample.'

Of course, doctors being human like to laud it not only over patients but over fellow doctors. That is why you may, in the corridors of the hospital, happen on two consultants involved in warring discourse. The first consultant is saying, 'Have you by chance read Thorngren and Gustafson on the effects of eleven-week increase in dietary eicosapentaenoic acid on bleeding time, lipids and platelet aggregation?' And the second consultant, with fugitive eyes, is flexing his head gently in a most non-committal modest way.

3

There are words used in certain contexts that have become inert, even dead. We sit down to write a letter, and address a friend, a stranger, or even an individual we actively dislike, with a 'Dear'. 'Dear Fred' we write, or 'Dear Mr Smith', or 'Dear Fred Smith', or 'Dear Smith', when Smith F. is not dear to us at all, never has been, never will be. We write 'Dear' with as little sincerity as those authors of the Tel Armana letters who, more than 3000 years ago, commenced their letters with a 'Seven times by seven times I fall at your feet'. But those once inert words, because they are no longer used, have become alive again. A meaningless formal ceremonial beginning to a letter has become a line of a poem.

If we are ignorant of the ceremonial language gestures of a particular society we are likely to react to them freshly. I recall the first time I visited the USA. When served my first breakfast by an attractive American waitress I felt I was in a movie. When she passed me the orange juice I automatically thanked her. 'You're welcome,' she replied. How sweet of her, I thought, to react like that and at this time of the morning. I wished to thank her for saying I was welcome, to show my gratitude for her generosity of spirit. So I said again with warmth, 'Thank you,' and again she responded, not looking at me now, 'You're welcome.' This time I repeated my 'Thank you,' less ardently. 'You're welcome,' she said, like a taped answering service. I was just beginning to experience a mild depression when, suddenly, all was dazzle and sunlight once more. For, with remarkable open warmth, the waitress even as she handed me the bill said, 'Now you have a nice day.'

The Americans use a vivid phrase: 'She came on a bit strong.' But all Americans, as far as we British are concerned, come on a bit strong. It doesn't matter a jot, of course, providing we understand the nuances of their statements: that what they say they don't necessarily mean any more than we do. I used to be pleased when an American friend wrote, 'Thank you for your good letter.' Later, though, several other American correspondents thanked me for my good letters and gradually I realized that they no more meant it than I did when I asked them to convey my greetings to their *good* ladies whom I secretly suspected may well have been bitches or harlots.

Yet the ancients came on more strong than any contemporary American. Here is the opening of a letter dictated by Abimelech of Tyre to Amenhotep IV about 1370 BC,

> To the King, my lord, my pantheon, my Sun-god say: Thus Abimelech, thy servant. Seven and seven times I fall at the feet of the King, my lord. I am the dirt under the feet of the King, my lord. My lord is the Sun-god who rises over the lands day by day, as ordained by his gracious father: who sets the whole land at peace by his might, who utters his battle-cry in heaven like Baal so that the whole land quakes at his cry . . .

This is but the beginning of the letter, or, as we say nowadays, 'That's just for starters.' All Abimelech has to tell Amenhotep is: 'I am guarding Tyre until you, the King, arrive.' The rest is wrapping. It makes the American, 'You're welcome,' and 'Have a good day,' perfunctory, even rude.

Our own verbal insincerities are so commonplace we do not notice them and those we address know we know that they know we do not mean what we say. 'Do call in on us when next you visit Reading,' said Fred Smith to my wife and me. And supposing one evening, about dinner time, we did happen to be in Reading with our three children, and did knock on his door to announce, 'We're here. Hello, Fred!' I can imagine the candid traumatic look on his face. Ah, but he would find the right, inert, dead words soon enough, the correct ceremonial response that would allow him legitimately to pretend to feelings he did not own or to conceal feelings he would rather not openly display. 'Yes,' he would say blandly, 'how very nice to see you,' and call his stunned wife from the kitchen where several pots on the stove were about to overbrim. She, too, shaking hands with my family, and despite her headache and sore throat, would respond to our 'How are you?' with a smile and a 'Fine. *Fine*, thank you!'

The Experiment

We are told by Plutarch that Julius Caesar surpassed all other commanders for in his campaigns in Gaul, over a period of a decade, he stormed 800 cities and subdued 300 nations. He slaughtered 1,000,000 men and took another 1,000,000 prisoners. We may be taken aback by the sheer size of these figures but we feel very little. All that suffering, for which, of course, we were in no way responsible, occurred such a long time ago. We can neither respond deeply to the plight of Caesar's victims nor enthusiastically admire Caesar's victories. History has become a storybook, albeit bloody, but all that blood has rusted, is too old, ancient. Indeed the crucible of centuries has transformed it into mere theatrical red paint: great distance, the long perspective, the blurring of faraway scenes, makes even the worst savagery appear ritualistic, almost decorous.

We feel otherwise about the wars and victims of our own century. Some men become hoarse shouting about them. In *The Times* today, I read that Senator George McGovern has made a speech in Beverly Hills, California. Despite the location, despite the proximity of the synthetic dream factories of Hollywood, he most earnestly shouted, 'Except for Adolf Hitler's extermination of the Jewish people the American bombardment of defenceless peasants in Indo-China is the most barbaric act of modern times.' In 1947, Jung had already maintained, echoing others, that 'in Germany, a highly cultured land, the horrors exceeded by far anything the world has ever known.'

But, of course, there is no competition: the man-made catastrophes of our times have only different names. Wherever modern man has been a wolf to modern man, whatever the roll call, call it Buchenwald or Vietnam, whatever the name of the horror, there we are involved and there we must respond.

Even the First World War has not yet become an opera or a prettified musical like, say, *Fiddler on the Roof*. We could not accept quite such a vulgarization or trivialization of that piece of our history *yet*. *Oh, What a Lovely War* at least owns a sardonic bite and is indeed a moral piece of theatre. After all, our fathers or grandfathers kept their heavy rainbowed medals in the bottom drawer of the bureau. We remember too the anecdotes they told us and the songs they hummed or whistled – the same songs that assault us so poignantly when we hear them today, played by some blind or crippled accordionist amongst the muffling traffic of a busy metropolis: 'Roses of Picardy', 'It's a Long Way to Tipperary', 'Smile, Smile, Smile'. We are moved by the silly heroism recounted in such First World War books as Robert Graves's *Goodbye to All That*, or Edmund Blunden's *Undertones of War*, and the poems of Siegfried Sassoon, Wilfred Owen and Isaac Rosenberg continue to engage us in a meaningful, contemporary way. In short, the suffering of the First World War is still real to us – is not merely an epic tale told in a dark shadowy hall to the accompaniment of a melancholy harp. The pain and the suffering, though not our own but our fathers', or our fathers' fathers', was an expensive matter. So we hold on to it like a possession and we want no one to change it, to tarnish it.

If the public calamities of our fathers' time are dear enough to us, our own seem barely supportable. We hardly think about them but they are always with us. We are all involved, every one of us, however far removed from those scenes of bleak, pale crimes. We are, metaphorically speaking, survivors because of them. We have lived through Auschwitz and Belsen, Hiroshima and Nagasaki and we did not know the enormity of the offence. We were not there. But with the passing of the years these catastrophes do not recede into history, do not become a tale in a storybook. On the contrary, something odd happens, the reverse happens, they come nearer and nearer, they become like scenes in a dream advancing towards us, on top of us, big, huge.

For with the passing of the years we hear more and learn more significant details. The actual survivors tell their terrible stories of gold from teeth and lampshades from human skin and so gradually the abstract geography of hell becomes concrete: we see the belching smoke of the chimneys, we hear the hiss of the gas and the dying cries of the murdered. We may not be able to hold steady, in the front of our minds, the enormity of the offence for very long, the picture slips away in the silence between two heartbeats; we cannot continually retain in our minds, as we perceive the natural beauty of the earth, or as we are touched by the genuine tenderness of lovers and friends, the psychotic savagery of our twentieth-century life. We have to shrug our shoulders finally or make a grim joke like Cioran – 'What would be left of our tragedies if a literate insect were to present us his?'

No, we cannot look too long at the searchlights of Auschwitz or at the coloured, intense flash of light over Hiroshima. We repress the horror. It becomes a numb disaster. In order to continue living as happily as possible, the more capacity we have for empathy the more we need to make it numb. It is not wrong to do that, indeed we have no choice. All the same we do have a continual headache that we rarely discern.

So who can tell what psychic devastation has really taken place within us, the survivors, especially for those of us who were brought up in an optimistic tradition, heirs of the nineteenth century, who believed in the inevitability of human progress, and who thought that the soul of man was born pure? Norman Mailer has said, 'Probably, we shall never be able to determine the psychic havoc of the concentration camps and the atom bomb upon the unconscious mind of almost everyone alive in those years.' And he goes on to ask, as others before him have done, remembering the millions killed in the concentration camps, 'Who can ignore the more hideous questions about his own nature?' For Mailer has apprehended, as others have also done, that it was not the German people alone who were capable of such stupendous crimes.

Social psychologists may point out that the 'typical' German may be self-important, insecure, over-respectful to authority, over-docile to superiors, and a little tyrant to his inferiors in the social scale, but we are not convinced that their faults are peculiar to them alone. The Germans may have that unattractive gift for planning meticulously, they may have a need for obsessional organization – and this, analytically speaking, does point down to suppressed powerful forces within of anarchy and division. Because of such suppressed forces, needing order, they may well have responded with a particular facility to Hitler's confident promise of A New Order. It is true that when the horns of the hunters were blowing in the dark the German nation of eighty millions, with terrible banners unfurled, followed their raving, hysterical Führer with 'a sleep-walker's confidence.' But despite their so-called national characteristics, their particular institutions, their history, despite Hitler and the Nazis, whose

jackboots left footsteps trailing away from Auschwitz and Buchen-
wald, despite all this, of course they are not a special people with
different chromosomes any more than the Jews, or others are, whom
they butchered.

To read Hannah Arendt's book on the trial of Adolf Eichmann is a
depressing experience if only because we learn that, with a few
important exceptions, nation after nation turned on its scapegoats
with a mercilessness and brutality that sometimes shocked in its
openness even the German SS. The willingness of apparently
ordinary people to obey evil commands is not a specifically German
phenomenon but the record of Germany remains, and it is a
shameful one. Some will forgive and most will feel no longer
vengeful, if only because, with Heine, they may say, 'Mine is a most
peaceful disposition. My wishes are: a humble cottage with a
thatched roof, but a good bed, good food, the freshest milk and
butter, flowers before my window, and a few fine trees before my
door; and if God wants to make my happiness complete, he will grant
me the joy of seeing some six or seven of my enemies hanging from
those trees. Before their death I shall, moved in my heart, forgive
them all the wrong they did me in their lifetime. One must, it is true,
forgive one's enemies – but not before they have been hanged.'

2

We have no inborn tendency, Germans and non-Germans alike, to
obey orders. On the contrary, we are born saying 'no' to civilization's
imperatives. But from babyhood on, we are conditioned to say 'yes',
to obey. We are trained by punishment and reward, by threat and
promise.

When we were small our parents proscribed our instinctual
actions because they wished us not to be antisocial or because they
were worried lest we damaged ourselves. If we obeyed them no harm
would befall us; we would be rewarded; our parents would smile
upon us and love us. If, however, we rebelled, atrocious things might
happen to us physically and we would lose the love of those two
people we most needed. There was no actual choice of course. We,
the little barbarians, had to become civilized or else.

Or else we would be unloved, castrated, killed. 'If you touch that,'
the six foot high voice said, 'you will be electrocuted. Come away,
this minute. I'll beat you. I will not love you any more. Come away I
tell you or you will be killed.' Or more simply, bluntly, to the point,

'Stop that. It will come off!' That six foot high voice knew best. It was omnipotent and respectable. It was law and order. It was the voice of spoilsport bearded Moses coming down the mountain, barefooted, with the Ten Commandments slipping from his hand, shouting 'don't' as we danced so happily, with such clear vivacity and happiness around the golden calf.

From the beginning, then, disobedience is associated in our minds with fearful consequences, even death. No wonder most people hardly operate their consciences as they react to a command – they do not think of its moral coloration. The conflict is not there, necessarily. Besides, the effect of an imperative may be too remote, too abstract. So we press down a lever or turn up a switch, obey this order or that order in My Lai or in Ulster. Consciences even where they are in operation are remarkably soluble. Worse, too often evil commands allow us to satisfy certain instinctual aggressive needs. Can we be sure that even without fear of the punitive consequences of disobedience there would have been neither the searchlights of Auschwitz nor the intense light over Hiroshima? Could we say simplistically with Alex Comfort, 'For the lack of a joiner's obedience the crucifixion will not now take place'?

Some years ago a play of mine, *In The Cage*, was produced at the Questors Theatre, Ealing. In it, I had peripherally touched on this question of obedience to an evil command. More recently I had wanted to take up that theme again, in dramatic terms again, but in a different way, and more centrally. So when the Questors Theatre offered to commission another play from me for their New Plays Festival, I accepted and told them how I would like to set *The Dogs of Pavlov* in a psychological laboratory.

For I had, not long before, read about a most remarkable experiment that had taken place at Yale University. This experiment had been devised by a Professor Stanley Milgram who was interested scientifically in 'the compulsion to do evil' and how men would obey commands that were in strong conflict with their conscience.

In my view, it is dubious whether his simple but brilliant and terrible experiment should have been carried out. I would like to take up this point later. For the moment, I merely wish to comment on how the strategy of his experiment led to fascinating and disturbing results – results which may instruct us and warn even the most sanguine of us about our natures. The conclusions we must draw from the experiment underline for us again the ironic, indeed holy, practice of James Joyce taking for his slogan Satan's '*Non Serviam*' ('I will not obey').

3

Supposing you, the reader, had agreed to take part in Professor Milgram's experiment. You had seen an advertisement in a New Haven newspaper. It seemed volunteers were required to participate in a study of memory and learning at Yale University. So you had volunteered – glad to be of use, to be used in the service of a scientific inquiry; besides, it would probably be interesting and, moreover, they even offered to pay each volunteer a small sum of money which would amply cover expenses. Others had already responded to that advertisement – high-school teachers, engineers, salesmen, clerks, labourers. All these people were between twenty and fifty years of age.

So one evening you had arrived at the laboratory in Yale and, along with another volunteer, a forty-seven-year-old accountant, you had been introduced to a younger man in a technician's grey coat. He evidently was a scientist. Imposingly he explained to you both, 'We know very little about the effect of punishment on learning. No truly scientific studies have been made of it in human beings. For instance, we don't know how *much* punishment is best for learning. We don't know how much difference it makes as to who is giving the punishment – whether an adult learns best from a younger or older person than himself – many things of that sort.'

The accountant nodded his head and you too, no doubt, listened attentively as the youngish scientist in the grey coat sternly continued, 'So in this study we are bringing together a number of adults of different occupations and ages. We're asking some of them to be teachers, some to be learners. We want to find out what effect *punishment* will have on learning.'

Perhaps, at this juncture, you had vaguely thought that, on balance, you would have preferred to be the teacher, the one who doled out the punishment, rather than the learner who received it. However, you made no awkward objections, did not say, 'I want to be one rather than the other.' After all, you had freely volunteered and everybody had been so courteous and you wanted to do your best to help them in this worthwhile experiment that was being carried out at such a *fine*, such a reputable university.

The scientist pushed forward a hat in which there were two slips of paper. It seemed like a child's game, a lottery. You pulled out one slip of paper; the other volunteer, the accountant, extracted the other. You opened your slip; he opened his. You read the word on it, 'TEACHER', smiled, then both of you were taken to an adjacent room. There, the accountant was strapped into an electric chair while you were being placed in front of an impressive shock generator which had a formidable row of lever-switches.

The accountant was given 'a learning talk'. He had to remember a series of paired words. When one word was spoken, the paired word had to be supplied by the accountant in the electric chair. If he made a mistake you were to give him an electric shock by pulling down one of the levers. *With each successive mistake you were to give him a stronger shock.*

You looked down at the thirty levers of the shock generator – these levers were set in a horizontal line and each of them was clearly labelled fifteen volts, thirty volts, forty-five volts and so on, going up in fifteen-volt increments to the extreme right-hand side of you where the last lever was labelled four hundred and fifty volts. You also noticed that these levers were arranged so that, in addition to the voltage label underneath, different groups were marked SLIGHT SHOCK, MODERATE SHOCK, STRONG SHOCK, VERY STRONG SHOCK, INTENSE SHOCK, EXTREME INTENSITY SHOCK, DANGER: SEVERE SHOCK. And, finally, the two levers on the extreme right-hand side had been designated, minatorily, with the symbols XXX.

'Before we start, we'll have a run through,' said the scientist in the grey coat. 'And also perhaps the teacher had better have a shock to feel the kind of punishment he is doling out.' So you were given a forty-five-volt shock when the Yale scientist pulled down the third lever of the generator. It was hardly of consequence, still it no doubt reinforced your feeling that you were lucky to have pulled out the slip of paper on which was written the word *teacher* rather than *learner*.

The accountant had been firmly strapped into the electric chair and he was having electrode paste applied – 'to avoid blisters and burns,' the scientist said. It made you feel apprehensive though you noted that your accountant colleague seemed relatively calm. Perhaps you were somewhat reassured when the scientist remarked, 'Although the shocks can be extremely painful they cause no permanent tissue damage.'

Because the experimenter apparently wanted to study the effect of punishment on memory you were going to be commanded to pull down successive levers which would cause the man in the electric chair an increasing amount of pain every time he made a mistake. How far along those levers do you think you would have gone? Each time you pulled down the lever a pilot light of bright red came on, an electric buzzing could be heard, an electric blue light labelled 'voltage energizer' flashed, the dial on the voltage meter swung to the right and various relay clicks sounded, and all the time the accountant in the chair objected more and more.

'Whether the learner likes it or not,' the scientist said sternly, 'you must go on until he has learned all the word pairs correctly. So please go on.'

At seventy-five volts the accountant had grunted, at one hundred and twenty volts he had complained verbally, at one hundred and fifty volts he demanded to be released from that chair, indeed from the experiment.

But the scientist had commanded you emotionlessly to continue nevertheless, and had added, 'The experiment requires that you continue,' and later, 'It is absolutely essential that you continue.'

You pulled down the levers, the shocks escalated, the protests of the accountant became louder, increasingly strident, more urgent, even desperate. He was pleading, 'Get me out of here! I won't be in the experiment any more! I refuse to go on,' until at two hundred and eighty-five volts he had screamed in agony.

Would you have stopped then? You are absolutely sure you would have stopped then, if not before, though the Yale scientist was again calmly ordering you to continue, urging you with the positive commands of a hypnotist, 'You have no other choice. You *must* go on.'

I suspect that you the reader, even if you had agreed to volunteer for such an experiment in the first place, believe that you would never have cooperated to any great extent with the experimenter, would never have really hurt the accountant, that mild stranger strapped in the electric chair. You are sure, I know you are sure. But what about your next-door neighbour? Supposing you were in that electric chair, are you certain that your next-door neighbour would not have responded to those clear commands? Would he have said, '*Non Serviam*'?

The results of the experiments carried out at Yale are hardly reassuring. Let Professor Milgram speak for himself. 'The initial reaction a reader might have to the experiment is: why would anyone in his right mind even bother to administer the first shocks at all? Why would he not simply get up and walk out of the laboratory? But the fact is, no one ever does. Since the subject has come to the laboratory to aid the experimenter he is quite willing to start-off with the procedure. There is nothing very extraordinary in this, particularly since the person who is to receive the shocks seems initially cooperative, if somewhat apprehensive. What is surprising is how far ordinary individuals will go in complying with the experimenter's instructions. Indeed, the results of the experiment were both surprising and dismaying. Despite the fact that many subjects experience stress, despite the fact that many protest to the experimenter, a substantial proportion continue to the last shock.'

The reader may be startled that so many submitted to the commands of the Yale scientist in a technician's grey coat and that when the experiment was repeated at other places, at other American universities, the results were basically the same. It may be equally incredible to the reader that scientists at Yale, and elsewhere, could allow volunteers to be so grossly shocked, to endure such dangerous levels of electric current. Well, they didn't. You the reader were had, hoaxed, fooled. That electric chair was never really wired up. Right from the beginning you were taken in. That accountant was collaborating with the Yale scientists. He was in on the secret. He was an actor. They were not a bit interested in the relationship of learning and punishment. That was bullshit, a cover story. They were intent on devising a laboratory situation where you had increasing conflict as you were commanded to electric-shock (or so you thought) a fellow human being. You, not that accountant–actor, were the victim. They wanted to know how much, to what degree, you would submit to a respectable, apparently reasonable authority – despite the pain and agony of your 'victim' and your slowly awakening conscience. They discovered that you often expressed disapproval – you even denounced, sometimes, the experiment as absurd, stupid. Yet, frequently, you obeyed even to the last lever for you could not be defiant enough to disengage.

Consider again what happened. The so-called accountant and you both chose a slip of paper from a hat. You did not know both pieces of paper had written on them 'TEACHER'. You were cheated. You were taken to a shock generator – but despite its elaborate dials and general convincing construction, it was a fraud. Only when the third lever was pulled could it generate a shock, a small shock, a forty-five-volt shock. You were the one who was shocked, you remember. It was you who were cheated. The accountant in the chair had been smeared with a grease to stop burns, the man in the grey coat had said. That too was a lie, part of the pretence. You were cheated. Those lines the accountant spoke were part of a prepared script. Those groans, those screams, were all counterfeit. You were cheated. Like any man conned, in my view, you have a right to feel angry. Yet, you may say – when your anger settles to leave a nasty little scar, a small infarct in the soul – thank heavens anyway that accountant was only an actor, that nobody really did get hurt. Or did they?

4

To have a play on, in front of strange juries in rows of plush chairs, is a time of self immolation, even martyrdom. Each time I have watched, from some inconspicuous seat in the back row of a theatre, a first performance of one of my own plays, I have, when it is a comedy, laughed more than anybody else in the auditorium; when a tragedy I have cried more than anybody else; and, either way, when the curtain has come down and the house lights have gone up, I have been more exhausted than anybody else. I have always staggered backstage feeling shot at, anaemic as a St Sebastian. Then, arrows barely removed, I have gone through the usual theatrical routine of brushing my lips against the cheek of the leading actress, 'Thank you . . . sweetie . . . wonderful,' shaking hands with the leading actor, 'Thank you, terrific . . .' and then the others, 'Thank you, superb, thank you, marvellous, you certainly gave me a plus, thank you, ta, I told you they'd laugh at that, thank you all,' to end up hugging the bastard director who actually had the impertinence to cut some of the best lines. 'Well you really pulled it off, Ted, Bill, Peter, Ken, Ronnie, thanks, thanks.' At the same time the few compliments returned are accepted gratefully like so many pints of pure blood.

The New Plays Festival at the Questors Theatre takes place annually. Each night, after each performance, there is a discussion about the play. The chairman who leads the discussion is someone well thought of in the theatre, someone like E. Martin Browne or Martin Esslin. The author is expected to attend these discussions and sometimes they can prove to be an ordeal in themselves – especially if the play has not had good notices; for even theatrically informed audiences on such occasions tend to form group attitudes. They like or do not like; they attack or praise. A pack formation does seem to occur and whether they bite or lick depends not only on what went on inside the theatre itself but what has happened outside – the reviews, the word-of-mouth, the attitude of the chairman to his own personal experience of the play, and so on.

Oscar Wilde once remarked that he knew his play was a success – but the question was, would the audience be one? The audience at the Questors Theatre for *The Dogs of Pavlov*, though it included some friends and relations, passed with distinction. Soon after the opening night, the 'FULL UP' signs appeared and I found all kinds of people began telephoning me at my home to see if I could wangle them seats. This small 'success' was helped by the fact that a couple of respected critics on national newspapers had trekked out to Ealing and had been kind to the play. Also BBC2 had filmed a scene from it and a tangential discussion had followed afterwards. I mention all this mainly, of course, in order to boast – but also to indicate reasons why the nightly discussions after the performance of *The Dogs of Pavlov* were not too much of an ordeal – not as they had been, for instance, for an earlier play of mine that had been performed at the Questors.

The after-performance discussions would focus initially on the play itself, on the characters in the play, their interrelationships, on dramatic devices in the play, on such matters as tension and pace and density, on other technical matters such as the film sequences and lighting and so on. But, after a while, the themes touched on in *The Dogs of Pavlov* were grittily engaged and attitudes about power and manipulation, racial prejudice and victimization, and even scientific experimentation itself were ventilated. I discovered more things in my play than I had thought I had put in.

Yet people on the whole preferred to discuss things other than the gut-aching historical outcome of man's willingness to submit to evil orders. 'Human kind cannot bear very much reality.' Certainly, there were those who amazingly saw only a very indirect relationship of the laboratory experiment (as played out on the stage) to what had happened so recently in Europe. I remember one articulate member of the audience in particular, who brilliantly enlarged on one man's need to dominate others and who did not see the relevance of that to anti-Semitism or colour prejudice. He quoted amusingly Dr Jean de Rougemont: 'If my neighbour is stronger than I, I fear him; if he is weaker, I despise him; if we are equal, I resort to subterfuge'; he pointed out (correctly) how I had been influenced by W. H. Auden's essay on Iago, 'The Joker in the Pack'; he touched on other academic points with great clarity and intelligence – yet he seemed to think the Nazi holocaust an irrelevance to the play that he had just seen performed. He was not alone in this.

I have said at the beginning that the worst savagery of our own time has not yet become blurred to a more ritualistic pattern as centuries-old violence has done. 'We are all involved,' I argued, 'every one of us, however far removed from those scenes of bleak, pale crimes. We are, metaphorically, survivors because of them.' I exaggerated. There are many who know little about Auschwitz or feel utterly estranged from that 'foreign' happening. We cannot feel ourselves to be survivors unless we feel some empathy for the victims of these pale crimes, unless we have, too, some sense of history. 'According to the wishes of the Reichsführer SS, Auschwitz became the greatest known extermination factor of all time,' wrote Rudolf Höss, the Auschwitz commandant. 'When in the summer of 1941 he gave me personal orders to prepare a mass extermination site in Auschwitz and to carry out this extermination, I could not in the slightest degree imagine its extent and consequences. . . . I didn't waste time thinking it over then – I had received the order – and had to carry it out. Whether the mass extermination of the Jews was necessary or not, I could not allow myself to judge. As the Führer himself had ordered the "Final Solution of the Jewish problem" there was nothing for an old Nazi to think about.'

Question: Who was Rudolf Höss? *Answer:* Not a monster but a man like you and me. That is the kind of question and answer that triggered off Professor Milgram's experiment at Yale. It is the question that has nagged many contemporary writers – some Jews, others not – into writing novels, film scripts, poems and, very occasionally, plays. It was the same question and answer that is, as far as I am concerned, the central theme of *The Dogs of Pavlov*.

If, sometimes, the after-performance debates about this central theme seemed hesitant, the sub-topic, the rights and wrongs of using humans as guinea-pigs for a scientific inquiry, generated much confident dialogue and passion. This was particularly true the night Michael Billington of *The Times* chaired the discussion for he seemed to think that human guinea-pig experimentation was the dominant proposition of *The Dogs of Pavlov*.

It is a subject, in any case, that interests many people. It is relevant to them not so much because they recall how doctors in Nazi Germany experimented vilely on concentration camp victims but rather because of publicity, more recent, about human guinea-pig experimentation at major teaching hospitals. There have been disquieting headlines in the newspapers and feature programmes on television. People are quite properly shocked and feel angry when they hear of doctors transgressing the spirit of the Hippocratic oath. Certainly, at the Questors Theatre, there were those who felt strongly about even such experiments as those carried out at Yale. 'Not ethical,' one man at the back thundered.

I do not know whether actual criteria exist for judging whether any particular human guinea-pig experiment is deemed to be ethical or not. I am not a lawyer nor a philosopher but surely commonsense dictates that these experiments should be judged to be ethical or not according to (a) the conscious motives of the experimenter; (b) the free consent of the subject experimented on; and (c) the harmlessness or likely harmfulness, physical and mental, that results from the experiment on the subject.

(a) *The conscious motives of the experimenter.* The scientist will usually maintain that his quest is to seek out new knowledge that can be used in the service of humankind. Or as Francis Bacon (who should be first in the pantheon of social psychologists) wrote once, 'The end of our foundation is the knowledge of causes and secret workings of things . . . to the effecting of all things possible.' Supposing though, instead, the experiment has been primarily devised for personal gain or publicity or for the personal advancement of the experimenter (to secure, say, promotion, through publication of a scientific paper) would we not judge the whole experiment rather more harshly?

(b) *The free consent of the subject experimented on.* Obviously to choose *freely* to participate in an experiment the subject must be old enough, intelligent enough and sane enough to make that choice after the facts of the experiment have been explained to him truthfully. He must not, therefore, be hoaxed.

(c) *The harmfulness or harmlessness of the experiment on the subject.* The interests of the patient experimented on cannot be casually ignored. He must not be used as a counter. It is true that the outcome of an experiment is not always foreseeable but this does not mean that should harm result the experimenter can disclaim responsibility.

Let us turn for a moment to an undisputed case of unethical human guinea-pig experimentation that took place in New York in 1965. On that occasion, highly qualified medical specialists, experts in cancer and viruses, had injected live cancer cells into debilitated patients without their knowledge. When live cancer cells are injected into a healthy human being the body rejects these cells as they do other foreign transplants. The medical researcher wanted to ascertain whether a debilitated human body, debilitated by chronic disease other than cancer, would also be able to reject the foreign cancer cells.

Laudably, the research doctors were trying to find a means of immunizing patients against cancer. But the patients injected with live cancer cells would not have agreed to such a measure – so they were lied to. They were told that the injections were simply a part of the treatment they needed.

On hearing of this experiment, three other doctors on the staff of the same New York hospital resigned in protest. An investigation followed. The research doctors were found guilty of unethical conduct and the investigatory committee recommended that their medical licences be suspended. We are not surprised by such a judgement because though (a) the conscious motives of the experimenters were impeccable, (b) the patients did not give their free consent to the experiment and (c) there was a distinct possibility that the outcome of the experiment would be harmful to them.

To be sure, the experiments that are taking place in psychological laboratories all over the world are not unethical like that New York medical experiment cited above. Yet it seems right, and in the public interest, that the spotlight be shone from time to time not only on experiments going on in the sick wards of hospitals but also on those in psychological laboratories so that their usefulness and ethical content can at least be questioned. Diana Baumrind, a research psychologist at the University of California who has written aggressively about the Yale experiment in the *American Psychologist*, has also commented, 'It has become commonplace in sociopsychological laboratory studies to manipulate, embarrass and discomfort subjects.' Isn't it time then that the general public knew about these studies?

When we spotlight the experiment that took place at Yale I suspect many will be grossly offended by the hoax element necessary for the experiment to take place in the first instance. They may feel that in order to demonstrate that subjects may behave like so many Eichmanns the experimenter had to act the part, to some extent, of a Himmler. Others may even believe that the documents of history can teach us the consequences of destructive obedience better than any laboratory experiment, however cleverly conceived.

Of course, Professor Stanley Milgram, in setting up his experiment, was actuated by the highest of motives. He had hopes that his work would lead to human betterment. Besides, as he has put it, 'enlightenment is more dignified than ignorance', and 'new knowledge is pregnant with humane consequences'.

Nevertheless, the volunteers who came to the Yale laboratory were placed under formidable stress and were divested of their human dignity. As the scientists stared through their one-way mirrors at the guinea pigs responding to the commands of the man in the technician's grey coat, they saw highly charged, dramatic conflict occur. I quote directly from Milgram's paper, 'Behavioral Study of Obedience'. 'Many subjects showed signs of nervousness in the experimental situation and especially upon administering the more powerful shocks. In a large number of cases the degree of tension reached extremes that are rarely seen in sociopsychological laboratory studies. Subjects were observed to sweat, tremble, stutter, bite their lips, groan and dig their fingernails into their flesh. These were characteristic rather than exceptional responses to the experiment. One sign of tension was the regular recurrence of nervous laughing fits. . . . The laughter seemed entirely out of place, even bizarre. Full blown uncontrollable seizures were observed in 3 subjects. On one occasion, we observed a seizure so violently convulsive that it was necessary to call a halt to the experiment.'

Here is a further description of another subject by an observer other than Professor Milgram: 'I observed a mature and critically poised businessman enter the laboratory smiling and confident. Within twenty minutes he was reduced to a twitching stuttering wreck who was rapidly approaching a point of nervous collapse. He constantly pulled on his ear lobe, and twisted his hands. At one point, he pushed his fist into his forehead and muttered, "Oh God, let's stop it." And yet he continued to respond to every word of the experimenter, and obeyed to the end.'

Prior to the laboratory experience neither Professor Milgram nor his colleague could envisage that their experiment would induce such harrowing and startling effects on their volunteer subjects. When they could foresee what might happen they were confronted with the choice of continuing their experiment or stopping it. They decided to continue. Professor Milgram felt there was no evidence of durable injurious effects on the subjects. 'In my judgment,' he has written, 'at no point were subjects exposed to danger and at no point did they run the risk of injurious effects resulting from participation. If it had been otherwise, the experiment would have been terminated at once.'

Indeed Stanley Milgram believed that some of his volunteers had

been enriched by the experience. By musing on their ugly perform-
ances in that Yale laboratory they might have received valuable and
startling insights into their own personalities. To be sure, if Socrates'
absolutist command of 'Know thyself' is invariably a wise one who
can quarrel with Professor Milgram's conclusion? Still, isn't it also
plausible that for some people, partial self-knowledge, anyway, could
be the knowledge forbidden to Adam and so its revelation could lead
to the re-enactment of the Fall, and to a personal, living damnation?
Who can be certain? Montaigne once inscribed on his mantelpiece,
'Que sçaise-je?' ('What do I know?')

Statements by the human guinea-pig subjects do suggest that a
number of them subjectively felt they had benefited from the
experiment; others seemed pleased that they had helped along a
piece of scientific research. It should be mentioned, too, that after
each experimental session the volunteer–subject was informed that
the electric shock treatment had been a hoax and, apparently,
friendly reconciliations then took place between the subject and the
accountant–actor who had once sat in the unwired chair. 'The
experiment was explained to the defiant subjects,' Milgram has
written, 'in a way that supported their decision to disobey the
experimenter. Obedient subjects were assured of the fact that their
behavior was entirely normal and that their feelings of conflict or
tension were shared by other participants.'

It is evident that post-experimentally Professor Milgram was most
concerned for the welfare of his human guinea-pigs. Hence those
reconciliations, those lengthy talks about the experiment after each
session and so on. He even sent the volunteers a follow-up question-
naire about their participation in the experiment so that they could
express their thoughts and feelings about how they behaved. 92 per
cent returned the questionnaire. Of these, 84 per cent maintained
they were pleased to have participated; 15 per cent were neutral; and
1.3 per cent 'indicated negative feelings'. Professor Milgram found
reassurance in the answers to that questionnaire. 'The replies to the
questionnaire confirmed my impression that participants felt posi-
tively towards the experiment,' he wrote replying to Diana Baum-
rind's earlier attack on the Yale study in the *American Psychologist*.

Professor Baumrind had written: 'From the subject's point of view
procedures which involve loss of dignity, self-esteem and trust in
rational authority are probably most harmful in the long run and
require the most thoughtfully planned reparations, if engaged in at
all. ... I would not like to see experiments such as Milgram's

proceed unless the subjects were fully informed of the dangers of
serious after effects and his corrections were clearly shown to be
effective in restoring their state of wellbeing.' I would go further than
Professor Baumrind because I for one, even if I was certain that
post-experimental reparations were 100 per cent effective in 100 per
cent of the subjects, would still feel most uneasy about the Yale
experiments – as I would feel about any experiments based on a hoax,
that causes men to lose their dignity, to twitch, to suffer seizures, to
reach the point of almost nervous collapse. How can such experi-
ments be happily sanctioned by an informed public though carefully
conducted, though supervised by men of impeccable morals,
though performed for the most idealistic of reasons? Certainly
such experiments would not have been sanctioned by those disin-
terested people who were articulate in the after-performance dis-
cussions of *The Dogs of Pavlov* at the Questors Theatre.

6

At the last after-performance discussion of *The Dogs of Pavlov*, one
lady, concerned about the morality of human guinea-pig experi-
ments, gently asked why I was not absolutely accurate about the
details of those experiments as outlined in my play. 'For instance,'
she asked, 'why did you make the minor characters of Dr Daly and
Dr Olwen Jones research doctors instead of research psychologists?'
I told her that I was marginally happier writing about doctors – since I
was one myself – than about psychologists but that, in any case, I was
interested in writing a fictional piece of theatre with fictional charac-
ters. Indeed, I was more interested in how these fictional characters
related to each other in human terms rather than in any abstract idea
– even if that idea was about the destructive consequences of
obedience. For a play is not an essay nor, for that matter, a
dramatized moral tract.

Prior to writing *The Dogs of Pavlov* the only thing I had read on the
Yale experiment was an interesting essay by a Stanley Milgram called
'The Compulsion to Do Evil' in the journal *Patterns of Prejudice*. This
essay I found suggestive but *The Dogs of Pavlov* is, of course, a work of
imagination as is the experiment outlined in it. But when asked to
write this introduction I read for the first time Professor Milgram's
original papers, 'Behavioral Study of Obedience' (*Journal of Abnor-
mal and Social Psychology*) and 'Some Conditions of Obedience and
Disobedience to Authority' (*Human Relations*) and in the process of

discovering additional details about the Yale experiment and its variations I found the results even more profoundly disturbing.

Professor Milgram speaks of a painful alteration in his own thinking as a consequence of his Yale laboratory studies. Far too frequently, he witnessed good people 'knuckle under to the demands of authority' and these same people perform actions that were utterly callous. 'What is the limit of such obedience?' he asks. 'At many points we attempted to establish a boundary. Cries from the victim were inserted: not good enough. The victim claimed heart trouble: subjects still shocked him on command.'

Nobody can feel sanguine about the statistics of the Yale experiments. These statistics, like the recent documents of history, are red lights warning us how a coercive government today could command its subjects to perform evil acts, and these subjects would not feel themselves to be morally guilty in obeying such commands. Rather they would regard themselves as innocent agents of a legitimate authority. In Milgram's post-experimental interviews, when asked why they continued to shock the accountant in the chair 'all along the board' they characteristically replied, 'I wouldn't have done it by myself. I was just doing what I was told.' We have heard that story before – not only at Nuremberg – and, alas, we shall hear it again. For as Professor Milgram says, 'It would be wrong to think of it as a thin alibi concocted for the occasion. Rather, it is a fundamental mode of thinking for a great many people once they are locked into a subordinate position of responsibility.'

On the other hand, we ought to remind ourselves, for it is the same part of the truth, that over one-third of the participants did not fall into the category of 'obedient' subjects. There were those who were utterly defiant. There were those, also, who managed to 'cheat' the experimenter in a humane way: thus they assured the experimenter (not wishing to offend him) that they were progressively raising the voltage shock level whereas, in fact, they surreptitiously continued to pull the first lever of the generator giving the accountant, they thought, only the mildest of shocks! Even those who did pull down all the levers – at least many of them – did exhibit high levels of conflict, as has already been indicated. This demonstrates, at least, that their consciences were being strenuously exercised. Hardly true solace, you may think, for any real victim!

Perhaps for small solace one should go back to the actual documents of history – to Berlin, for example, in 1942, to the Gestapo headquarters at Prinz-Albrechstrasse. There a Gestapo official said to Dr Baeck who was President of the Representative Council of German Jews, 'Surely not even you can deny that the whole German nation is behind the Führer's measures regarding the Jews?' Dr Baeck replied, 'I wouldn't like to be dogmatic about that. I would though like to say one thing. When I go home from here . . . with my yellow star, nothing bad will happen to me. . . . On the other hand, here and there someone will try and push his way over to me, a stranger; he will look around nervously and press my hand. He might even push an apple into my hand, a bar of chocolate, or a cigarette. Apart from that, nothing will happen to me. I don't know whether the Führer, in my place, would have the same experience!'

There is the parable of the three wise men who walked past a dead dog. The first uttered, 'What a terrible sight!'; the second, 'What a terrible smell!'; but the third, who was the wisest of all, remarked, 'What beautiful white teeth has that dead dog!' We must find our consolations where we can.

Part Three

A Voice of My Own

Different poets were invited to discuss their own work under the title of
'A Voice of My Own' on Radio 3

At the top of the report my name, *D. Abse*; my address, *Mayim,
Windermere Avenue, Roath, Cardiff*; my age, *15½*. Opposite English
Literature, in red ink, the tidy handwriting of our English master, Mr
Graber: *He has a voice of his own.* My parents would be puzzled by that
remark. 'He means,' I would tell them uselessly, 'that I have a style of
my own.' I recalled how, some years earlier, my brother Leo had
brought home his school report and that next to his Latin mark of 25
(out of 100) a master had written, *He is in a class of his own.* Leo's
oratorical and persuasive gifts were such that he had managed to
convince my innocent parents that Latin was not his worst subject
but his best, that the Latin master's comment had not been deroga-
tory but a startling and honourable compliment. Only quite recently I
heard my mother declare, when a neighbour was discussing the
Latin temperament, 'Our Leo was always excellent at Latin.'

Reading my report my father's lips moved silently before he finally
lifted his face from the page to blindingly search mine, 'Everybody's
got a voice of his own,' he grumbled. 'Everybody's face is distinctive.
I don't see that your English master's praising you.'

I fumbled until, inspired, I said, 'It takes time even to grow into
your own face.'

Ever since I had been *so high*, cheek-pinching fussy visitors with
strong thumbs had pondered, 'Who does he look like?' The
Shepherd side of the family said with an 'alas' that I resembled an
Abse; the Abse side, though, insisted that I, poor boy, looked like a
Shepherd. That kind of luminous conversation would always con-
clude with my mother reminding everybody that she had once been
the prettiest girl in the Swansea valley and that when she had married
my father the neighbours had called the newly wed couple Beauty
and the Beast.

One wry aunt, not listening to this true but worn story, and staring
at me as if I were in a cage, pronounced that I looked like nobody in

particular. This was a most fearful and scandalous metaphysical judgement. Yet she was right. My face was not then, nor yet at 15½, my own. Similarly my English master was wrong: I did not yet have a voice of my own. All I had was an accent. And when I started to write my schoolboy poetry, in 1941, even that suggestion of individuality was soon submerged as I caught, like a happy infection, the intonation of the poets I had read at school and at home.

I had become interested in poetry after reading one of Leo's books, *Poems for Spain*. Stephen Spender, in the introduction to that book, declared:

This collection of poems about the Spanish War written and translated by English writers is a document of our times. . . . The fact that these poems should have been written at all has a literary significance parallel to the existence of the International Brigade. For some of these poems, and many more which we have not been able to publish, were written by men for whom poetry scarcely existed before the Spanish War.

Until I read that book, poetry scarcely existed for me. For matriculation I had studied and liked Tennyson's 'Lotus Eaters', Keats's 'St Agnes Eve', Wordsworth's 'Lines at Tintern Abbey'. Earlier, at home, sometimes in the corners of an evening, Leo would also read me poems. I particularly enjoyed hearing him recite Browning. And when I played tennis, and was losing, I would rouse myself into a proper aggressive stance by mouthing lines from 'The Lost Leader'. Wordsworth had sold out, Leo had told me years earlier – become Poet Laureate. Wordsworth, it seemed, was a turncoat like Ramsay MacDonald. So as I endeavoured to serve an ace I would mumble to myself, 'Just for a handful of silver he left us.' *Smash* . . . OUT. 'Just for a riband to stick in his coat.' *Smash* . . . DOUBLE FAULT. 'Blot out his name, then, record one lost soul more.' *Smash* . . . OUT.

Poetry, then, had its uses but it moved into the centre of my preoccupations gradually, and that movement only commenced after I had read my contemporaries in the urgent, yellow-jacketed anthology, *Poems for Spain*. Here I read for the first time poets whose adult moral concerns and protestations engaged my own wrath and indignation. Their voices had a passionate immediacy and their language was fresh, of the twentieth century. The raw political poems of the Spanish peasant poet, Miguel Hernandez, moved me to express my own indignation about the horrors of war in verse. I had begun to write verse voluntarily, not as an exercise for school. I hardly thought about technique at first or worried about owning a voice of my own. Looking back now, I realize that, as I wrote, I was beginning to exchange the collective tone of the nineteenth century – Wordsworth, Keats, Tennyson, Browning – for that of the twentieth – Hernandez, Auden, Spender. And, naïvely, I wanted to make political statements.

A few years ago, my *Collected Poems 1948–1976* was published. A reader lingering over these poems would discover occasional references to the most important public events of our time – events in Nazi Germany, or war in Vietnam, or man landing on the moon. For instance, a first visit to Germany in 1970 prompted lines like these:

> Can't sleep for Mozart,
> and on the winter glass
> a shilling's worth of glitter.
>
> The German streets tonight
> are soaped in moonlight.
> The streets of Germany are clean
> like the hands of Lady Macbeth.
>
> (from 'No More Mozart')

A few years earlier, lying on a foreign beach, after reading an English newspaper with its news of Vietnam I looked up at a single cloud in a blue sky and thought how Euripides had made Helen say, 'I never went to Troy. Only a phantom went.' To which the messenger, according to Euripides, replied, 'What's this? All that suffering for nothing, simply for a cloud?' And soon, still thinking of such things as Vietnamese women newly widowed, I wrote:

> Later, I walk back to the hotel thinking:
> wherever women crouch beside their dead,
> as Hecuba did, as Andromache,
> motionless as sculpture till they raise their head,
> with mouths wildly open to howl and curse,
> now they call that cloud not Helen, no,
> but a thousand names, and each one still untrue.
>
> (from 'On the Beach')

As for man landing on the moon, the news that those computer-speaking astronauts – bleep bleep bleep, *over* – had brought back some moon material to be examined by scientists made me write a poem called 'Moon Object'. You could pronounce that title as 'Moon Ob*ject*', if you wish. Addressing a scientist examining samples of moon rock I continued:

> Blue eyes, observe it again. See its dull appearance
> and be careful: it could be cursed, it could be sleeping.
>
> Awake, it might change colour like a lampshade
> turned on, seething – suddenly moon-plugged.
>
> Scientist, something rum has happened to you.
> Your right and left eyes have been switched around.
>
> Back home, if you dialled your own number now,
> a shameless voice would reply, 'Who? Who?'
>
> (From 'Moon Object')

So, over the years, I have managed to write lines like these, poems such as these; but I've never managed to make an overt political poem of the platform variety such as Hernandez once so passionately wrote. For that early resolve to write direct political verse dissolved after a year or two – long before I served my long apprenticeship in learning how to write. Perhaps I realized even then that a voice shouting loses its distinctive quality. The voice of, say, John Smith speaking is his own but John Smith shouting becomes the raised voice of anonymous humanity.

But I see that I am immodestly suggesting that by not shouting I have at last achieved what Mr Graber once falsely claimed – a distinctive style, a voice of my own. Style, though, is something more unconscious than deliberate. Poetry depends upon unconscious engenderings and proliferations. Poetry is written in the brain but the brain is bathed in blood. So a writer intent on recognizing what distinguishes his own poetry from that of his contemporaries is confronting a dilemma. He looks into the mirror but sees no one there. To put it another way: style is like an odour in a room he has lived in for so long that it is not recognizable to himself – only to visitors.

That is why someone with the integrity, for instance, of Victoria Sackville-West could happen on a typescript of a poem among her papers called 'St Augustine at 32' and could believe that it was one of her own discarded efforts – not a poem by Clifford Dyment who, as a young poet twenty-two years younger than she, had sent it to her for appraisal many years before. Not knowing her own style she read it as if it were her own – critically, yes, but with that especial tolerance proper and common to authors examining their own work! With cosmetic changes, she decided, this neglected draft could be rendered into serviceable verse. Soon the poem bore a new title, 'The Novice to Her Lover' and some months later a puzzled and irate Clifford Dyment read it in the *New Statesman*.

But if style is truly unconscious how, in another issue of the *New Statesman*, could one of those competitions which directs its readers to write a paragraph in the style of Graham Greene be won by Graham Greene himself, when he entered under a pseudonym? I think a writer while not able to apprehend the matrix of his own style can become aware of its superficial elements – the audible mannerisms and visible devices – and it was these that Mr Greene supplied. I would now, therefore, like to change my metaphor of a writer in search of his own style being one who looking into the mirror sees no one there, to one who because of mannerisms and devices looking into the mirror sees clothes with no one in them – clothes without an Emperor!

Every writer, some time or another, is likely to ponder the question of literary influence: of who has influenced him and whom he has influenced; what are just and proper borrowings and what is a too overt imitation. Perhaps writers generally feel sympathy with the Lacedemonians who used not to punish theft so much as the inability to conceal it. But it is better to sin than to be sinned against. For imitations debilitate, somehow, the power of the original; they cheapen the original. True, when fashion changes, and changes again, the original work of art discharges once more its old energy, whereas the imitations seem poor, inert reproductions with only as much resemblance to the original as handwriting has to its rough reflection on blotting paper.

When I look back at my earliest published work of the late 1940s I discern not only the then fashionable manner of neo-romanticism, but the unpremeditated influences, too dominant, of Dylan Thomas and Rainer Maria Rilke. Whatever individual voice I owned had to make itself heard above such noisy echoes. It seems to me now, what is probably obvious to everybody else, that a poet's progress towards discovering his own voice is marked by the shuffling off of all discernible individual influences. In his youth, a poet reading this or that poem with admiration may often murmur, as I did, 'I wish I had written that.' Later he will never articulate such a wish for he will realize that only one man can write one particular poem, that the style of that poem cannot satisfactorily be borrowed, and that without that style the poem cannot exist. This man's gift, that man's scope, may continue to be admired, but the mature poet will know it is better to be that ill-defined thing, himself, rather than the second Rainer Maria Rilke or the second Dylan Thomas. A true poet may envy another poet's material success, the winning of awards, the adulation of critics, but he cannot envy the other poet's poetry. To put it another way, as Eliot would have said, and indeed to quote Eliot, there are 'men whom one cannot hope to emulate, *but there is no competition*'.

Those poems of mine marred by the too intrusive accents of Rilke and Dylan Thomas I left out of my *Collected Poems*. And if some of the earliest poems in that volume seem to me half-successful it is not because I now find my own individual voice in them. On the contrary, it is because they imitate everybody and in doing so sound like nobody in particular. That is to say they belong to an anonymous tradition. Here, for instance on page 2 of my *Collected Poems* (the poems in this volume are arranged more or less chronologically) is a poem called 'Epithalamion' which belongs, I think, to the central English lyrical tradition:

> Singing, today I married my white girl
> beautiful in a barley field.
> Green on thy finger a grass blade curled,
> so with this ring I thee wed, I thee wed,
> and send our love to the loveless world
> of all the living and all the dead.
>
> Now, no more than vulnerable human,
> we, more than one, less than two,
> are nearly ourselves in a barley field –
> and only love is the rent that's due
> though the bailiffs of time return anew
> to all the living but not the dead.
>
> Shipwrecked, the sun sinks down harbours
> of a sky, unloads its liquid cargoes
> of marigolds, and I and my white girl
> lie still in the barley – who else wishes
> to speak, what more can be said
> by all the living against all the dead?

Come then all you wedding guests:
green ghost of trees, gold of barley,
you blackbird priests in the field,
you wind that shakes the pansy head
fluttering on a stalk like a butterfly;
come the living and come the dead.

Listen, flowers, birds, winds, worlds,
tell all today that I married
more than a white girl in the barley –
for today I took to my human bed
flower and bird and wind and world,
and all the living and all the dead.

I was trying to say earlier that a shout becomes less particular in character than a level speaking voice. The voice of John Smith talking is his own, but John Smith shouting is the raised voice of anonymous humanity. That direction towards anonymity is also evident, is it not, in the singing voice? I think it no accident that as the years pass by I use more and more a conversational tone rather than a singing one. Could it be, incidentally, that the poet's general tendency to be more lyrical in youth is related to his own existential doubt, his own falterings about his immature and unstable identity?

I find a letter addressed to me by T. S Eliot, when I was a medical student and publishing poems for the first time, more enlightening now than I once did. I had sent him a number of poems including one by an imaginary Israeli poet. In 1948, the state of Israel had come into existence and I wrote a song which I purported was by a young Israeli called Dov Shamir. Eliot, who did not know about my impersonation, liked my 'Dov Shamir' poem and he wrote to me more or less saying that I should do more Dov Shamir translations because they were better than my own work! I still think that judgement ironic and amusing, but I realize now that Eliot was at least right about the song for Dov Shamir. It was better than the others I had sent him. The others had unintentional bits of Dylan Thomas and Rainer Maria Rilke in them, whereas the Dov Shamir song could have been written by anyone – even by Dov Shamir himself! For that is the point I am trying to make. A pure song has no particular voice in it. It merely waits for a particular voice to sing it.

So if I have found eventually my own voice it would be more evident in the later rather than the earlier pages of the *Collected Poems*, in those poems conversationally directed. I stare now at these pages and try to assess the poems on them rather like some frowning critic. I see they are rooted to the time and the country and the tradition in which the author works. I note certain recurring preoccupations and evidence to confirm the autobiographical facts that the poet is a married man practising as a doctor in a city in the twentieth century. I might even be able to guess (as if I didn't know) that one of the author's favourite precepts about aesthetics is that of Han Fei who, in the third century BC, maintained that it was too easy to paint a ghost but most difficult to paint horses or dogs! Playing the part of a sympathetic critic, all this and much more I can apprehend. Further, I hear no particular alien voice in them – those intonations of Dylan Thomas and Rainer Maria Rilke having faded entirely. I hear no voice at all that sounds particularly like someone else's. Only in this negative way can I conceive that I have, in fact, a voice of my own. And the only other confirmation I have in this is when others tell me they can recognize my way of saying things or when, occasionally, I am confronted by imitations of my own work. Then I think, 'Why, that's, damn it all, like me.'

But, of course, it's not for me to make any judgement about such a matter. Strangers less prejudiced in my favour must arrive at their own conclusions. It seems sensible, then, to help them in this by ending with a poem. The last one in my *Collected Poems* should do as well as any other. It does not seem eccentric compared with many of those that precede it, nor do I think it better or worse than them. It's called 'The Stethoscope'.

> Through it,
> over young women's abdomens tense
> I have heard the sound of creation
> and, in a dead man's chest, the silence
>   before creation began.
>
> Should I
> pray therefore? Hold this instrument in awe
> and aloft a procession of banners?
> Hang this thing in the interior
>   of a cold, mushroom-dark church?
>
> Should I
> kneel before it, chant an apophthegm
> from a small text? Mimic priest or rabbi,
> the swaying noises of religious men?
>   Never! Yet I could praise it.

        I should
by doing so celebrate my own ears,
by praising them praise speech at midnight
when men become philosophers;
        laughter of the sane and insane:

        night cries
of injured creatures, wide-eyed or blind;
moonlight sonatas on a needle;
lovers with doves in their throats; the wind
        travelling from where it began.

On Rhyming
and Not Rhyming

This was a contribution to a symposium – this time initiated by
Poetry Wales – where six poets were asked to tell why they do or don't
use rhyme, and to provide a new poem with their comments!

I

As you read this prose-note your expectancy will be that I shall not
rely on words that regularly or irregularly rhyme. On the contrary, as
I write, should a word here or there inadvertently and frankly rhyme
it may interfere with the clear progress of the sentence, and I, aware
of the sound words make (as all writers are whether of prose or
verse), will accordingly substitute another word for the rhyme-
obstruction.

Of course, there are occasions when the writer of prose will
deliberately borrow devices that are commonly associated with
poetry: false rhymes, pararhymes, assonance, alliteration, parallel-
ism and so on. I take down a book from the nearest shelf. Because it
happens to be *The Oxford Book of Welsh Verse in English* edited by
Gwyn Jones and I wish for the moment to dwell on prose I turn to the
introduction. Almost at once I discover what I am looking for:

> The two centuries ran their course, fashions rose or were adopted;
> fashions fell or were adapted; by 1800 the poetic landscape showed a
> visible shortage of tall trees, and the ninth wave had ceased to roll
> and thunder . . .

It is perhaps amusing to note that Gwyn Jones's reliance on such
poetic devices as parallelism and pararhyme – 'fashions rose or were
adopted; fashions fell or were adapted' – prompted him, probably
unconsciously, to borrow immediately a second property of poetry,
namely metaphor. The ostentatious *aural* pattern is followed by
visual metaphors, albeit mixed! I am not, need it be said, criticizing
the quality of Gwyn Jones's prose. What I am endeavouring to point
out now, no doubt laboriously, is how often any writer of prose with
half an ear deliberately uses – pick up any book from any shelf – all
the devices associated with verse *except true, frank rhyme*.

There are, of course, many living poets who follow prose writers in this and just as stringently eschew rhyme in their verse. It is not because they, like Milton, recall with reverence the non-rhyming parings of the Latin or Greek tongue or the august high seriousness in the non-rhyming poetry of the ancient Hebrews. Rather it is because they feel rhyme is too obviously an artificial device and that such transparent artifice contradicts Wordsworth's still modern proposition that poets should keep as far as possible to a selection of language really used by men. In addition, some small number mistakenly feel that, with the advent of the modern movement more than half a century ago, rhyme became dated, old-hat – and this despite the example of the best poets writing since T. S. Eliot.

What has *genuinely* become dated though are those limitations on the use of rhyme that once governed poets in their employment of it. My father, soon after the First World War, bought a set of encyclo-paedias from a travelling salesman. These encyclopaedias, published by the defunct Gresham publishing company, at present adorn my bookshelves, and I confess that before beginning this note I took down volume IX, PHO–ROM, to look up *Rhyme*. I discovered much prejudice about rhyme that no longer endures. For instance:

> English writers have allowed themselves certain licences and we find in the best English poets rhymes which strike an accurate ear as incorrect. In some instances such as *sky* and *liberty*, *hand* and *command*, *gone* and *alone*, the correspondence in the letters makes what may be called a rhyme to the eye which supplies, in some measure, the want of correspondence in sound. In other instances, however, this is not the case, as in *revenge* and *change*, *remote* and *thought*. Such rhymes may be tolerated if they only occur at rare intervals, but they must certainly be regarded as blemishes, and are carefully avoided by all who wish to write harmoniously.

Autres temps, autres moeurs. The fact is, whatever may be the case in prose, there are no immutable laws of when and where not to use rhyme in poetry or what kind of rhyme is legitimate and acceptable.

When I look back at my own work I discover that sometimes I have used regular rhyme, sometimes irregular rhyme, sometimes internal rhyme, and sometimes no rhyme at all. I should like now to refer to two poems I wrote more than a decade ago which have cooled in that distance allowing me some measure of objectivity. Both poems have an autobiographical basis; both indeed arose from harrowing experi-ences, though of a different kind; both were informed with a more than ordinary emotional charge. One of anger, one of grief. Neither were poems that resulted from emotion remembered in tranquillity.

One poem was called 'In Llandough Hospital' and was written in rhymed quatrains, the other 'A Night Out' consisted of three unrhymed, eleven-lined paragraphs or stanzas. Both poems can be found in my *Collected Poems* so I shall not reprint them here. I would like, though, to say why I felt it necessary to use rhyme in one poem and no rhyme at all in the other.

'A Night Out' relates the experience of going to a cinema and being surprised by a too lifelike Polish film about a concentration camp in Hitler's Germany. The film assaulted me as a matter of fact. I quit that cinema in London's Oxford Street in an undefined rage and needed, soon after, to write a poem about the experience. Such was the charge of my emotion that rightly or wrongly I felt that I did not wish to make any pretty artifice out of it. I did not want to be lyrical about such a theme. I wanted to be as truthful as possible, to avoid all kinds of artificiality, to say what I felt and to say it plainly. I wanted the *verisimilitude of prose* – and so wanting that I used rhythms associated with prose and of course, as prose writers do, I eschewed rhyme.

'In Llandough Hospital' is a poem about the death of my own father when I, as a doctor, also happened to be in attendance some of the time at his deathbed. I have written a little elsewhere about that poem – in my autobiography *A Poet in the Family* – and perhaps I may be allowed to quote from that book here:

> I started to write a poem about that recent experience in Llandough Hospital. Then I put my pen down listlessly. To convert that raw finale into a mere wordy resemblance of it seemed wrong. Why should I allow myself to pull back the curtain on a scene so intimate to me? Yet since poetry was my raison d'être – my ambition, I had said often enough, was to write the next poem – then surely not to try and make a poem about that urgent eye-brimming experience would be to admit that poetry-making was a trivial act, a silly useless fiddle with words, and that my own life, its direction and centre, was silly and useless too? I began to feel I must write a poem called 'In Llandough Hospital'. I had written poems about a stunted tree, about a railway shunter, about a piece of chalk even, about the halls of houses, about odours, about a hundred things, hundreds of things, so not to write about my father's death would be an insult to my father's memory. . . .

What I did not go on to say was that when I began the poem I was oppressed by the need – as much as one may be at a funeral – for some ceremony in the diction, for the poem itself to own the formality of ceremony. Nothing too elaborate. A simple form and simple rhymes. Not the intricacies of the *cynydd* or any English approximation of it. No, a quatrain say, with line-endings *abca*. What could be more simple, appropriate? (And more difficult!) Not a choir then, but one voice, and that single voice on this occasion not too colloquial.

Ridiculous pressures, feelings? Maybe. Perhaps another poet experiencing that Polish film in the way I had done or the trauma of a father's death may have made poems of and about these experiences with the discipline of a contrary technique? No rhyme in this poem but in the other. Or no rhyme in either. Or rhyme in both. It is all subjective, is it not? There are no laws. And what seems, in the end, inevitable, was at one time probably not so.

2

Looking back at the poems I have written during 1978 I observe once again that some depend on regular rhyme, some on irregular and internal rhyming, and some eschew rhyme altogether. The poem I choose to print here, 'In the Gallery', was finished but a month ago. It is irregularly rhymed and I select this poem rather than another because its genesis is eccentric for me in that it is rooted in a rhymed couplet, or to be exact two rhymed couplets of a sort.

A little while back in writing an introduction to my *Collected Poems* I remarked, 'For some time now my ambition has been to write poems which appear translucent but are in fact deceptions. I would have a reader enter them, be deceived he could see through them like sea-water and be puzzled when he cannot quite touch bottom.' This comment has provoked a number of people to ask me to elaborate on it. On one occasion I was called upon to do so after a poetry reading and perhaps too succinctly I replied, 'Think blue, say green.' My response doubtless did not satisfy my interlocutor but I liked my own suddenly made-up phrase. Indeed, later, going home, it occurred to me that *Think Blue, Say Green* might well be a good title for my next book of poems! The trouble was soon another line occurred to me: 'Squeeze apple-pips from a tangerine.' So there I was now stuck with two lines of a poem:

> Think blue, say green,
> squeeze apple-pips from a tangerine.

At regular intervals these two lines came into my head and were as regularly dismissed because I did not know what lines could follow or precede them. More recently, while watching a programme on BBC television about Schubert, I saw a shot of birds flying up from a waste of snow. The commentator spoke of snows and crows, unintentionally presenting a rhyme, and almost at once I thought:

> Four hoofmarks in the snows
> flew away. They must have been four crows.

Like 'Think blue, say green . . .' these two lines also focused on deception, a visual deception. Perhaps each of these 'couplets' though rhythmically different, had something to do with each other?

Now I have long believed that poems should arise out of experience, true or imagined, rather than from naked ideas. An image itself or a musical phrase can be a kind of experience but to set lines authentically ticking and onward I needed a further and more concrete experience and this was given to me when I accepted an invitation to a party at an art gallery.

I do not propose to talk about the meaning of 'In the Gallery' for it is about deceptions as any reader could perhaps have predicted from what I have already said. I shall draw attention, though, at any rate briefly, to the rhymes in the poem or rather some of the rhyming problems that exercised me as I worked on the different lines. Certain parts of the initial conception of the poem had to go – including 'Think blue, say green/squeeze apple-pips from a tangerine.' That 'couplet' I eventually discovered did not belong to the poem; as for 'four hoofmarks in the snows' this image became separated from 'they must have been four crows' because I wanted the last two lines of 'In the Gallery' not so much to rhyme as to each end with the same word – that is with *crows*.

I do not know why I wanted such a conclusion. Shakespeare, I can reason, concluded scenes with a rhyming couplet sometimes when he had used no rhymes earlier. But in 'In the Gallery' I had employed irregular rhyme throughout so to finish the poem with a rhyme would hardly have been surprising. On the other hand to repeat the word-sound exactly is a small surprise for that repetition is a variation that could, as it were satisfactorily, snap shut the poem finally.

Any image in a poem should be alive and to be alive it needs to be both surprising and apt. So it is with rhyme though, I think, to a lesser extent since there is something satisfying also in predictability of sound patterns. How then can predictability and surprise both be present in one rhyme? That apparent contradiction can be solved in different ways. For instance, in the lines:

> Outside it is snow snow
> snowing and namelessness is growing

I hope it is accomplished by the placing of *snowing* at the beginning of the second line rather than at the end of the first line where the reader may justly expect it to be. It is a small adjustment and only changes the sound pattern by the briefest of hesitations. In other lines I trust the problem is solved by using hidden, internal and approximate rhymes with a consistency – *chandelier, weather, sculptor, straw, forever, anywhere* – that the authoritative contributor to the old *New Gresham Encyclopaedia* (vol IX) would have baulked at.

Of course, there were temptations to use additional frank rhymes, to write for example, 'Her name is forgot' rather than 'forgotten' so as to allow *forgot* to chime more loudly with *spot, not* and perhaps *bolt*, but that temptation was resisted because *forgot* is an archaic mode and a discerning reader would have sensed that I had merely been ruled by rhyme rather than being the master of it. Besides, I wanted a three-syllable word, *forgotten*, at this point in the context of the lines that immediately followed it, for these also are end-stopped with three-syllable words (namely *disputed* and *forever*), for such a sequence, though short, can set up a pleasing aural pattern. All this may be of small matter to the reader and I wish to avoid becoming tedious. In other words it is time for me to conclude. So please turn to 'In the Gallery' and do read the poem the second time anyway without noting its rhymes if you can. It wasn't written to demonstrate any technique or lack of it.

In The Gallery

I

> Outside it is snow snow
> but here, under the chandelier,
> there's no such thing as weather.
> Right wall, a horse (not by Gericault);
> left, a still life, mainly apples;
> between, on the parquet floor, a box
> or a coffin which is being opened.

Through a gold-framed mirror,
the Director, dressed as if for mourning,
observes the bust
of an unknown lady
by an unknown sculptor
being lifted out of the straw
by a man in overalls.

II

The apples do not rot, the horse will not bolt,
the statue of the lady
cannot breathe one spot
of tissue paper on the mirror.

Her name is forgotten,
the sculptor's name is disputed,
they both have disappeared forever.
They could have been born
in the North or the South.
They have no grave anywhere.

III

Outside it is snow snow
snowing and namelessness is growing.

Yesterday four hoofmarks in the snows
rose and flew away.

They must have been four crows.
Or, maybe, three of them were crows.

A Meeting with
Robert Graves

I think Sam Wanamaker, the American-born actor, sometimes stands at a window of his house in Southwark, Bankside, and sees his immediate environs not as they now are but as they were in Shakespeare's time. Certainly he imagines Southwark as it may be in the future, as it ought to be. Mr Wanamaker's vision is that of a Bankside once again thriving, bustling with denizens of London in search of serious entertainment – the Globe Playhouse itself, reconstructed. To realize that vision Sam Wanamaker formed the Globe Theatre Centre and since 1972 has encouraged contemporary poets, each year, to honour on the page and on the platform the supreme poet and dramatist of all time. For one of the centre's commendable aims was, and is, 'to create a Shakespeare Birthday Fund which will commission new works of music, poetry, drama and art to be presented annually as the most appropriate tribute to Shakespeare's memory'.

In April 1972 Sam Wanamaker accordingly planned a concert in Southwark Cathedral. Nine contemporary composers were commissioned to contribute music, thirteen contemporary poets to write poems and speak them. I remember being somewhat pleased *and* worried when Christopher Hampton, on Mr Wanamaker's behalf, asked me to be one of the poets – pleased because Mr Hampton had invited, or intended to invite, a number of poets including W. H. Auden and Robert Graves whom I admired but had not met and now would meet; worried because I knew that poetry is something that cannot be willed, that I could not will a poem into existence, that I might not be able to keep a promise to provide a new poem for the occasion. As Shelley once wrote, 'Poetry is not like reasoning, a power to be exerted according to the determination of the will. A man cannot say, "I will compose poetry." The greatest poet even cannot say it; for the mind in creation is as a fading coal, which some invisible influence, like an inconstant wind, awakens to transitory brightness. . . .' Nevertheless, persuaded by Christopher Hampton, I accepted the commission and eventually, armed with a new poem, I went along to Southwark Cathedral to read it.

I suppose many of us have wished sometimes, frail and silly wishes, that we could turn back the clock, be transported if only for an instant to a certain place, at a certain time. Driving over towards Southwark, I wished uselessly that I could have attended a Shakespeare play at the original Globe Theatre – perhaps *Julius Caesar* – for I had read a description by a Thomas Platter of an evening at the Globe when he saw that play. 'After dinner, at about two o'clock, I went with my party across the water,' wrote Thomas Platter. 'In the straw-thatched house we saw the tragedy of the first Emperor Julius Caesar, very pleasantly performed, with approximately fifteen characters; at the end of the play they danced together admirably and exceedingly gracefully, according to their custom, two in each group dressed in men's and two in women's apparel.' Yes, it would have been interesting to have travelled across the water in that party; as a guest from another century it would be like being a stranger in a foreign land.

Instead I drove through twentieth-century London towards London Bridge in my Austin 1300. It was a lovely, fresh April day; it was good to be alive. Soon, before me lay Southwark Cathedral where that afternoon I would discover, I hoped, one more sweet beginning and no unsavoury end. I parked the car, then walked into the cathedral to meet, at once, Christopher Hampton who told me that Cecil Day Lewis was seriously ill, was in fact dying; also that W. H. Auden would not be with us for he was in New York.

'You'll be reading your poem in the second half, after an interval,' Christopher said. 'Is that all right? Let me show you where I want you to sit.'

As I followed Christopher I saw, near the door in the north aisle of the nave, Sam Wanamaker talking to Stephen Spender, Peter Porter, and an elderly man whom I did not know. Could it be Robert Graves, I wondered.

'Yes,' said Christopher, 'he looks pretty fit, doesn't he? He's seventy-six now, you know.'

I recalled Graves's own self-portrait:

> Crookedly broken nose – low tackling caused it;
> Cheeks, furrowed; coarse grey hair, flying frenetic;
> Forehead, wrinkled and high;

Jowls, prominent; ears, large; jaw, pugilistic;
Teeth, few; lips, full and ruddy; mouth, ascetic.

I paused with razor poised, scowling derision
At the mirrored man whose beard needs my attention
And once more ask him why
He still stands ready, with a boy's presumption,
To court the queen in her high silk pavilion.

His face had softened with age evidently, but he still looked sprightly
enough to chase that same queen and catch her. In the choir stalls
Christopher pointed to the seat he wanted me to occupy, immediate-
ly after the interval. 'Between Graves and Adrian Mitchell, all right?'

I had liked Robert Graves's poetry for many years: it was always
well-organized and lucid, always an internally directed soliloquy that
the reader, as it were, was privileged to overhear. He composed
poems in the central English lyric tradition and he used a conserva-
tive diction and a logical syntax without display, though not without
the power to surprise. His was an essentially romantic sensibility with
its belief in phantoms and miracle; in the terrifying and terrific
supernatural; in his interest in myth as a living, operative power even
in our so-called rational societies; and not least in his preoccupation
with the creative and destructive element that waxes and wanes in a
man–woman relationship. Yes, I looked forward to meeting Robert
Graves; besides, his reputation as a man was intriguing. I had heard
how he could be iconoclastic, anti-academic; how he was quick to
deflate lofty pretensions, how he could be wittily bitchy about his
most celebrated contemporaries.

I was introduced to him in the Harvard Chapel, which lay behind
the north choir aisle, as the buzzing audience were returning to their
seats in the nave after the interval. 'John Harvard,' Robert Graves
told me, 'was baptized here in 1607.' I assumed John Harvard was the
gentleman who emigrated to Massachusetts to make a fortune and to
found Harvard College. I was not sure, though, and not wishing to
boob I said nothing. Soon Robert Graves was telling me, as we took
our seats in the choir, all kinds of esoteric information about the
cathedral. He seemed anxious to instruct me. My knowledge of the
cathedral was small, my ignorance large – and even if I should have
dared to pronounce on that which I did know, it would have been
without confidence, like a blind man naming the colours in a

rainbow. Instead, I told him the names of the poets who, one by one, faced the very large audience, for he was most eager to identify them. 'Who's that?' he would spit out to me.

'Vernon Scannell,' I'd say and as soon as Vernon had finished his poem and the next piece of music commenced – by Richard Rodney Bennett or Lennox Berkeley or Peter Maxwell Davies or John Tavener – Robert Graves would generously impart to me his next small piece of scholarship: 'Edward Shakespeare, William's youngest brother, was buried in the churchyard here.' He pulled out a snuffbox, an antique, from his pocket and surreptitiously showed it to me. I learnt a few quick facts about that snuffbox, its provenance, before the music ended. 'Who's that?' asked Robert Graves a minute later. 'Peter Redgrove,' I said.

For the next twenty minutes we bartered information for information. His numerous facts for my one name. He mentioned Hollar's drawing of the Bankside three centuries past and I believe if the musical pieces had been more prolonged I would have learnt of 'the colouring of Titian, the grace of Raphael, the purity of Domenichi-no, the *corregiescity* of Correggio, the learning of Poussin, the airs of Guido, the taste of the Carracci, or the grand contours of Michel-angelo'. I began to feel that my contribution to the whispered dialogue was insufficient. I tried to think of some relevant piece of recondite information *I* could drop; but all I could think of was a conversation I had once with a man who worked at London Zoo who had told me that tortoises often died of diphtheria. Somehow, to state baldly there and then, 'Tortoises frequently die because of diphther-oid organisms in their throat,' did not seem right and proper.

In any event, suddenly, a whole group of strangers descended upon us and began to sing a song for Shakespeare's birthday, 1972. Robert Graves seemed pleased: he had written the words for it. We both listened intently as a maniacal conductor waved his arms and the choir *so near, so loud*, sang:

> When Will sat forging plays with busy friends
>   He wrote no worse than they;
> When he sat writing for his loves, and us,
>   Such play outshone all play.
>   And still it does today.

I had the sense *not* to say, 'That was pretty awful.' I smiled like a hypocrite when the audience applauded enthusiastically as the immoderate choir scurried away and Robert Graves stood to his feet.

He raised two hands like a triumphant boxer who had knocked his opponent out. It was certainly hard to think of him as one aged seventy-six. Back in his corner, I mean his seat, he whispered to me, 'That was the best thing we've heard all afternoon.'

'Who's that?' Robert Graves asked.

'George MacBeth,' I replied.

Eventually it was my turn to walk the twenty-two yards to the scaffold and face all those seated figures in the soaring, elongated nave (rebuilt, I think Robert Graves said, in 1897 to replace the, er, thirteenth-century nave destroyed, er, in 1838). It is not easy to read one poem only. As soon as you become used to the stressful situation, the hundreds of upturned faces, the different sources of light, the unfriendly microphone, the whole thing is over. You have been bowled out, the audience are clapping out of habit but you are walking back to the pavilion pulling off your batting gloves; knowing that you have made a duck. I sat down and took my own pulse.

Music began – by Harrison Birtwhistle.

Robert Graves leaned over towards me. I thought he was going to say, 'Well done,' or 'That was a good poem' – something sensible like that. Instead he whispered more confidentially, 'He nodded at me, you know.'

'What?' I asked, wondering.

'He nodded at me.'

'Who?'

'The Prime Minister.'

I paused. When I was reading, I had spotted someone in the front row, in spitting distance, a man with a red, adipose, shining face who did, come to think of it, look very familiar.

'Edward Heath?' I asked.

'Of course,' Robert Graves said irritably, as if I were a dunce and did not know with certainty even the name of the present Prime Minister.

For my part, I felt irritated with Robert Graves. He was supposed to be a rebel, a nonconformist; and now here he was full of ridiculous pride, *hubris*, because the Prime Minister, a *Tory* Prime Minister (whom, of course, *I* did not vote for) had nodded at him.

'What did you do?' I whispered.

'I nodded back,' Robert Graves said.

At this point, Adrian Mitchell who had just arrived, late – at least he looked as if he had just parked his motorbike at the South transept door – took the empty seat on my left-hand side.

'Adrian,' I said quietly, 'Mr Graves is on nodding terms with our Prime Minister.'

I explained to Adrian that the Prime Minister was sitting in the front row. This information activated Adrian Mitchell – his skin, eyes, horns altered. 'Is Heath here?' hissed Adrian between bared teeth, his face contorted, vivid with displeasure. Evidently Adrian regarded Heath as an amalgam of Caligula and Hitler.

Just then Birtwhistle's music ceased and the audience applauded again.

'Yes,' said Robert Graves benignly, cheerful, leaning over me towards Adrian Mitchell, 'Mr Heath's sitting in the front row.' But now it was Adrian's turn to read his poem. He almost ran towards the microphone.

'Who's that?' asked Robert Graves, startled.

There are those who hardly know what they think until they express it either vocally or on the page. That is not true of Adrian Mitchell. His political views are not shaded. They inform and energize his work, they translate him as a man, they draw him, as it were, as clearly as a pencil can draw a profile. I have a feeling that Adrian perceived no human being occupying that chair in the front row but a monstrous cartoon figure, one responsible for all the treachery in the world, all the injustice, coercion, easy manipulation, casual greed, inequality, unnecessary pain. Now, at last, here was a chance of a lifetime to confront bluntly that one who had previously stood in the shadow, that cartoon figure, that prime adversary. Adrian boiled with rage. He began to abuse Edward Heath, accused him of being partly responsible for the chemical warfare in Vietnam and those at the back of the nave, far away, clapped while those somewhat wealthier, in front, nearer to the presence of the Prime Minister, sat dumbly. Then Adrian Mitchell read his poem and afterwards, in reverse, curiously pale, rushed past us through the choir to disappear down the South transept whence he had come.

Some music started up – by Elizabeth Lutyens, I think – and Robert Graves said, 'You've seen the tomb of Lancelot Andrewes? He was buried originally in the Bishop's Chapel, you know.'

The concert was almost over, this was the last musical composition and all the poets had read their commissioned poems. Sam Wanamaker had arranged for the concert to conclude with a reading by the actress Diane Cilento. She had been asked to recite the epitaph by John Milton on the Admirable Dramatick Poet, W. Shakespeare. The attractive blonde actress moved to the microphone and I happened to glance at Robert Graves who seemed to be following her progress with exceptional interest – rather, I thought, as the elderly King David must have looked upon, for the first time, the beautiful Abishag. Before the microphone Miss Cilento recited without book:

> What needs my Shakespeare for his honour'd bones
> The labour of an age in piled stones?
> Or that his hallow'd reliques should be hid
> Under a starry pointing pyramid?
> What need'st thou such weak witness of thy name?
> Thou, in our wonder and astonishment
> Hast built thyself a live-long monument . . .

The Milton poem over, Diane Cilento bowed to the applauding audience with pleasing grace. 'Who's that?' asked Robert Graves once more.

'Diane Cilento,' I told him.

Robert Graves hesitated, furrowed his brows, nodded his head.

'Cilento,' he said.

'Yes.'

'Cilento. Quite a gifted poet,' he said.

'She's an actress,' I explained.

'An actress?' he asked.

'The poem was by Milton.'

'Quite. Ah yes, I thought that poem sounded familiar.'

I did not laugh. Robert Graves had made the sort of boob that I could have made. I looked at him with growing affection; he looked at me, puzzled.

Later, at the reception that followed the concert, near the entrance, I met Sam Wanamaker. 'Let me introduce you to Robert Graves,' he said. I looked across the crowded room and saw Mr Graves deep in dialogue with Mr Heath. 'It's okay,' I said. 'We've met. In fact, we've had quite an intermittent, instructive conversation. We both enjoyed the music so much.'

A Weekend in Toronto

> 'Brezhnev arrived in Washington on June 16th. Somewhat of a hypochondriac, he turned the necessity of getting used to the time change into an obsession. He wore two watches, one set at Moscow time, the other for Washington time. He kept forgetting whether Moscow was ahead or behind Washington. When he reached San Clemente and three more hours were added, he gave up keeping track of the time difference but never ceased his grumbling about it.'
>
> Henry Kissinger

In the autumn of 1980 I accepted an invitation to visit Canada. Three Canadian poets were to tour Britain, three British poets to tour Canada. It did not seem a fair exchange.

'Who else will be going from Britain?' I asked Pamela, the director of the Poetry Secretariat.

'We were thinking of Adrian Henri and Fleur Adcock,' she declared.

I knew Fleur Adcock and liked her; Adrian Henri I hardly knew at all but I had been told that he was easy-going – 'very difficult to quarrel with'.

'It's an arduous schedule,' Pamela admitted, 'from coast to coast.'

I learnt that our first reading would be in Toronto on a Saturday night, that we would leave London Thursday and depart from Toronto for Vancouver on Monday morning. I thought, I'll have Thursday night, Friday night, Saturday night, Sunday night, to catch up on sleep – a long weekend to become accustomed to Toronto time, recover the five hours lost before the next long haul to the Canadian West Coast where everybody once again would be programmed younger, shouting eagerly, 'Have a nice day,' and 'You're welcome,' as we staggered dehydrated, our baggage growing heavier, our arms longer, into the foyer of some overheated hotel. After that it would be easy: each flight eastward, homeward, and the clock would be turning clockwise.

As we progressed across the Atlantic towards Toronto I considered the three Canadian poets – George Johnston, Susan Musgrave, and Bill Bissett – who at this very hour would be flying over the Atlantic in the opposite direction. I looked out of the Jumbo Jet window.

Because my knowledge of Canadian poetry was somewhat limited I had not heard of these three poets. In order to reduce, in some measure, my ignorance I leafed through an anthology of Canadian poetry I had brought with me. Later, trying to ignore a 'movie' flickering to the left of my eyes I browsed through a small reference manual put out by the League of Canadian Poets which offered biographical details of living Canadian poets – a selected bibliography, quotes from reviews, that sort of thing. I looked up first Bill Bissett.

I had got it wrong. It was bill bissett, a lower-case man. Under the heading, WHAT CRITICS SAY, I read, ' "Like Blake, bissett is a visionary, mystical poet who makes his own rules of poetry as he goes along." *Queens Quarterly.*' I felt somewhat dwarfed by the knowledge that Canada was sending us this blake-like, visionary figure. Nobody had called *me* blake-like. I felt certain too that neither Fleur Adcock nor Adrian Henri had been described as such. A little depressed, I turned the pages to discover Susan Musgrave. There she was – her photograph, I mean: attractive. Moreover, under WHAT CRITICS SAY I read, 'Musgrave explores sexuality at the primal level of bone-hurt.' I looked out of the window again.

The critical remarks about George Johnston seemed more enigmatic. Lawrence Jones in *Canadian Literature* had written of him, 'Surely an anomaly among the present generation of Canadian poets.' And then it came to me, after six weary hours in the plane, a revelation of sorts – the reason why we particular three had been invited to Canada: why I had been asked, why Fleur Adcock had been asked, why Adrian Henri had been chosen for this jaunt. It was to match these three Canadian poets, blow for blow. Had I not seen, a month or so ago, a lower-case advertisement for an Adrian Henri poetry reading? That was it: adrian henri for bill bissett; our best-looking poet, Fleur Adcock, for Canada's best-looking poet, Susan Musgrave; and therefore, I pondered gloomily, QED, me for George Johnston whom they bloodily well called 'an anomaly'.

At Toronto airport we were met by Arlene Lampert, executive director of the League of Canadian Poets, who handed us envelopes with expenses money in, a more detailed itinerary for us to study, and

forms to sign. It seemed the first reading would be at the Harbour
Front where we were part of an International Festival Week, organ-
ized by one Greg Gatenby. That very evening Arnold Wesker and
other dramatists were featured at the Habour Front and on Saturday
night we would be reading with the Polish poet Czeslaw Milosz.
Soon we discovered that the early posters which advertised the event
had recently been supplanted by new ones. 'THREE BRITISH POETS:
DANNIE ABSE, FLEUR ADCOCK, ADRIAN HENRI with Czeslaw Milosz',
the original posters had proclaimed. But Milosz had then been
awarded the Nobel prize for literature, so quickly new posters were
printed. The copy had been altered to: 'CZESLAW MILOSZ with three
British poets: Dannie Abse, Fleur Adcock, Adrian Henri'. At least
we had not been downgraded to lower case.

At 9.30 p.m. I decided to go to bed for it was now 2.30 a.m. real
time, and I was tired. With luck I would sleep for five or six hours
before the clock in my head foolishly woke me up. As I walked
towards the lifts, or rather elevators, I heard the familiar pleasant
voice of Arnold Wesker talking about a new play of his. 'It begins with
an orgasm,' he was saying. 'And no doubt ends with a bang,' another
writer interrupted him.

In my room on the twenty-eighth floor I lay in the dark. The TV
set waited in the same dark lifelessly. So did the radio, the ironing
board, the central-heating radiators, the telephone, the shower,
the lav, the armchairs, the writing desk, the wardrobe, the whole
caboodle. What did they say the name of this hotel was? I thought of
Big Ben far away, striking the hour on the hour, the *right* hour, every
hour. I decided this was Hotel Insomnia. However, eventually I must
have fallen asleep because I woke up startled by the clamour of an
active telephone. I struggled to put the light on, to focus my eyes on
my wristwatch which read 1 a.m., i.e. 6 a.m. real time. Puzzled, I
fumbled for the receiver. A Canadian voice, a man's, asked twangily,
'Is that you, Ginger?'

'What?'

'Ginger?'

'Ginger?' I repeated, dazed.

'Yeh. That you, Ginge?'

'No,' I said, 'I'm not ginger. In fact I'm going greyer every second.'

Annoyed, the anonymous caller grunted, 'Jesus,' and slammed the
phone down. I did not sleep much that night. So the next night, after
meeting some old friends who had emigrated to Canada a decade
earlier and after visiting the museum to see the enormous and

multiple Henry Moores etc., once more I decided to have an 'early' night. I was too tired even to read. I would, before sleep, have welcomed some consoling music perhaps, but nothing too loud, orchestral. What sometimes is engaging is to hear a solo composition, not in a concert hall or on the radio, but unexpectedly, fortuitously – an accordion in a street, a flute in a night train, a mouth organ in a field, picnic-time. None of that was possible. I fiddled with the radio and lost. So, resigned, I went to bed, turned off the lamp.

I did not expect a replay of the previous night. But again the telephone woke me up. Furious, I picked up the phone to shout at that heavy breather who wanted to talk to Ginger in the middle of the night. 'Hello,' the voice said. It was Arnold Wesker. Besides I saw that it was only 11 p.m. (Toronto time). 'Dusty and I are going to Niagara Falls tomorrow,' Arnold said generously. 'There's a car picking us up. Would you like to join us?' Afterwards, again I found it difficult to fall asleep.

The next day there was a cloudburst or rather clouds burst one after the other over Toronto. Niagara Falls, as if summoned, had come to us. The car did not arrive. I was disappointed. I wanted to see the Horseshoe Fall, which I gathered was 149 feet high, width 2100 feet. But I had to imagine it all, the river below the falls rushing with great velocity down the sloping bottom of a narrow chasm for a distance of seven miles. We would not, in that strenuous rain, have seen very much anyway – merely heard the smoke that thundered.

Dusty, Arnold's wife, was a fan of the actor Walter Matthau. That afternoon we went to the cinema. I could have been anywhere, in an Odeon in London or Llantwit Major, Jerusalem or Pontardawe, as I sat with friends staring at a big screen, at the shagged face of Walter Matthau.

The rain stopped before the evening concert. I was surprised by the numbers who had come to the Harbour Front, almost a thousand I should think: every seat taken. No doubt people were curious to hear the new Nobel prizewinner.

I knew Milosz's work a little. A line of his had stuck in my head: 'When you leave your native land don't look back, the Erinyes are behind you.' How desolate to be a perpetual exile as Milosz was, to be separated from your own language, the true nationality of a poet. Bolingbroke, in his 'Reflections on Exile', suggested that that which is most valuable cannot be taken away from us, is out of reach of any political power, any tyranny. 'There is no part of the world,' declared

Bolingbroke, 'from whence we may not admire those planets which roll, like ours, in different orbits round the same central sun; from whence we may not discover an object still more stupendous, that army of fixed stars hung up in the immense space of the universe, innumerable suns whose beams enlighten and cherish the unknown worlds which roll around them; and while I am ravished by such contemplations as these, whilst my soul is thus raised up to heaven, imports me little what ground I tread upon.' Consolations these are, but we are not elevated to the stars most of the time, and so the ground we return to and stand upon generally matters more and long.

In the dressing room behind the stage I spoke briefly to Milosz – in particular about the work of his compatriot Zbigniew Herbert who, of my contemporaries, is one of those I admire most, and whose work I knew first because I had read Milosz's translations. I recalled the first poem of Herbert's I had come across. Was it in *Encounter*? (Present events in Poland make it seem even more relevant and immediate.) The poem begins:

> 'Our fear
> does not wear a nightshirt
> does not have owl's eyes
> does not lift a casket lid
> does not extinguish a candle
>
> does not have a dead man's face either
>
> our fear
> is a scrap of paper
> found in a pocket
> 'warn Wojcik
> the place on Dluga Street is hot'.

A thousand years ago the bard sat at the right hand of his prince and spoke for the prince; now princes, such as they are – disguised with other names – have no use for bards, at least not in our part of the world. And elsewhere, in Chile or Argentina, or in Eastern Europe, the bard is more likely, being subversive by nature, to be thrown into a dungeon or mental hospital by those who have the power of princes, than to sit honoured at their polished tables. Camus wrote that 'the writer's role is not free of difficult duties. By definition he cannot put himself today in the service of those who make history; he is at the service of those who suffer it.' He must do this because he is not separate from those who suffer the active decisions of the princes. He suffers them himself and by being vocal about his own predicament, may speak for others also.

> our fear
> does not have the face of a dead man
> the dead are gentle to us
> we carry them on our shoulders
> sleep under the same blanket
> close their eyes
> adjust their lips
> pick a dry spot
> and bury them
>
> not too deep
> not too shallow.

I did not get back to the hotel till the early hours of the morning. After the successful reading at the Harbour Front there had been a successful party. And there was a party too next evening, on the Sunday, given by Arlene Lampert so that Adrian, Fleur and I could meet such considerable Canadian poets as Earle Birney, Patrick Lane and Eli Mandel. By 9.30 p.m. I was exhausted and knowing that I had to be up early to catch the flight to Vancouver I planned to slip away. A young poet, Giorgio Di Cicco, offered to drive Fleur (who was also very tired) and me to the hotel. We left Adrian Henri behind as our energetic representative whose glands obviously secreted natural Benzedrine. Or perhaps, simply, he had no telephone in his room.

Returned to my room, I could not resist looking up Giorgio Di Cicco in my little reference manual of Canadian poets. Under WHAT THE CRITICS SAY I read, ' ". . . a visionary in his own right . . ." *Joe Rosenblatt*.' Curious, I turned to Eli Mandel to see how he was described. The *Winnipeg Free Press* labelled him as '. . . a would-be visionary'. There was no point in looking up other Canadian poets I had happened to meet earlier that evening: they were all, doubtless, visionaries or would-be visionaries or visionaries *in their own right* – blake-like figures every goddam one of them. I went to bed. Absurdly my watch read only 10.20 p.m. but my brain knew the real time – that which is recorded perpetually by the cenotaph clocks in the suburbs of hell: 3.20 a.m. I decided to take a Mogadon, a sleeping tablet, something I rarely need to do.

It seemed to me that I had only been asleep some five minutes when I was awakened by a noise much louder and more frightening than a frenetic telephone. I sat up in bed astonished. *It was a fire alarm*. I closed my eyes, squeezing the eyelids tight, thinking, 'This can't be true, I'm dreaming this.' The fire alarm continued on and on. 'This is the twenty-eighth floor,' I thought. I jumped out of bed and shifted smartly to the door, reaching for a dressing gown. In the corridor, outside their doors, stood several people looking anxious. The alarm bell ceased and a voice on a Tannoy said sedatively, 'Please be calm. A fire has been reported on the twenty-sixth floor. We are trying to confirm whether this is really so.'

'Hey,' one of the men said along the corridor, 'you can smell smoke, can'tcha?'

I sniffed. I smelt nothing. Since all was silent now I decided to get dressed.

'Nobody can get to the elevators,' the man was saying, 'it's not possible.'

I managed to dress in 40 seconds flat and I was about to reach for my shoes when suddenly the Tannoy blared again. 'The fire on the twenty-sixth floor is being investigated. Nobody need be alarmed. We will come back to you as soon as we have definite news.'

I put on my shoes and stood again at my open door. The man who earlier could smell smoke now said, 'Hey, look, you can *see* smoke down there near the elevator, right?'

I looked down there. We all looked down there. I could not see any smoke. Somewhere, further along beyond the elevators, was Fleur Adcock's room. Possibly she would be anxious. I decided to call on her but near the elevators a fire barrier had descended obstructing the way through. I had to turn back and as I did so a door was flung open in front of me. A lady in a nightdress faced me, wildly shouting, 'He's looking at a pornographic movie in there and he won't fuckin' well come out.' I nodded sympathetically and returned to my own room as the Tannoy once more announced that the fire was being investigated on the twenty-sixth floor.

'Investigated?' said the man with the wonderfully acute senses, who, visionary as any Canadian poet, could smell nonexistent smoke, see nonexistent smoke. 'Jesus Christ, who're they trying to fool? They're trying to put it out, that's what. An' they're having problems.'

Maybe he was right. Inside my room I imagined a fire below, growing tall, taller, blue and black whirling smoke among bouquets of glowing geraniums, proliferating neon wreaths of red roses. Then the Tannoy's bland voice told us that the *minor* conflagration on the twenty-sixth floor had been dealt with, that now all was well and all manner of things were well. 'We are sorry,' the voice said, 'that you have been disturbed.'

I went back to bed. I tasted the age in my own mouth, closed my eyes. My weekend in Toronto was over.

David Wright, Maverick

This piece was initiated by *PN Review*, who invited a number of writers to salute David Wright on his sixtieth birthday

I

In 1947, when living in digs at Swiss Cottage, I would occasionally make excursions to the Soho literary pubs – the Fitzroy Tavern, the Wheatsheaf, the Black Horse. I was a medical student who the previous June had had a first book of poems accepted for publication by Hutchinson. In certain moods I wanted to talk to others with similar literary pursuits – something I could hardly do at Westminster Hospital Medical School. 'Good conversation makes a home,' Ezra Pound wrote. There were occasions when I felt homeless.

One evening I entered the Black Horse with a girl and observed John Heath-Stubbs, whom I had met some months earlier, a dozen yards away at the bar. He was talking in a peculiar way – his mouth moved in slow motion – to a tall, burly individual who had some resemblance to Yeats, or at least to the photographs of Yeats, and who, abruptly, would burst out laughing in a peculiar, uninhibited way.

'A blind man talking to a deaf man,' my companion remarked.

John Heath-Stubbs was not completely blind; but David Wright, the tall, burly individual, it became evident, could not hear a word. Blind man, deaf man, later left the pub together. I cannot remember much else about that evening but the image of those two friends engaged in their unusual posture of dialogue persisted.

Soon after, I happened on a terse poem by David Wright called 'On Himself' – published, I think, in *Poetry Quarterly* – in which he spoke of his own deafness:

> Abstracted by silence from the age of seven,
> Deafened and penned by as black calamity
> As twice to be born, I cannot without pity
> Contemplate myself as an infant;

> Or fail to speak of silence as a priestess
> Calling to serve in the temple of a skull
> Her innocent choice. It is barely possible
> Not to be affected by such a distress.

Those post-war years I often heard, as I walked the wards of Westminster Hospital, many a patient complain of some unenviable distress. None spoke as eloquently as this. The economy of pain generally allowed only a threadbare vocabulary: *Oh dear, doctor; oh God; oh dear, oh dear; hell, doctor; oh God, oh dear; oh dear God.* I read other poems of David Wright in such magazines as *Poetry London* and the *Windmill*. All his poems had the opposite of a threadbare vocabulary.

What a paradox it is that the language in David Wright's poetry 'flies'. For any conversation with David has to *crawl*. The mouth has to undertake its theatre slowly, else the voice is grounded on scraps of paper, key words jumbled on them endeavouring to clarify what was only vaguely understood. On the page, though, David Wright's voice is all velocity and height. The earth-bound dreamer flies at night. It is hardly surprising that David Wright admires Milton's Latinized eloquence.

The eloquence of his verse points to another paradox. Conversation with a deaf man tends to be functional; it is much too laborious to relate, with the mouth moving slowly, a shaggy-dog story or some green allegory. Only necessary statements are uttered – cautious qualifying adjectives are exiled. In short, sentences become straight lines. But, in poetry, David Wright's lines slope and curl. Much of his work is decoration – it delights in ornament, in description elaborate and curved. It is not short-winded. He has 'swallowed a dictionary' and yet the multisyllabic words are not superfluous and his verse still remains a form of conversation:

> What I like about art, and what you might call nature,
> Is, in the last resort, their absolute absence of
> Adumbration of information, propaganda,
> Of even, pace the romantics, moral uplift.
>
> A tree or a mountain is there, being itself,
> Not responsible for emotions of the beholder
> Or whether a shift of light, moonrise or rain falling
> Should make him feel good, resolve at least to do better.
>
> Their inveterate superfluity lets them speak
> As do paintings, carvings, and the collocation

Of words or noise or both (i.e. poetry, music)
On matters about which there is no communication . . .

A faint echo in the tone of T. S. Eliot in that last line? Perhaps. But most of his work is entirely in his own manner: dryly humorous, anecdotal, elegant – yet still laced with colloquialisms and, most mysteriously, since David Wright has been completely deaf since seven years of age, not only aurally correct but aurally adventurous.

On hearing David Wright speak the listener cannot help but notice that, from time to time, he will pronounce occasional words peculiarly, putting the accent on the wrong syllable. After all, there are many words in his large vocabulary that he has never heard pronounced. How then, one may well ask, can he write rhythmic verses with such assurance and subtlety? David Wright, in the autobiographical section of his book *Deafness*, draws attention to that inexplicable quality in poetry which allows it to survive in different pronunciations. 'It is known that the pronunciation of English has changed over the centuries,' David Wright reminds us. 'If we had a record of Pope reading 'The Rape of the Lock' he would sound queer, and Shakespeare speaking one of his sonnets queerer yet, while Chaucer might be unintelligible. But the sound-effects of their verse do not seem impaired by modern pronunciation.' I have never heard David Wright read his own poems – such an occasion might make me mistake him for Chaucer for all I know. What I am certain of is that his poems, when read out loud by others, give no hint that the author is a deaf man any more than the late music of Beethoven suggests that that composer was similarly afflicted.

2

It was while editing *Mavericks* in 1956 with Howard Sergeant that I first read David Wright's poems with more than ordinary attention. I admired, in particular, his second book of poems, *Moral Stories*, which had been published two years previously, as well as the current poems he was then writing, such as 'Monologue of a Deaf Man', which I encountered in magazines or in manuscript. To understand why I responded so acutely to some of David Wright's poems at that time it is perhaps necessary to say, briefly, something about the anthology *Mavericks* and the critical and biographical reasons for its coming into existence.

The poems published and acclaimed in such journals as the

Spectator in the mid-fifties had a certain commonality of style and tone: a reticent, small-gestured, plain diction, a paraphrasable content, a visible, often symmetrical structure – the poems by those, among many others, later designated as the Movement. Poets ostentatiously not conforming to such a strategy of writing, who reached for more, were pejoratively labelled 'romantic' or 'pretentious'. I think Howard Sergeant felt some sort of mild conspiracy was going on and that the widely publicized advancement of the Movement was a PRO job. He argued that while some of the Movement poets were indisputably gifted, others outside the fashionable poetry circuits, also talented, were being neglected.

I agreed with him and suggested we coedit an anthology to be entitled *Mavericks*. (I had recently used the word *mavericks* in a poem. It meant an 'unbranded steer' in the USA; in Britain it was a term generally unknown at that time.) There were a few mavericks, I believed, who wrote involving but unfashionable poetry – one of these being David Wright, whose work I would now examine more closely.

I was very open to the poems of David Wright for in 1956 I had certain theoretical assumptions about poetry – not all of which, by the way, have proved stable. While a medical student, and earlier, I had responded to those whose work was an unmistakable reflection of some urgent personal predicament. Some of the best poems of the Second World War were such. Then there were the poems of 'patients' – John Clare's lucid declarations about his insanity, the poems of poets confronted by tuberculosis, Keats's 'Ode to a Nightingale', D. H. Lawrence's 'Ship of Death'. Liking such poems I could hardly share the New Critics' contempt for autobiography. And David Wright's *Moral Stories* were nothing if not unashamedly autobiographical. They were about his birthplace, South Africa; about his friends – many of them Soho poets like George Barker, Roy Campbell, John Heath-Stubbs; about his deafness; about himself, as can be seen in 'A Funeral Oration':

> Composed at thirty, my funeral oration: Here lies
> David John Murray Wright, 6′ 2″, myopic blue eyes;
> Hair grey (very distinguished looking, so I am told);
> Shabbily dressed as a rule; susceptible to cold;
> Acquainted with what are known as the normal vices;
> Perpetually short of cash; useless in a crisis;
> Preferring cats, hated dogs; drank (when he could) too much;

Was deaf as a tombstone; and extremely hard to touch.
Academic achievements: B.A., Oxon (2nd class);
Poetic: the publication of one volume of verse,
Which in his thirtieth year attained him no fame at all
Except among intractable poets, and a small
Lunatic fringe congregating in Soho pubs.
He could roll himself cigarettes from discarded stubs,
Assume the first position of Yoga; sail, row, swim;
And though deaf, in church appear to be joining a hymn.
Often arrested for being without a permit,
Starved on his talents as much as he dined on his wit,
Born in a dominion to which he hoped not to go back
Since predisposed to imagine white possibly black:
His life, like his times, was appalling; his conduct odd;
He hoped to write one good line; died believing in God.

Reading such poems, recalling so many others by other poets dead
or alive, I could not agree with T. S. Eliot who, in 1919, in his
influential essay, 'Tradition and the Individual Talent', lauded the
impersonality, even anonymity, of significant art.

Later, in 1940, he radically modified his view when he wrote an
essay on Yeats. In extolling Yeats's late work he acknowledged the
vivid expression of personality in it and suggested that it was better
than his earlier work for this reason. It is Eliot's 1919 essay, though,
that is the more often recalled and quoted. It seems that it is Eliot's
youthful, over-refined attitudes to anonymity and impersonality that
the literary critics find most congenial. They do so today and they did
so in the 1950s.

I do not myself think that personal poems and impersonal ones
compete with each other or that one mode should be elevated, the
other deflated. But in the mid-1950s, so many of the poems published
eschewed personality and had no urgency about them at all. Too
many versifiers were counting not the heartbeats but the syllables!

But I have digressed too long. What of the mavericks and David
Wright in particular? To want to include in an anthology poems that
were personal, urgent, written as a result of some pressing, human
predicament, poems where music moreover served the sense but did
not neurotically dominate it, was one thing; to find young poets
writing such poems was another. No wonder I suggested to Howard
Sergeant that we should select poems by David Wright. Had he not
written most affecting poems that had sprung (or would spring) from
his personal predicament of deafness: tersely in 'On Himself';

touchingly in such poems as 'By the Effigy of St Cecilia' or 'The Musician'; triumphantly in such a fine poem as 'Monologue of a Deaf Man'?

> In whatever condition, whole, blind, dumb,
> One-legged or leprous, the human being is,
> I affirm the human condition is the same,
> The heart half broken in ashes and in lies,
> But sustained by the immensity of the divine.
>
> Thus I too must praise out of a quiet ear
> The great creation to which I owe I am
> My grief and my love. O hear me if I cry
> Among the din of birds deaf to their acclaim
> Involved like them in the not unhearing air.

The affirmative note evident in these lines is one that is refreshingly present in many of his poems and appears to be the expression of a celebratory religious sensibility. Perhaps it is his deafness, his own sense of otherness, that allows him, with greater facility than some, to identify with those living on the margins of society, with the one-legged and the leprous, with the self-exiled Soho bohemian, with the different and the hurt. David Wright was and is a true maverick.

Long after the publication of *Mavericks* his removal from London to the country in Cumberland led him to a new source of imagery, but the same quality of reasoning compassion that informed his earlier work has operated in this new context to allow him to write poems like 'Swift' or 'Rook'.

David Wright has always been the man outside and he will always surely continue to be the sly observer with a decorative verbal gift, one who is, moreover, willing to laugh at himself and at us. I trust that he will also continue to write poems impelled out of actual autobiographical pressures and without disguise, for then I believe he is at his best. He may say that he is committed to his notion of the absurd (any man born in South Africa is entitled to say that) but beyond such a stance, when he himself is directly and feelingly involved with that which he is witnessing, his poetry becomes more than mere electric description and decorative comment, for it reaches out instead to its broadest and true dimensions.

The Sincerity of 'I'

Not too far down the Englishman's list of 'Don'ts' is 'Don't say *me* all the time.' No doubt, in early life, some visitor, an uncle perhaps, underlined the virtues of reticence as he relentlessly bored nephew and niece alike with 'I fixed it,' and 'He couldn't put it over on me,' and 'So I showed 'em.' That boasting visitor, all unknowingly, had assisted many an Englishman into a crippling diffidence and into the tortuous word *one*. One has had an article published in a learned journal; one has played cricket for one's school; one works in the Foreign Office; one has one child.

There are occasions, of course, when society gives us sanction to say *I* nakedly, unashamedly. A patient, for instance, in a doctor's consulting room, does not say, 'One has a lump here.' No, he's encouraged to be flagrantly self-directed, self-absorbed, to utter *my* back, *my* throat, *my* knee. An autobiographer, too, must begin his work with *I* and end with *me*. His book would fail as an autobiography if he insisted on being truly impersonal in his approach – if he did so, it would be something else. Yet I suspect serious literary critics feel more comfortable when autobiography is successfully disguised as novel, short story, play or poems. Perhaps they feel confessional prose belongs more appropriately to the doctor's consulting room. They find congenial T. S. Eliot's early belief in the impersonality of poetry, the anonymity of significant art. 'The progress of an artist,' asserted T. S. Eliot in 1919, 'is a continual self-sacrifice, a continual extinction of the personality.'

T. S. Eliot was a reticent, secretive man. He did not display himself in his poetry or write anything as seemingly brash as an autobiography. But fellow poets since 1919, despite the climate of critical opinion, have frequently left us with memorable records of their lives. Two of Eliot's contemporaries, Edwin Muir and the American doctor–poet William Carlos Williams, have written auto-biographies that I find particularly affecting and which some readers may think deserve that high-flying appellation 'significant art'.

It was the poems of William Carlos Williams that tempted me to read his autobiography. His poetry has the purity of immediate experience as for instance in this short poem, this short note, perhaps left to his wife on the mantelpiece and called 'This is Just to Say':

> I have eaten
> the plums
> that were in
> the icebox
>
> and which
> you were probably
> saving for breakfast
>
> Forgive me
> they were delicious
> so sweet
> and so cold

A simple autobiographical note, and yet at the same time a slight genuine poem. In his autobiography too, William Carlos Williams is content to present his direct experiences to the reader in a very spontaneous, very fresh way. His book sprawls, goes off in all directions and, as in the short poem quoted, it is always conversationally pitched. Poets, as a breed, do seem to be anecdotal creatures. Their amiable, tall conversations amble along as it were, in late summer evenings, in open doorways of public houses, anecdote after anecdote, some credible, some incredible. Carlos Williams's anecdotes are arresting and always artful. Judge for yourself:

> Once at a small lake near Esopus, New York, I was deeply in love with a girl's legs I met underwater there. Their father was suspicious of me. I was a well-intended enough young man, but he damned well kept his eye on us as we played around that week in the barnyard and closely adjacent parts of the old place where the family lived. Ah those summers at the age of fifteen and seventeen! And perhaps a bit later!
>
> One rainy day those white legs and I found the barn, with a full hayloft, and under that rattling roof lay quietly together listening. But tiring of that, we began to burrow deeper into the hay. Our bodies were thrown close together there. It was very exciting as we must soon have acknowledged, but they began looking for us and we were chased out with loud calls and told never to go there again. How can a pair of legs defy their father under such circumstances?
>
> One day we all went fishing together. The old man was portly and

wore a straw hat. He fished from the end of the pier while we held
our poles out over the water not far off – or perhaps he was in a boat
or on a point under a protecting tree. It was a beautiful hot day. The
water crystal clear, the bottom weedy, with small fish swimming over
it. Those lovely white legs were hanging in the water side by side with
mine, good enough legs for a guy about my shape, moving a little
back and forth in the cool lake.

   But, by accident perhaps, after a moment one of my legs touched
those others in the water. They were not withdrawn – not withdrawn!
and the sun and the clouds meeting over our heads did a seraphic *pas
de deux*, so that I thought the world a paradise. It didn't take me long
to rub my legs underwater with those others, to twine them about the
others as best I could. If I should see that lake or pond today, I'd
think it a mud-hole.

I can imagine listeners to Williams all sipping from their pint glasses
as the doctor turns away and looks pensively out of the open saloon
door! Not all the incidents that Carlos Williams conversationally
relates are as charming, though many of them have a similar sexual
energy to them. He writes as a physician as well as a poet, of suffering
patients as well as of fellow authors like Ezra Pound, James Joyce,
Gertrude Stein, Ford Madox Ford.

   When he speaks of medical matters, of some of his patients'
tribulations, he does so graphically, dramatically. For instance, he
tells of a mountain of a woman giving birth to twins, so vividly that I
can imagine myself in attendance when she is delivered of her two
baby boys who came into the world, it would seem, not so much
screaming as cursing. Those who know William Carlos Williams's
poetry cannot help but be struck by its visual precision, by the way
things have looked to his rinsed eye. Critics of his poetry have
referred to his 'concrete presentation' and to 'data brought back
alive'. There are many startling visual evocations in the autobiogra-
phy too, snapshots of the ordinary or of the unusual.

   Once, after visiting Ezra Pound at St Elizabeth's Mental Hospital
in Washington, he was walking in the grounds of that institution
when he looked up from the mud, from where he was somewhat
carefully stepping. Williams wrote:

   I saw this man naked, full on and immobile, his arms up as though
   climbing a wall, plastered against one of the high windows of the old
   building like a great sea slug against the inside of a glass aquarium,
   his belly as though stuck to the glass that looked dull or spattered
   from the bad weather. I didn't stop, but kept looking up from time to
   time. I glanced around to see if there were any women about. There

was no one in the grounds at that point but myself. The man's
genitals were hard against the cold (it must have been cold) glass,
plastered there in that posture of despair. When would they come
and take him down? After all, it was glass, window glass, bars though
there were beyond it. The white flesh like a slug's white belly
separated from the outside world, without frenzy, stuck silent on the
glass.

I said earlier that William Carlos Williams's poetry led me to his
autobiography; so it did, but I can imagine the reverse process
occurring for another reader. A reader who has never read his poetry
cannot fail to be engaged by his memoirs and I suspect, afterwards,
he would be likely to investigate the poetry itself. So it would be too,
surely, with Edwin Muir's autobiography, published in 1954, a book
which has been described by J. C. Hall as 'a small masterpiece'.

Edwin Muir relates how he, a country boy, a boy used to farm
life in the Orkneys, emigrated to the squalor of town existence – in
Glasgow, at first, and its environs. In remarkably modulated and
vivid prose Edwin Muir, in meditating on the progress of his own life,
acknowledges the fable of Innocence and its Fall. He is more
reflective than Williams, at least more willing to ponder on ideas. It is
not surprising, somehow, that after fifty pages or so he asks himself
why he's writing his autobiography. 'There is a necessity in us,' he
writes, 'however blind and ineffectual, to discover what we are.' He
continues, 'Human beings are understandable only as immortal
spirits. They are immortal spirits distorted and corrupted in count-
less ways by the world into which they were born.'

In describing the world into which he was born Muir seems also to
be engaged in a religious quest, in that philosophical imperative,
Man, Know Yourself – for in writing an autobiography a man may
find one more pathway towards self-revelation. Edwin Muir, in
short, looks into his soul to write. And he does believe in the soul. It is
inconceivable to him that men are animals wearing, as he puts it, 'top
hats and kid gloves, painting their lips and touching up their cheeks
and talking in heated rooms, rubbing their muzzles together in the
moment of lust'. He cannot bear the concept that man is an animal
furnished with human faculties.

Nevertheless he's haunted by that very possibility:

> One summer evening in Glasgow in 1919 I was returning in a tramcar
> from my work; the tramcar was full and very hot; the sun burned
> through the glass on backs of necks, shoulders, faces, trousers, skirts,
> hands, all stacked there impartially. Opposite me was sitting a man

with a face like a pig's, and as I looked at him in the oppressive heat
the words came into my mind, 'that man is an animal'. I looked round
me at the other people in the tramcar; I was conscious that something
had fallen from them and from me; and with a sense of desolation I
saw that they were all animals, some of them good, some evil, some
charming, some sad, some happy, some rich, some well. The tramcar
stopped and went on again, carrying its menagerie; my mind saw
countless other tramcars where animals sat or got on or off with
mechanical dexterity, as if they had been trained in a circus; and I
realized that in all Glasgow, in all Scotland, in all the world, there
was nothing but millions of such creatures living an animal life and
moving towards an animal death as towards a great slaughter-house.

His description and exploration of his life of ritualistic order in the
Orkneys and his life of chaos in the great cities is, in part, embarked
on to contradict that vision, his own. We follow Edwin Muir outside
the gates of Paradise to an evil-smelling bone factory (for glue) where
he is an employee and then to London and elsewhere; but he's always
able to look over his shoulder back to the little island of Wyre in the
Orkneys:

> I cannot say how much my idea of a good life was influenced by my
> early upbringing, but it seems to me that the life of the little island of
> Wyre was a good one, and that its sins were mere sins of the flesh,
> which are excusable, and not sins of the spirit. The farmers did not
> know ambition and the petty torments of ambition; they did not
> realize what competition was, though they lived at the end of Queen
> Victoria's reign; they helped one another with their work when help
> was required, following the old usage; they had a culture made up of
> legend, folk song, and the poetry and prose of the Bible; they had
> their customs which sanctioned their instinctive feelings for the
> earth; their life was an order and a good order. So that when my
> father and mother left Orkney for Glasgow when I was fourteen, we
> were plunged out of order into chaos. We did not know it at the time,
> and I did not realize it for many years after I had left Glasgow. My
> father and mother and two of my brothers died in Glasgow within
> two years of one another. Four members of our family died there
> within two years. That is a measure of the violence of the change.

Edwin Muir's autobiography, then, is that of a survivor and it
would be hard to imagine a more honest one. Yet autobiography
itself is a kind of fiction. It cannot be otherwise. The autobiographer
cannot but help omit so much of his life experience, as he edits his
life, his memories, as he shapes his text, as he tries for 'significant

art'. In the foreword to his autobiography William Carlos Williams
writes:

> Nine-tenths of our lives is well forgotten in the living. Of the part that
> is remembered, the most had better not be told: it would interest
> no-one, or at least would not contribute to the story of what we
> ourselves have been. A thin thread of narrative remains – a few
> hundred pages – about which clusters, like rock candy, the interests
> upon which the general reader will spend a few hours, as might a
> sweet-toothed child, preferring something richer and not so hard on
> the teeth. To us, however, such hours have been sweet. They
> constitute our particular treasure. That is all, justly, that we should
> offer.

What Carlos Williams does not remark on is how the autobiog-
rapher courageously destroys his past experiences by naming them.
The autobiographer does achieve an extinction of at least his
previous personality. For as soon as he has published his autobiogra-
phy he has irrevocably changed his own life. He has deleted it and
substituted it with artifice. Think of it this way. Think how you
looked when you were, say, sweet sixteen. 'I remember,' you say; but
you don't. What you recall is the image of your face not seen in a
looking glass of years ago but in that yellowing, cracked snapshot in a
drawer somewhere upstairs. And that snapshot did not resemble you
quite – it flattered or did not flatter you. Still, that's the image of
yourself, the face that you remember – nothing else. Yes, that
treasured photograph has powerfully blotted out the remembrance
of your real sixteen-year-old face, forever. In the same way, gradu-
ally, an autobiography, with all its approximate resemblances, buries
the real life of the autobiographer. The life that was real becomes
extinct.

Even so, autobiographies, though a deception like photographs,
do not give us the feeling when we read them that we are being
deceived. On the contrary, if well done, they seem authentic and
sincere. When we read William Carlos Williams's account of his life
we may think his writing uneven, wonderful, terrible, careless, we
may think his book sprawls, but we do not feel deceived. Nor do we
think, 'This is a beautiful, inspired lie,' when we read the more
ordered, the more literary-conceived autobiography of Edwin Muir.
The *I* in both books is no fictional mask, not a *persona*.

That the *I* nakedly represents the author himself, worries those
critics who still believe overtly, or vestigially, in the doctrine of
impersonality in art and who can neither accept confessional poetry

nor autobiography itself as a supreme act of the imagination. Such critics have not heard the news that Lionel Trilling broadcast in his book *Sincerity and Authenticity* (1972):

> Within the last two decades English and American poets have programmatically scuttled the sacred doctrine of the *persona*, the belief that the poet does not, must not, present himself to us and figure in our consciousness as a person, as a man speaking to men but must have an exclusively aesthetic existence.

Autobiography in the hands of such poets as Carlos Williams and Edwin Muir need not be adjacent to literature, it can be literature itself; and the more I think of T. S. Eliot's remark that the progress of an artist is a continual self-sacrifice, a continual extinction of the personality, the more absurd it seems. Indeed, the opposite strikes me as being true: the progress of an artist is a continual self-enlargement, a continual addition to the personality. And in enlarging himself by writing autobiography, in coming to know himself better, an author, despite inadvertently altering the true colours of his life, obliterating this, accentuating that, may ultimately not only give us pleasure but reveal to us more about the world we live in, and more about ourselves.

Pegasus and the Rocking Horse

(Notes on Originality and Imitation in Poetry)

A lecture delivered to the Institute of Psychoanalysis in London

I

I should confess, ladies and gentlemen, confess immediately, that I was somewhat puzzled when I was invited to address you here this evening for I have as little, and as much, interest in your discipline as I suspect some of you may have in mine. I am reminded of the prolegomenon to a lecture given by Robert Bridges in 1917, one dreary night in rain-swept, gas-lit South Wales. He said to the bemused members of the Tredegar and District Cooperative Society, 'I am here to talk about poetry and you little think how surprised you ought to be. I have refused many invitations to lecture on poetry; but most of us nowadays are doing what we most dislike.'

It is sibling rivalry, no doubt, that brings me here, that explains why I accepted your kind invitation: both my brothers are seriously preoccupied with depth psychology and would feel more at home in this Ernest Jones room than I. Indeed, I have been here once before. On that occasion, two years ago, I attended a lecture delivered by my psychoanalyst brother, Wilfred. So, as you see, I am in some measure imitating him. As for my other brother, Leo, he is, as some of you may know, the very original MP for Pontypool who relentlessly speculates on the psychodynamics of politics and the psychopathology of his Parliamentary colleagues – much to their chagrin.

My interest in psychoanalytic literature has been much more sporadic, much more confined, than that of my brothers so for this second Tolkien lecture I could only offer to compose for you some notes on originality and imitation in poetry, a subject that interests *me*. This theme, however, was welcomed as being appropriate and, further, it was generously suggested that I could illustrate what I had to say by referring to my own texts, my own poems. I propose to do exactly that towards the conclusion of this paper which, for reasons that will soon become clear to you, I have called 'Pegasus and the Rocking Horse'.

2

Indisputably, during the twentieth century, there has been, in the judgement of artistic works, an italic emphasis on the value of originality. Many feel that to imitate another is somehow a fraudulent exercise, that imitation stales the imagination rather than provokes it. Yet such imperious slogans as 'Keep It Spontaneous' and 'Make It New' are frequently misunderstood. At best, the artist can only engage in a deception: his work must *appear* spontaneous however many versions, drafts, rehearsals, have been gone through in its maturation; his work must *appear* new though the old, the traditional, have been called upon to be vividly refurbished.

In the autumn of 1971 there was an exhibition in London, called *Art into Art*, that illustrated the influence of earlier artists on the imagery and stylistic modes of later artists. In the exhibition's catalogue, Keith Roberts acknowledged that the activity of copying and imitating is not admired nowadays as once it was, that the spirit of the age is very much 'to do your own thing'. One impetus then, it seemed, for this exhibition was to act as a corrective: to dispel popular prejudice against imitation.

No one, I imagine, would have recommended that exhibition to his students – had they and he been alive – more than Sir Joshua Reynolds who, in his Sixth Discourse on Art, urged that novitiates and master craftsmen alike should engage themselves in the continual activity of imitation. 'Invention,' Reynolds suggested, 'is one of the great marks of genius; but if we consult experience we shall find that it is by being conversant with the inventions of others that we learn to invent; as by reading the thoughts of others we learn to think.' He then went on to describe and prescribe the means whereby admired inventions can be truly known – in short, by assiduously copying them. 'No man,' Reynolds dogmatically averred, 'can be an artist, whatever he may suppose, upon any other terms.'

Blake, no admirer of Reynolds – he felt he'd spent 'the vigour of his youth and genius under the oppression of Sir Joshua and his Gang of Cunning Hired Knaves' – even Blake, annotating Reynolds's Discourses, commented, 'The difference between a Bad Artist and a Good One is the Bad Artist seems to Copy a Great Deal. The Good One Really does Copy a Great Deal.'

To be sure, Reynolds's advice to painters was by no means unambiguous. By imitation he meant something far more than a mere mechanical copy, which he censured for being inferior, for being barren and servile. We today readily assent to such a censure. Tom, Dick and Harry will declare that a slavish copy lacks the genius of the original. Yet, pause for a moment: why shouldn't a forgery by a master craftsman be as powerful as its model?

One modern explanation of this conundrum has been supplied by Anton Ehrenzweig in his book, *The Psycho-Analysis of Artistic Vision and Hearing*, where he stressed the importance of unconscious perception in our appreciation of works of art. He argued, for instance, that when we look at a painting we are blind to certain details in it, we repress certain significant and disturbing forms that feed the painting with active energy. Copies, he asserted, are emotionally sterile because the unconscious has played little part in the making of them. But let me quote him directly: 'The conscious imitator of a great work,' he wrote, 'misses the chaotic, inarticulate structure of technique and the emotional impact of the original. He fails because he reproduces by a conscious effort what the master has created unconsciously. As he copies the erratic brushwork of the original, the gestalt process ruling his conscious form perception will inevitably straighten out and regularise what he sees; he will overlook the little gaps and vaguenesses as accidental and insignificant in which, however, the master's unconscious has symbolised itself most powerfully.'

Ehrenzweig reminds us how when we recollect a dream we disremember its incoherence, its vagueness, as we conjure it up in a more orderly manner. 'As our mind lingers on the dream memory,' he continues, 'it gains in clarity and compactness and those details which drop out first are sure to be the most important. Freud had only to observe which details would be suppressed first in order to know where he had to start his analysis.' In short, if we think of the original masterwork as the dream of the artist, then the imitator, because of the safeguarding reaction of his superego, cannot copy the dream itself, only the dream, as it were, that he remembers.

This argument seems to me to be almost persuasive – almost, not totally, because, in the history of art, forgeries, criminal and legitimate, are not always, *inevitably*, discernible. Certain copyists become so skilled, so in empathy with the original artist, that their mimetic gifts amaze and dazzle – to such an extent, indeed, that the viewer becomes blind to which is the original and which the copy. For instance, no critic more than John Ruskin knew so thoroughly the works of Turner or appreciated them as much or championed them more; but he insisted that those two extraordinary Turner copyists, William Ward and Isobel Jay, sign their 'Turner' watercolours (and he countersigned them) lest, at a later date, their versions be mistaken for the real thing, strange.

Nevertheless, despite the copyists' skills, in our judgement of them as works of art, we properly take into account the fact of primacy, we uphold the value of primacy. Offered a gift of a Turner watercolour or a Ward or Isobel Jay copy we would choose the Turner – and not only for monetary reasons. There is something in us, prim and primitive, childlike perhaps, that makes us respond to an imitation, albeit sub-vocally, 'Copycat, copycat!'

When I was a schoolboy I used to turn in essays every week to my English master, a Mr Graber. Every week Mr Graber gave me 8 out of 10. For a short time my ambition in life, apart from playing centre-forward for Cardiff City, was to ascend to the mark of 9 out of 10. I tried hard, harder, hardest. No use, still I was only awarded 8 out of 10. I told my elder brother Leo my problem – Leo had recently won first prize in the *Reynolds News* essay competition.

'No problem,' Leo replied. 'I'll write your essay for you. You'll get 9 out of 10 next week, you'll see.'

So Leo, six years or so older than I, the following week composed my essay on the set subject of sugar. It was brilliant. What a vocabulary! What a gift of the gab! Word for word I copied it out in my own handwriting and confidently awaited Mr Graber's response. Eventually the essay came back marked 7 out of 10 and underneath it in red ink Mr Graber warned, 'Do not use words you do not understand – like *aberration*.' Had Mr Graber intuitively recognized that my composition was a forgery? I think so, and in this way he alerted me to the value of primacy.

I would have come to appreciate that value anyway – as we all do. If we profoundly admire an original work of art and can discern the difference between it and its imitation, then we come to *resent* the copy. It is as if, in some curious way, it cheapens the model that inspired it. When one man's powerfully individual voice or style is caught like an infection – and usually just as unwittingly – often the imitator seems ill; his work has not the energy of health. Even if we should admire an imitation at first, not knowing it to be one such, when we do discover the original, immediately the copy becomes diminished for us. We experience a puritanical sense of outrage that one artist or poet has gone to another, if not like a thief in the night, at least like an absent-minded, plundering sleepwalker. Soon enough the imitation we admired and thought so fine becomes in our minds merely a derivative object.

Perhaps this is what Blake meant by saying, 'The Bad Artist seems to Copy a Great Deal,' and why Reynolds warned, 'Borrowing or stealing . . . will have a right to the same lenity as was used by the Lacedemonians who did not punish theft, but the want of artifice to conceal it.'

3

To become conversant with works of art, to copy them, may well be a part, and a good part, of the education of an apprentice painter. But what of an apprentice poet? Does he similarly need a wide knowledge of poetry? Should he also take models and imitate them consciously?

While no education in verse can activate, as it were, growth hormones to enlarge a dwarf talent, it is certain that no man or woman can make a real poem who has not read seriously the works of his contemporaries and something of that tradition which informed them. As the American poet, William Cullen Bryant, remarked in a lecture he gave in 1826, 'Whoever would entirely disclaim imitation, and aspire to the praises of complete originality, should be altogether ignorant of any poetry written by others, and of all those aids which the cultivation of poetry has lent to prose. Deprive an author of these advantages, and what sort of poetry does anyone imagine that he would produce? I dare say it would be sufficiently original, but who will affirm that it could be read?'

I remember some years ago talking to Stephen Spender about a biography of Robert Frost. Spender wondered, somewhat wickedly but not too seriously, whether Frost had wanted to be the only poet in the world.

'Would *you* like to be the only poet in the world?' Stephen Spender suddenly asked me.

I don't think he expected a reply but I said, 'Of course not. If I were, I would soon be locked up in a mental hospital. Besides, I would miss reading my contemporaries too much.'

In fact, all poets, apprentice ones as well as those somewhat riper, would be unlikely to be writing poetry unless, for years, they had enjoyed reading the stuff. Young aspiring writers know that their lives would be much poorer, much more threadbare, if poetry was not available to them. So they seek it out, to enjoy it, to be enlarged by it, and unconsciously they are influenced technically by what they read. They hardly need to be persuaded to read poems nor to write parodies as conscious exercises.

These days writing schools abound (in the USA they are illiterately called 'creative writing programs') and in some of them students are urged not merely to tackle forms – sonnets, sestinas, villanelles – but to 'write in the manner of——' It would appear that whole classes, hordes of young men and women, are in strenuous training to win prizes in those competitions hebdomadally set in the back pages of the *New Statesman.* I suppose there is nothing wrong in committing parodies. They prove the author's esteem for certain originals even as he gently mocks them. There have even been poets, Swinburne among them, who have deliberately parodied themselves, this act of narcissism neutralized by a humorous self-ridicule. The whole thrust of making a parody is to produce something comical. Even when composed by one as skilled as Wendy Cope, parodies are no more than music-hall impersonations – and I doubt whether many aspiring poets long to become the Mike Yarwoods of verse.

Besides, it's only the surface manner and the metre that can be *consciously* imitated, not the hidden inner lining of a great poem, not even the real sound of that inner lining. The real sound, its sum of cadences and silences – the musical matrix of a poem in which even punctuation plays a part – defies rational analysis. A metre allows us to know only the rough caricature of a poem's sound. Blake's line, 'Tyger, Tyger, burning bright' may own the same metre, have the same number of syllables as, say, Auden's 'Lay your sleeping head, my love,' but we do not have to be a Schoenberg to recognize that these two lines differ musically.

Whether an apprentice poet is urged to write parodies or not, soon enough he will become *unconsciously* influenced by what he admires, and in most cases overwhelmingly possessed by another man's voice. He may be unaware of having become a dummy to a great ventriloquist. He may believe he speaks with his own voice when others listening hear only the intrusive accents of Hardy or Yeats or D. H. Lawrence or Eliot or Dylan Thomas or someone else equally distinctive. It may take years before such dominant hauntings are recognized by the possessed aspiring poet and exorcized. Meanwhile he will 'sway upon a rocking horse and think it Pegasus'.

I look at the early work of my favourite contemporaries and recognize who possessed them. I go like a detective with a magnifying glass to find they are covered blatantly with the fingerprints of older, famous poets. I see in their verse crude transplantations, bloodstains from the underside of poems not theirs. I look at my own first published book – and wince. Some poets, genuine minor poets, even as they mature never entirely escape from the thraldom of their first masters. Recently, over breakfast, I glanced at the current issue of the *Times Literary Supplement* and read a review of a posthumous volume of poetry by Thomas Blackburn. The reviewer, a friend of Blackburn's, John Heath-Stubbs, justly praised his friend's talent but remarked:

> At times Blackburn had a lazy habit of quoting verbatim from other poets and not, as did Eliot, placing the quotations in a context which gives them a new dimension. Thus we find well-known phrases from Yeats and Eliot and even Ezra Pound's grammatically incorrect *contra natura*. Blackburn would have defended this practice by saying that other poets had expressed what he wanted to say so precisely that he could not alter it. But this will not do: the poet has always to 'make it new'.

But why is a distinctive voice in *poetry* so important to us in the enjoyment of it; or why, conversely, are recognizable imitations so irritating? The same criteria apply as in painting, not least the territorial claims of primacy. Consider for a moment those majestic lines of *English* poetry in Ecclesiastes that many of us may have known and valued for years – valued as literature, I mean.

> . . . Or ever the silver cord be loosed, or the golden bowl be broken, or the pitcher be broken at the fountain, or the wheel broken at the cistern. Then shall the dust return to the earth as it was and the spirit shall return unto God who gave it. Vanity of vanity, saith the Preacher, all is vanity.

In the New English Bible of 1972 we find a different translation from the Hebrew which the editors believe to be clearer, more readable, more accurate:

> . . . before the silver cord is snapped and the golden bowl is broken, before the pitcher is shattered at the spring and the wheel broken at the well, before the dust returns to the earth as it began and the spring returns to God who gave it. Emptiness, emptiness, says the Speaker, all is empty.

It is not possible for those of us attached to the older version to accept the recent rendering as anything but a paste copy of less value. Apart from its sense, 'Emptiness, emptiness' has a passable sound relationship to 'Vanity, vanity' but the final 'all is empty' seems faintly ridiculous because we hear a distinct aural error as we, reflexly, echo what we already know and admire. Only those totally new to both versions are able to make a more objective judgement about which is the better poetry; they, unlike us, have not to contend with the power of primacy. Translations, like original poems, if they are really fine, can inhabit us and, once accepted, all other versions, all other translations, whether objectively better or not, are dismissed by us as imposters.

Sir Joshua Reynolds's advice to apprentice-painters was complex: he warned them of the dangers of imitation though he recommended the practice of it. In poetry these dangers are even more acute. The power of primacy and therefore the importance of originality remain paramount. Certainly no metamorphosis of the wooden rocking horse can occur unless a new-made poem is active with originality, and paradoxically this originality can only subsist where there have first been models.

It is obvious that the work of some poets appears to be more original than that of others. Some, by being least imitative of the fashionable modes of the period – poets absorb generic modes as much as individual models – seem eccentric when they first attract the public's eye. They have been more rebellious, have adopted a more confident, pugnacious posture towards the dominant literary tradition than most of their colleagues. I recall Freud believed that 'a man who has been the indisputable favourite of his mother keeps for life the feeling of a conqueror, the confidence of success that often induces real success'. The aetiology of artistic confidence, a poet's risk-taking and adventurousness in technique, may indeed reside in early developmental entanglements.

I dare say a number of you would consider that some of, if not all, the hidden roots of a poet's technical rebelliousness – his overturning of models, his striving for marked originality – may find nourishment in the darkness of his Oedipus complex. Be that as it may, the general reader's initial response to blatant originality is one of hostility, a degree of hostility of greater moment than that directed against blatant acts of imitation which I commented on earlier. Poets who remark metre in an original way are particularly likely to irritate most poetry readers. What Robert Bridges declared about metre still obtains: 'It offers a form which the hearers recognize and desire, and by its recurrence keeps it steadily in view. Its practical working may be seen in the unpopularity of poems that are written in an unrecognized metre and the favour shown to well established forms by the average reader.'

It may be that Bridges privately, with a too complacent satisfaction, was thinking of his own fame – he was Poet Laureate – and of the contrasting neglect of his innovative friend Gerard Manley Hopkins. The irony, of course, is that with the passage of time it is Manley Hopkins who has found favour with poetry readers rather than Bridges whose diction, if not metre, seems stale to us. Yes, Bridges perhaps was too imitative of the poetic conventions of his day, while we can now see to what end Manley Hopkins confessed, 'The effect of studying masterpieces makes me admire and do otherwise.' In short, it is not a matter only of models becoming part of a poet's natural disposition like his heart that beats and his blood that throbs; he may go further, he may inventively react against such models so that the rocking horse gallops up the mountain and takes wing.

4

I should like to return to the reasons why some writers feel compelled to be innovative in an extreme way whereas so many others seem content to work within the constraints of a dominant literary convention. It may be that psychoanalysts have news to give us about this enigma other than the old headlines on page one about Oedipus. One text I discovered to be particularly audacious and rewarding is *Thrills and Regressions* (1959) by the analyst, Michael Balint. To be sure, he does not concern himself with the nature of originality, that is not his central theme, but I believe his propositions to be relevant to it.

A baby, Dr Balint suggests, may respond to the early traumatic discovery that important objects lie outside himself in one of two ways: (a) he may create a fantasy world where firm objects, though having now an independent existence, are deemed to be still benevolent and reliable; or (b) he may recreate the illusion of the world prior to the trauma – when there were no hazardous, independent objects at all, when there were only free, unobstructed, friendly expanses.

It seems the direction of these early responses persists, to a greater or lesser extent, into adult life. So there are those who, when their security is threatened, would *cling* to objects. These are the so-called ocnophils. Then there are those who are their antithesis – the so-called philobats who, finding objects hazardous, would reach for the free spaces between them. For the extreme philobat, objects are indeed objectionable whereas for the extreme ocnophil they are objectives.

In describing adult behaviour patterns, Michael Balint spotlights the philobat as one who prefers to be solitary, devoid of support, relying on his own resources – indeed, the further he is in distance (and time) from safety, from *mother* earth, the greater the thrill he experiences in proving his independence. That is why, Dr Balint suggests, some find it attractive to undertake solitary crossings of the Atlantic or remain aloft in gliders for long periods. Clearly the philobat, or rather the extreme philobat, for there are all kinds of mixtures and gradations, would be perceived by most of us as having the character of a hero. Such men live dangerously. They are, though, according to Dr Balint, bolstered by their feelings of their own potency by holding on to phallic objects, to a magic penis: the tight-rope walker carries his pole, the lion-tamer his whip, the skier his stick, and yes . . . the poet his pen!

It is odd that the poet, the true poet, should be conceived to be, like the trapeze artist or lonely mountaineer, or racing motorist, a philobatic hero. Michael Balint infers as much. Other analysts too have done so in the past and will continue to do so in the future. How romantically one such as Jung discusses the Poet with a capital P. 'Art', he writes in *Modern Man in Search of a Soul*, 'is a kind of innate drive that seizes a human being and makes him its instrument. The artist is not a person endowed with free will who seeks his own ends but one who allows art to realize its purposes through him. . . . To perform this difficult office it is sometimes necessary for him to sacrifice happiness and everything that makes life worth living for the ordinary human being.'

'Tosh,' one might say, but the fact is that this view of the poet as tragic philobatic hero-figure is commonplace and poets themselves have contributed to the making of this myth. 'Why,' asked Yeats, 'should we honour those that die upon the field of battle, a man may show as reckless a courage in entering into the abyss of himself?' And here's Rainer Maria Rilke pronouncing in a letter, 'I feel myself to be an artist, weak and wavering in strength and boldness. . . . Not as a martyrdom do I regard art – but as a battle the chosen one has to wage with himself and his environment.' As Robert Graves has justly remarked, 'Despite all the charlatans, racketeers, and incompetents who have disgraced the poetic profession an aroma of holiness still clings to the title "poet" as it does to the titles "saint" and "hero", both of which are properly reserved for the dead.' Nor does Mr

Graves demur from this popular belief.

It may be inferred from my remarks that I do! I certainly would not subscribe to the notion that the poet is a hero, that the writing of poetry is an heroic act. That notion seems absurd to me; yet when I look back at the poems I myself have written and at the few in particular that have taken as theme the creative process itself, I am surprised to see that my rational belief is contradicted by those very poems. I am even startled to discover that one of them, a poem written some years before the appearance of Michael Balint's *Thrills and Regressions*, actually spotlights the poet as trapeze artist, the very same figure Dr Balint characterizes as an extreme philobat.

I called my poem, 'Go Home the Act is Over'. It was written soon after Dylan Thomas died in 1953 and I had Dylan Thomas very much in mind when I wrote it. I subsequently suppressed the poem. I did not, for instance, include it in my *Collected Poems* (1977) because I did not think it good enough. However I should like to read it to you now for it does lucidly define what I am saying:

Go Home the Act is Over

Roll up, roll up, the circus has begun
and poets, freaks of multilingual Time, perform.
Fingers, ten dwarfs, beat thunder on a drum
and whizzing spotlights flash as in a storm.

Look, like a trapeze artist he flies with wires
above pedestrians who with iambics freeze.
To those with cold hands he offers fires
and sings the catastrophes.

Play gaudy drums then, let the lions roar,
the circus crowd is ready. You others
is it his death you're waiting for?
Where any poet sings, the vulture hovers.

Electricians above the balcony point the light.
Against the roof his two shadows dance
and somersault. He sings for our delight
but seeing gold he trips and loses balance.

The audience is hushed. The sawdust ring
is empty except where that singer lies.
Still, high in the air, two trapezes swing.
Does that last image leak from his two eyes?

Return now to that place. The grass, instead,
the wind and stars where once the spotlights shone.
His funambulists and jugglers are dead.
The show is over. The big tent gone.

It seems that each generation needs to create a martyr–poet: in the
fifties when I wrote 'Go Home the Act is Over', it was Dylan
Thomas, a generation earlier Wilfred Owen. More recently, Sylvia
Plath has been cast for that role. There are those who feel romanti-
cally – common reader, analyst, sometimes, as you see, the artists
themselves – that somehow the poet soars to forbidden heights,
steals the ambrosia of the gods, illicitly brings heavenly fire to earth.
What has been said of the public's attitude, in another context, about
drug addicts could equally describe general feelings about the *poète
maudit*: 'Prometheus, having illicitly brought the fire to earth, is
condemned to a millenium of being eaten alive; Tantalus, having
stolen the ambrosia of the gods, suffers a fate that makes his name a
symbol of an exquisite form of torture; Icarus, having sought the
forbidden heights, suffers the inevitable consequence of plummet-
ing to the depths.'
   And so the poet too, receiving merciless justice, becomes sacri-
ficial martyr and then is glamourized: Alec Guinness, incongruously
wearing a red wig, a curly red wig, impersonated a libidinous Dylan
Thomas on a Broadway stage; Glenda Jackson, of luscious propor-
tions, transformed slight, angular, flat-chested Stevie Smith in a
British film; and even as I'm speaking now, they are preparing in
Langholm, a small border town in Dumfriesshire, to erect a sculp-
ture–monument to honour their locally born Hugh MacDiarmid.
When MacDiarmid was alive, by the way, his poetry was of less
consequence to members of the Langholm council who declined to
grant him the freedom of the town – instead they honoured Neil
Armstrong, the astronaut, whose connection with Langholm was
somewhat more cosmic. In any event, dead, it seems MacDiarmid
has become as philobatic a hero as any astronaut alive.
   Indeed it is not unusual that the poet, elevated to pedestal after his
death, may have received scant attention from the public at large
during his lifetime, especially if his work has been conspicuously
original. The analyst, Phyllis Greenacre, in describing an individual's
reactions to strange events – events not poems – wrote, 'Any
experience which is so strange that there is little in his life to which he
can relate it, is felt as inimical, alien and overwhelming. On the other

hand, an experience which is only somewhat or a little bit new is pleasantly exciting.' As with external events, so with poems: if too strange (original) the poems may be felt to be inimical, if 'a little bit new' they may be welcomed as 'pleasantly exciting'. But I should like to qualify Dr Greenacre's proposition: the intensity of the experience, the poem's effect, depends surely not only on the gradation of its strangeness (originality) but on the ocnophilic or philobatic temperament of the individual, the particular reader. A strange experience, whether an event or a poem, may provoke in one person, at first, inordinate hostility or fear; in another it may merely promote curiosity or unease.

Most people have ocnophilic leanings. Accordingly they prefer that the pattern of any new poem be not too strange, the cadences and images and syntax not too strange, the organization, structure and theme not too strange. The word *ocnophil*, by the way, was suggested to Michael Balint because it stems from the Greek verb meaning to shrink, to hesitate, to cling. So the reader, with his ocnophilic tendencies, *clings* to the nourishing breast of proved traditional modes, to that with which he is most familiar. The avant-garde writer apprehends this: he expects resistance to his way-out inventions. William Wordsworth in his day, publishing the *Lyrical Ballads*, certain of the marked originality of his poems in style and theme – poems that were so different from those currently receiving general approbation – expected more derision than praise. And he was correct in this assumption. Thirty years after the publication of the *Lyrical Ballads* the common ocnophilic reader in England thought Wordsworth to be a fool who could write forty dull sonnets on one streamlet or go berserk about linnets, red-breasts, larks, cuckoos, daisies and 'the scenery of the English Switzerland'. That was generally the blunt response to a particularly original poet. Later in the nineteenth century, the same reader, or at least his great-nephew, would have been more comfortable with the poems of Robert Bridges than those of Manley Hopkins.

The paradox is that though the common reader may hanker for the familiar he also inwardly desires the poet to take heroic creative risks. This conflict is resolved eventually: strangeness endured ceases to be strange. As Dr Greenacre has pointed out in another context, the fear an individual may experience as a result of a strange event may in time give way to the triumph of recognition. It is sad that this recognition, in connection with fresh poetry, is so often postponed until after the poet's death.

Earlier I suggested that we are likely to resent an imitation of an admired model. I spoke of the claims of primacy, I remarked that something in us, prim and primitive, leads us to whisper, 'Copycat, copycat,' derisively. Perhaps at this point I can partially identify that something in us. For if we do, consciously or unconsciously, conceive the artist as hero, as one who takes philobatic risks, we will, with some irritation, discount the efforts of those who merely make replicas and imitations. For these imitators have not truly adventured, have avoided the thrilling risks that we admire, or will in time admire. We recognize that the imitator is no more philobatic than we are and so cannot, must not be acknowledged as poet–hero. On the contrary, he is a pretender and impudent. He is an imposter, and scorn, not honour, should be accorded him!

5

Ben Nicolson once told me that his mother, Victoria Sackville-West, on going through her papers came across a typescript of a poem called 'St Augustine at 32'. She had forgotten that its author was Clifford Dyment who when a youthful poet – he was twenty-two years younger than she – had sent it to her for comment and admiration decades earlier. She assumed that this poem about a man directed towards religious asceticism, yet beset by carnal temptation, was one of her own discarded efforts as she read it to herself critically, yet with that proper tolerance common to authors reading their own work.

St Augustine at 32

Girl, why do you follow me
When I come to the threshold of the holy place?
My resolution falters: it seems a death to enter
When, turning back, I look into your face.

I saw you when I lay alone
And ran from you as from a searching light
Into the gentle, acquiescent
Obscurity of the night.

I crave communion that is not words
And life fulfilled in my cell alone –
And you, you come with your lips and your gold hair
And at your feet is a leaf that the wind has blown.

Victoria Sackville-West must have thought, 'Not half bad,' and soon began to revise the poem, altering 'searching light' to 'hungry light'. Other cosmetic changes, she evidently felt, would save this neglected draft of hers and transform it into serviceable verse. For instance, 'gold hair' – that would not do, that was too romantic; nor was she keen on 'acquiescent obscurity of the night'. There were other details too. She worked speedily on the poem which soon miraculously bore a new title, 'The Novice to Her Lover'. Altogether more appropriate, she decided. At last she typed out the final version.

The Novice to Her Lover

Why must you follow me
When I come to the threshold of this holy place?
My resolution falters, and it seems death to enter
When, turning back, I look upon your face.

I could renounce you when I lay alone.
I ran from you as from a hungry light
Into the gentle, the infinite, the healing
Clemency of the night.

I crave an eloquence that is not words.
I seek fulfilment in the kiss of stone –
But you, you come with your mouth and your dark hair
And at your feet a leaf that the wind has blown.

Some months later, a puzzled and growingly irate Clifford Dyment read in the *New Statesman* a poem by Victoria Sackville-West called 'The Novice to Her Lover'. Knowing Clifford as I did, I can imagine what happened next. Hearing his wife, Marcella, moving about in the kitchen, I bet he rose to his feet, rushed hurriedly out of the room clutching the *New Statesman* and shouted hoarsely, 'Marcella, Marcella!'

Quite recently I stayed in a house in Yorkshire where my hostess, a devout Catholic lady, kept an interesting commonplace book. In it she had included, side by side, 'St Augustine at 32' by Clifford Dyment and 'The Novice to Her Lover' by Victoria Sackville-West; and being of a religious temperament, had done so, I suspect, because she believed the remarkable similarities between the poems gave witness yet again of some dual, sacred intervention. Awe is more elevating than scepticism, though less humorous, and she was somewhat disappointed by my mundane explanation of this apparent psychic synchronicity. Nor did she consider one poem to be better than the other.

In that, I agreed with her. So what of the so-called claims of primacy? Such claims only operate when the original is of genuine value, when it has, in turn, claimed something in and of us. If the original does not engage us in any durable way it will not necessarily be cheapened by an imitation. The fact is, neither 'St Augustine at 32' nor its imitation 'The Novice to Her Lover' are poems of any real consequence. One of them once served to decorate a column in a weekly paper and they both continue to give us, when we read them now, only momentary minor pleasure before each version becomes utterly unremembered. If Clifford Dyment's poem was not so easily paraphrasable, if it were more than a mere translation of prose into verse, if it were more than a statement without feeling, if it contained the inescapable entropy of live poetry, then Victoria Sackville-West's 'imitation' would not have equalled its model. For genuine poems, whatever else they may be, are made up of the right words in the right order and subsequent tinkerings with these words will only do the poems mortal damage. That is why, surely, Valery's suggestion that 'a poem is never finished, only abandoned' is wrong.

It has not been remarked on before that when Clifford Dyment published his *Collected Poems* in 1970 – the year he died – he included in it 'St Augustine at 32', keeping that title (his own) but adopting many of Victoria Sackville-West's cosmetic adaptations. A justified, ironic revenge, I suppose. For example, his 'light' was no longer 'searching' but 'hungry'. On the other hand I find it amusing to see that whatever else he plundered from Victoria Sackville-West's version, he did not dye the 'gold' hair of St Augustine's temptress to a darker hue.

Perhaps Victoria Sackville-West had apprehended the unconscious significance of hair colour. The virgin, asexual princesses of fairytales are always blonde – and so, maybe, that was one reason why she felt gold hair was inappropriate for the sexy temptress of a saintly man. Clifford Dyment must have felt otherwise – he saw St Augustine's vamp as a true blonde – and a true blonde she obstinately remained like his own charming wife Marcella! So 'St Augustine at 32' finally comes to rest as:

> Girl, why do you follow me
> When I come to the threshold of the holy place?

My resolution falters and it seems a death to enter
When, turning back, I look into your face.

I looked upon you when I lay alone
And ran from you as from a hungry light
Into the gentle, the infinite and healing
Clemency of the night.

I crave eloquence that is not words
I crave fulfilment in the kiss of stone –
And you, you come with your lips and your gold hair.
And at your feet is a leaf that the wind has blown.

6

I come now to my final note which will be, as promised, shame-lessly self-directed. I have already confessed that I wince when I examine those poems I published during my medical-school days. That apprentice work, apart from occasional echoes of Dylan Thomas – 'harp of sabbaths', 'choir of wounds' – obeyed too slavishly the worst dictates of the then fashionable neo-romantic school of poetry: my diction was too florid and approximate, my themes too arcane, too private. I did not perceive these faults at the time, of course. I was deluded – believing the poems to be original and momentous. I am reminded of Ernest Jones's anecdote in his autobiography, *Free Associations*, where he confesses that, as a boy, he thought he knew where Heaven was. All you had to do, he believed, was to look southwards from Swansea Bay across the channel. You see, he had misheard an adult say 'That's Devon.' In my long-ago green days I also, as it were, misheard my poems.

Eventually, though, I emerged from the amniotic sac of neo-romanticism to write, I trust, poems of a more original order. By then I had formulated my own theoretical concepts about the making of poetry and I recall these when I reread some clumsy embattled prose notes I contributed to *Poetry and Poverty*, a little literary magazine of the early 1950s. For instance I had come to believe passionately that Jung was correct in arguing that the private was a limitation, even a sin in the realm of art. He declared that a private form of 'art' 'deserves to be treated as if it were a neurosis'. I had decided that private poetry, though it might fraudulently present the appearance of being original, did not thrive as literature. If hermetic, however musical it might be, however much it might seduce a scattering of academic critics partial to shaped bombinations, it could not en-

duringly engage a real audience. I did not want myself to write poems
so neurotically involved with the sound of words that common sense
became obliterated. Yet, in the 1950s, I still wished to tell it slant and
to tell it eloquently, to tell it, indeed, not conversationally, flatly, but
with my voice not too far away from song.

I soon fell into the practice of devising markedly rhythmical
structures which progressed as an allegorical or symbolic narrative.
This allowed my theme, in a disguised way, to occupy, and to be
highly visible in, the centre of my poems. They were, in one sense,
parable poems.

Modern novelists have invented parables of one kind or another,
some fathomable, some less so: Kafka, for instance, symbolically,
George Orwell allegorically; but in Britain not one of my contempor-
aries consistently published short poems structured in this way. I
hardly felt I was engaged in strategies particularly original; I did
sense, though, that others began to regard me as a maverick, as one
now writing outside dominant modes, away from what has been
called 'the central English tradition'.

It was not that with each poem I wrote I would consciously
manipulate symbolic counters. Simply, I acquired the habit of
writing in this fashion. If I wanted to protest about the dire potentiali-
ties of the Cold War I discovered that I needed to refer to imaginary
individuals warring on an imaginary deserted island; or if I discussed
the opposition of the good and evil propensities in men I evoked as
realistically as possible a professional football game where the home
team did no wrong, the away side no right, and the referee, of course,
was in the pay of the devil; or, as you have already heard, if I wished to
focus on the relationship of a death-seeking poet and his salacious
audience then I described a trapeze artist in a circus. The theme of
the poem, in short, was abstract, the poem itself concrete.

By 1960 I feared that the framework devices that I had used
repeatedly and half-unwittingly would become surface contrivances.
I believed, and still believe, that style, one's own voice, as it were, is
not truly knowable to oneself. The moment a man, while speaking,
can actually hear his own voice it alters and loses power. In this one
sense, self-knowledge, for a poet, can be dangerous: instinctive
manners may become mannerisms. And as Sir Joshua Reynolds
admonished, 'He who resolves never to ransack any mind but his
own, will soon be reduced, from mere barrenness, to the poorest of
all imitations; he will be obliged to imitate himself . . .'

So I began to dismantle that symbolic or allegorical framework.

Gradually I wrote altogether more directly. An epigraph to that symbolical poem *The Rime of the Ancient Mariner* warns us against allowing our minds to become accustomed to the minutiae of daily life; but it was these very minutiae that increasingly intrigued me. My pitch of voice became less obviously musical, more conversational, my subject matter more rooted in common reality – no less mysterious for being common to us all. In brief, I looked outward to start from the visible and I was startled by the visible. And I still tried to write lucidly without losing depth. Abstract ideas as a partial source for poems ceased to interest me; instead my poems were nourished by experiences, imagined and factual, my own and others', ordinary and extraordinary.

Every poet, of course, has the obligation to be original: no genuine poem can exist without it being so. There are occasions, however, when the poet, on completing what he may feel to be a successful poem, experiences a particular satisfaction because he sees his poem to be cast in an uncommon way – not only technically. For instance, I do not set out, necessarily, to write a poem of celebration or one of lament, one optimistic or pessimistic, but if, when the poem is concluded, I see that I have somehow struck what I think to be a truthful, affirmative note, then I am particularly pleased. For so many poems gather the images of despair; so few celebrate and affirm.

It's the same with subject matter. I happen to be a doctor. Now there have been many physician–poets but few have called upon their medical experience in the making of their poems. John Keats, for example, a student at Guy's Hospital, assisted a celebrated butcher of a surgeon when, as you know, no anaesthetics were available. His dramatic medical experiences, nevertheless, hardly infiltrated into his wonderfully rich poems. In consequence, when I do refer in a poem to my medical experience I am not dogged by the feeling that I am going over worn ground. I am encouraged by the absence of that feeling and all the more prepared to write such poems. 'Chance favours the prepared mind,' asserted Louis Pasteur, speaking of inspiration, and chance has favoured me with a number of medical poems over the years. Here is one such, a recent confessional poem called 'X Ray'.

X Ray

Some prowl sea-beds, some hurtle to a star
and, mother, some obsessed turn over every stone
or open graves to let that starlight in.
There are men who would open anything.

Harvey, the circulation of the blood,
and Freud, the circulation of our dreams,
pried honourably and honoured are
like all explorers. Men who'd open men.

And those others, mother, with diseases
like great streets named after them: Addison,
Parkinson, Hodgkin, – physicians who'd arrive
fast and first on any sour death-bed scene.

I am their slowcoach colleague, half afraid,
incurious. As a boy it was so: you know how
my small hand never teased to pieces
an alarm clock or flensed a perished mouse.

And this larger hand's the same. It stretches now
out from a white sleeve to hold up, mother,
your X ray to the glowing screen. My eyes look
but don't want to, I still don't want to know.

Freud saw himself as an extreme philobat. He once wrote, 'I am
not really a man of science ... but a conquistador ... with the
curiosity, the boldness, and the tenacity that belong to that sort of
person.' Perhaps many of us wish we could claim as much; but I for
one, as you see in my poem 'X Ray', have confessed to ocnophilic
tendencies; with which modesty, after so many boastings, and
hearing the neighing outside of an impatient horse, not wooden, I
trust, I shall decently end.